Advance Praise for
The American Imperative

"Development is an underrated but mighty power. It opens the opportunity for freedom and self-sufficiency. With *The American Imperative*, Daniel Runde reminds us that both good and bad actors can fill vacuums in the world. By making a case for a renewed foreign policy agenda that emphasizes broad-based economic growth and good governance for the developing world, this book outlines how the United States can lead for good."

–Henrietta H. Fore, former Executive Director of UNICEF
and former Administrator of USAID

"An absent America will mean ceding burgeoning economies, emerging technologies, influential institutions, and the very values of work and governance to authoritarians with no interest in the words and propositions of the Declaration of Independence. In *The American Imperative*, Runde provides the playbook, one in which America leads with the tools of diplomacy and development to advance democracy and opportunity the world over, not at the point of a sword but with a helping hand. It is time for policymakers to read it, get off the sidelines, and put it into practice."

–Senator Todd C. Young, U.S. Senate

"The United States has a unique role to play in the world today. Of course, it will need military power to play that role. But most of the challenges facing America require harnessing other forms of power. In *The American Imperative*, Dan Runde explains the importance of non-military power and provides a blueprint for a long-overdue bipartisan consensus on how the country can strengthen these other instruments of national power."

–Stephen J. Hadley, former United States National Security
Advisor

"The rise of China under the rule of the Communist Party poses perhaps the greatest threat to the United States and our way of life that we have ever seen. To prevail and ensure that we enjoy another American century, we must use every tool of national power. Dan Runde is one of the nation's preeminent experts on international development. In *The American Imperative*, Runde gives us a guide for how America can complement its military strength with diplomatic, cultural, and economic power to ensure victory in the long struggle ahead."

–Robert C. O'Brien, former United States National Security
Advisor

"If, as Clemenceau said, 'War is too serious to be left to the generals,' global development is too important to be left to well-meaning philanthropists and multinational development agencies. Hard-headed realists miss the point when they categorize a coup in a developing country by Putin's Wagner Group of paramilitary mercenaries as hard power while a different country falling into a debt trap by Xi Jinping is treated in the category of 'soft power,' when the consequences of the latter may in fact have a greater impact on the hard subject of great power competition. *The American Imperative* is the first book that I can recall reading by someone with deep experience and involvement in the issues of global development policy who addresses that subject from the hard-headed perspective of whether U.S. policies—and those of the multinational institutions that pretend to be apolitical but which often serve to compete for national and commercial interests—do in fact serve the interests of the American taxpayers who fund them."

–Paul Wolfowitz, former President of the World Bank Group and former United States Deputy Secretary of Defense

"Will competition with China for world leadership mean military conflict? Dan Runde explains how to fight—and win—peacefully by making our policies and bureaucracies fit for the twenty-first century. In the struggle for influence in the developing world, Runde tells us what cards we hold—and how to play them."

–Elliott Abrams, Senior Fellow, Council on Foreign Relations, former Deputy National Security Advisor for Global Democracy Strategy

"Dan Runde is one of our nation's foremost scholars of international security. In *The American Imperative*, he takes us inside the global competition playing out in the developing world between the United States and our values and our authoritarian adversaries and their values. This is a competition we cannot ignore and one we must win in order to safeguard our own security. Policymakers would do well to study Runde's book and put it into action."

–Representative Mike Gallagher, U.S. House of Representatives

"Dan Runde shows that soft power doesn't have to be soft-headed. Facing a determined, often ruthless, Chinese foreign policy, America needs to deploy all the instruments of its national power far more effectively. Runde's suggestions should launch an important debate on the role and objectives of U.S. foreign economic assistance."

–John Bolton, former United States National Security Advisor and former U.S. Ambassador to the United Nations

THE
AMERICAN
IMPERATIVE

THE
AMERICAN
IMPERATIVE

Reclaiming Global Leadership through Soft Power

DANIEL F. RUNDE

Post Hill
PRESS

Published by Bombardier Books
An Imprint of Post Hill Press
ISBN: 978-1-63758-200-8
ISBN (eBook): 978-1-63758-201-5

The American Imperative:
Reclaiming Global Leadership through Soft Power
© 2023 by Daniel F. Runde
All Rights Reserved

Cover Design by Tiffani Shea

Interior Design by Yoni Limor

BOMBARDIER
BOOKS

Post Hill
PRESS

Post Hill Press
New York • Nashville
posthillpress.com

Published in the United States of America
1 2 3 4 5 6 7 8 9 10

For Sonia, Danny, Ben, and Alex

Table of Contents

Introduction

WHO WILL LEAD?

Our adversaries are intensifying their efforts in the entire under-developed world. Those who oppose their advance look to us and I believe, at this dangerous moment, we must respond.

—John F. Kennedy, upon the signing of the Foreign Assistance Act of 1961

In 1992, the year after the collapse of the Soviet Union, the political scientist Francis Fukuyama published *The End of History and the Last Man*. This seminal work of political philosophy argued that civilization had reached "the end-point of mankind's ideological evolution and the universalization of Western liberal democracy as the final form of human government." The world was experiencing a wave of democratization, not just in the former Soviet states in Eastern and Central Europe, but also in Africa, Asia, and the Americas. Fukuyama believed, as I do, that market democracies are the best foundation for moral, social, and economic progress, and that the "liberal world order" that had come into being after the Second World War—which I believe has kept humanity free from global conflagration for seventy-five years—would be cemented as the fundamental organizing principle of geopolitics.

World events have shocked the world out of the complacency that followed Fukuyama's optimistic prediction. After several years spent observing with concern the "democracy recession" around the world, the US and its partner nations saw the liberal world order come under all-out attack in 2022 with Russia's barbaric, catastrophic invasion of Ukraine. What had been a sleepy multilateral system roared back to life, brandishing the weapons of diplomatic, economic, and cultural connections.

When I set about writing a book about great-power competition and the growing threat to the liberal world order, I focused my attention primarily on China, or more specifically, the Chinese Communist Party. China's rapidly spreading influence has made it the second largest economy on the planet. But even as Beijing hosted the 2022 Winter Olympics, Russia, in the authoritarian grip of Vladimir Putin, grabbed the headlines.

I fervently hope that we are not at the beginning of a second Cold War, but without question, the great-power competition facing the United States has become more complex and more urgent. Russia and China are going to be challenges for the next twenty or thirty years, but they are not one and the same. Each has its own intentions and motivations, and the response of the US and its partners will have to be multifaceted and draw on every tool at our disposal. Our long-term goal for US leadership is a world based on broadly shared liberal values and ideals, not those of China or Russia, and we should work to pull as many countries as possible toward that liberal international order, assuming those countries want to join.

The world is, for the moment, distracted by Moscow's aggression, but we need to be careful not to take our eye off the ball. Russia may be a local bully, reasserting its presence in the former Soviet space, but it has neither the economic might nor the ability to set global standards that China has achieved.

Yes, Russia insists on being recognized as a global force. The great-power competition currently taking shape is not going to play out in Beijing or Moscow, though, but rather in places like Kyiv and across the developing world from Central Asia to Africa and Latin

America. Before the Ukraine invasion, we assumed this competition would not be fought with armies, but rather with ideas and economic engagement. In the words of former Defense Secretary Robert Gates, "If we can avoid war with Russia and China, our rivalry with them will be waged using nonmilitary instruments of power—the same kind of instruments that played a significant role in winning the Cold War: diplomacy, development assistance, strategic communications, science and technology, ideology, nationalism, and more."

I think about the United States' relationship with the world as being supported by a tripod of three Ds: diplomacy, defense, and development. My field is development, which is linked inextricably to the other two elements as a critical component of statecraft. A great deal of attention is going to be paid to military and security issues, with many already arguing for a revitalized, technologically advanced military. I don't believe, though, that global leadership is going to be asserted primarily on the battlefield, but rather through economic and other soft-power tools. The international response to Putin's assault on Ukraine has been a testament to the importance of diplomacy, as democracies have reinvigorated their commitment to liberal principles and have made clear their united opposition to Russian aggression. At the same time, the human tragedy in Ukraine should make us reflect on our assumptions about how we engage with the world—and how we apply various forms of power in concert with our allies.

In Ukraine, the tools of soft-power and development will be needed to help restore the functionality of institutions and respond to the humanitarian crisis—and later to help a war-torn country rebuild and have deep long-term political, economic, and people-to-people relationships with the West. Every American—from elected policy makers in Washington to informed citizens everywhere—needs to understand the full array of tools and opportunities available to us to exercise American leadership in these international undertakings.

In a March 3, 2022, statement, Robert Gates wrote persuasively of the need "to awaken democratic governments to the reality of a new world." In that statement, he pointed out:

> Another crucial nonmilitary instrument—as we
> have seen in recent days—is our alliances and the
> power inherent in acting together. Two of the most
> important agencies during the Cold War were
> the United States Information Agency (strategic
> communications) and the U.S. Agency for Inter-
> national Development (economic assistance). We
> need creatively to reinvent both—and other critical
> nonmilitary instruments of power—for the global
> struggle in which we are now engaged.

While Russia licked its wounds for thirty years, the rise of
China as an economic and geopolitical force was so swift that the
governments that traditionally dominated the world stage were
essentially caught napping. The end of the Cold War seemed to
offer a lull—a "peace dividend"—that allowed the West to reorder
its priorities, which meant relaxing its guard. China rushed in to
fill the empty spaces created during that time of transition. Before
the United States and its allies opened their eyes, the once insular
China had reached out and established its presence on every continent, and it had begun systematically building its own future with
the world's resources.

Twenty years ago, many observers viewed China as a developing nation, culturally and politically isolated and opaque. By
the early 2020s, however, China could boast of being the leading
trading partner for 124 countries, while the United States could
claim only 76. Chinese companies have built infrastructure and
invested in energy projects throughout the developing world while
also setting up new multilateral development banks and actively
competing with the US and the West for influence and authority in
global organizations.

I've watched this taking shape over my twenty years in development work. Now I feel I must raise the alarm. The discussion of
soft-power and how we use it needs a major refresh, and we also
need a reset of all our assumptions for this new post-post-Cold
War landscape.

This is an entirely new kind of superpower competition. Over
the course of this book, I will detail the economic and demographic

forces driving Beijing's hegemonic agenda as well as the tools and techniques it uses to achieve its goals. To see this new dynamic as a return to the perilous days of the Cold War would be misguided.

Russia may be hoping to reclaim past glory, but China isn't looking to export ideology or gather military allies into its camp. Rather, Beijing has engaged in the multilateral system and is seeking to reshape it according to its needs. It is an exaggeration to say that Chinese leadership has set a goal of upending the liberal world order, but both China and Russia have been working to revise it in ways we are not going to like—unless you're a fan of rigged plebiscites, systemic corruption, unfettered pollution, and religious persecution as state policy. Should the current world order become obsolete, it won't be the result of some nefarious Chinese plan to sabotage the West; it will be due to the West's, and particularly the United States', inattention, complacency, and lack of deep examination into what motivates the next great superpower and its Russian partner.

With China ascendant in the 21st Century, I believe that there is now one great, overarching goal of American soft power: to enable a better alternative to all that China is offering to the developing world as a means of preserving the multilateral system that sustains prosperity. This will not happen overnight, and it cannot be addressed by short-term thinking, planning, or budgeting. I expect a thirty- to forty-year marathon, which will involve reinvigorating global alliances and promoting the strengthening of economies and governance in more and more countries so that they will have broadly shared the interests and values and also be able to share the burdens of meeting global challenges. I envision a prosperous world that is increasingly democratic, in which people can achieve their individual dreams and societies can achieve their deepest hopes and aspirations. In that world, the United States should lead an updated liberal international order. While this order will need to include some burden-sharing shifts among our friends and allies, it also requires that the US continue to play a leadership role and accept the costs and responsibilities of maintaining global leadership.

Our response to the current Russia challenge could offer a roadmap for our approach to China. Even though Russia offers no compelling economic vision, the United States and its allies can offer a meaningful development alternative based on freedom and prosperity. That vision has suffered some setbacks in recent years, after our problems in Iraq and Afghanistan, the global financial crisis, the widespread democracy recession, and troubles at home. But warts and all, we must continue to stand up for these ideals. That's going to require efforts across multiple fronts: democracy, human rights, and governance; continued reform of the state sector; market-based economic reforms, continued reform of the energy and power sectors; and many other forms of soft-power engagement. Additionally, we must remember that our rivalries are with government regimes, not with civil populations—it is with Vladimir Putin and the Chinese Communist Party and not with the Russian or Chinese people. The US should also find ways to support civil society and human rights in Russia and China. Our policy should not be regime change, despite Putin's deeply inhumane policies, but rather to support and give voice to the millions of Russians and Chinese who wish for a better future based on openness and fundamental freedoms.

In the chapters that follow, I will show how important it is that the United States organize and lead global coalitions of the willing while remaining a standards *maker*, not a standards *taker*. I will offer a brief historical perspective, explaining the steps and missteps that brought us to this present juncture, to better inform our strategy for the immediate future. If the keys to enduring peace and prosperity are political and social stability, economic vigor, and self-sufficiency for a continually increasing number of countries, development offers the best path forward. Foreign assistance is only one small piece of the puzzle, but it is critical in that it catalyzes progress in what I believe are the two most important factors in development: a strong private sector—often working in partnership with public institutions—and effective governance operating in a context of democracy.

If we have learned anything in 2022, it's that the United States cannot afford to turn its gaze inward. The mechanisms of the multilateral system may operate outside the realm of most people's consciousness, but there is no overstating the extent to which we all rely on that system and, therefore, need to ensure that it functions well. We will likely need to go back to the drawing board, not only on our use of multilateral financial institutions, but on energy policy and commercial diplomacy as well. The rules of the game may not yet be perfect, but one thing is certain: we would not like the rules as China would rewrite them. It is time to reconsider our international relationships, with our traditional allies as well as with countries with which we've had fraught relations.

The challenges ahead are substantial and require both immediate attention and persistence over the coming decades. Meeting those challenges will require committed leadership. But who will lead? I believe that will be the United States, which has demonstrated its positive impact repeatedly in the past and is uniquely capable of carrying out that responsibility. No other nation has the clout and commitment to do so. Our efforts in foreign affairs, our use of soft power, and our engagement in the multilateral system should seek to ensure that the United States continues to lead through the rest of the 21st century. In the chapters that follow I am going to offer specific solutions and specific steps that the United States must take. The United States must move swiftly and boldly, but wisely, efficiently, and with international support, to build the global future based on common security, shared democratic values, sound economic principles, and broadly inclusive opportunities.

PART I
THE ASSESSMENT

Chapter 1

THE WIND FROM THE EAST

China on the March

Beijing did not leverage its growing economic wealth for the sake of greater political freedom. It did not use its entry into the so-called rules-based global order to play by the rules. It did not mean what it said when it promised Hong Kong "one country, two systems." It could not be trusted to honor business and academic partnerships without stealing intellectual property on a massive scale. It has not turned its development schemes in vulnerable foreign countries, from Ecuador to Montenegro, into lasting foundations for mutual good will, rather than one-way exploitation.

—Brett Stephens, *New York Times*, 7/5/21, "China Won't Bury Us, Either"

When the leaders of the Myanmar military deposed the democratically elected government in a coup d'état on February 1, 2021, it made me rethink my own assumptions about the US approach to development. As someone who built my career on the premise that support for development is a critical component of foreign policy, the coup struck me at once as a huge setback for both statecraft and development, and also a confirmation of so much that I had observed and believed in my work. It's tempting to try and draw conclusions and learn lessons from the events in Myanmar, but perhaps the only obvious lesson is that any assumptions that big powerful countries might make about smaller, weaker, and poorer countries are likely wrong and arrogant. Leadership on an international level requires vigilance, care, and flexibility, as well as highly specialized knowledge, resources, and tools that vary and adapt to unique cultures, circumstances, and moments in history.

Having secured its independence from British colonial rule in 1948, Myanmar was kept politically and culturally isolated from the global community by its ruling military junta. If Myanmar, or Burma, existed at all in the consciousness of the average American, it was most likely as the misty setting of a grainy old black-and-white movie. In reality, the country is larger and more significant in geopolitical terms than many realize. It shares a border with China on its northeast and with India to its north and west. Myanmar offers a critical entry point into the Bay of Bengal and the Indian Ocean. For decades, the international community heard very little about numerous and often bloody insurrections, in which the state armed forces, the Tatmadaw, fought to gain control over various ethnic groups seeking self-determination. The conflict with the Karen ethnic group has been going on for over sixty years and has been labeled by some as the world's longest-running civil war, although a fragile cease-fire was signed by the recently deposed civilian government. There is also a significant population of ethnic Chinese, a growing influx of Chinese nationals, and, of course, the widely publicized conflict with the Rohingya ethnic group, referred to by some observers as genocide in progress.

For most of the period of its independence, American diplomats and development workers kept their distance from Myanmar, at least until the charismatic pro-democracy activist Aung San Suu Kyi rose to international prominence in the late 1980s, focusing the world's attention on Myanmar's secretive government and earning the 1991 Nobel Peace Prize in the process. Of course, she spent most of the next twenty years under house arrest, despite global outcry and appeals from prominent heads of state and two different UN secretaries-general.

During that time, the United States pursued few, if any, of the soft-power options it traditionally rolled out in other comparable countries. There were no specialists on the ground from the American foreign service; no educational exchange programs bringing the best and brightest of Myanmar's future leaders to the US for study and training; few, if any, American corporations setting up economic partnerships, entrepreneurs creating new enterprises, or NGOs establishing an operational foothold; no advisors sharing expertise in engineering, agriculture, environmental science; and no cultural exchange programs. We brought limited or no influence to encourage public or private financial institutions to invest in Myanmar's economic growth. These are the means by which the US has provided support and assistance to many nations to begin climbing the ladder of development, simultaneously exposing people in those countries to values and knowledge while remaining supporting actors in those nations' internal dramas. Having come to Washington in 2002, during the George W. Bush administration, I had completely bought into his ambition to promote democracy in the developing world, which President Bush spoke of in his second inaugural address. It had been a cornerstone of our foreign policy since FDR and had been reiterated by Ronald Reagan, who established the National Endowment for Democracy in the early 1980s. I had made it a central part of my work at USAID. Countries at the second or third tier of perceived importance to the US national interest became something of a specialty for me. My particular development work, putting together multi-stakeholder partnerships with philanthropies, organizations, and corporations, covered all sorts of development issues, including inclusive economic growth, democratic governance, human rights, and the rule of law in such countries.

The US, for the time being no longer driven by the dictates of global superpower competition, may have had its back turned, but Myanmar's great and powerful Asian neighbors did not. With its economy crippled by decades of trade and investment sanctions, Myanmar welcomed Chinese support. The Chinese government, for its part, didn't share the West's qualms about authoritarian governments and didn't hesitate to step in, pouring in financial, technical, and human resources. China supplies Myanmar's military and makes enormous investments in industries like oil and gas, mining, and agriculture—from which China itself stands to benefit greatly—not to mention the infrastructure needed to harness and transport those resources: roads, railways, pipelines, and power installations. China further supports Myanmar's economy by supplying a ready market for raw materials such as rubber and lumber. And in contrast to the majority of the international community, China has refrained from condemning the abuses attributed to the Tatmadaw and has assumed the role of Myanmar's defender at the UN and other international organizations.

One might expect that after so much bilateral trade, a cozy relationship would have developed between China and Myanmar's ruling generals, but here is where assumptions begin to break down. In time, the military leaders in Myanmar began to grow suspicious of China's motives and concerned about the growing—and perhaps irreversible—dependence on China. They resented being bullied by China, or any other outside power, for that matter. Even a casual observer of recent Chinese relations with lower- and middle-income nations would know those concerns were real and legitimate. China has established a track record of investing in massive infrastructure projects in smaller countries, projects that tend to serve its own needs more than the needs of the recipient country, in the form of natural resources, strategic position, or work for its own labor force.

A case in point is the Hambantota port project in Sri Lanka, for which China provided virtually all the funding, beginning in 2015. The new port was a priority of Sri Lanka's leader at the time but was considered something of a white elephant by most potential investors. When the port proved as unprofitable and unsuccessful as had been predicted and became an economic burden to Sri Lanka, China renegotiated its terms, securing for itself the rights to manage the port and adjacent facilities under a ninety-nine-year lease, similar to that which was extended to the United Kingdom for the territory of Hong Kong. The port added to Sri Lanka's already massive debt burden. The Hambantota project may have had little value to Sri Lanka, but to China, it represented a toehold along the coast of the Indian Ocean, enabling shipping access to the South China Sea through the Strait of Malacca. The port would be a critical piece of China's "string of pearls" strategy, a planned series of ports (and potential naval bases) linking its eastern coast. The financial performance of the port has indeed improved somewhat under Chinese management, but it still was perceived by many China observers as the poster child for China's "debt-trap diplomacy," to use a phrase coined by Brahma Chellaney, an Indian geopolitical expert. When I was asked to provide a briefing to Senator Romney in 2019, his staff gave me five questions, one of which was, "the senator would like to know more about the port in Sri Lanka." Hambantota is far from the only example; similar predatory lending practices helped precipitate debt crises in a string of African nations.

In 2011, the Myanmar government suspended work already in progress on a massive China-sponsored hydroelectric project, the Myitsone Dam. The junta's motives and intent are always shrouded in secrecy, so it's difficult to tell exactly what prompted this move. There had been an enormous public outcry in response to the dam along the Irrawaddy River, often called "the lifeblood of Myanmar." With several other proposed dams, it would permanently alter the nation's central watershed, possibly displacing countless fishermen and farmers. Just as significantly, about 90 percent of the power generated by the dam would be channeled back across the Chinese border into Yunnan, and the dam was to be built using imported Chinese labor, further limiting its contribution to the local economy. We may never know for sure if Myanmar's secretive generals had actually been moved by public opinion.

At roughly the same time, the United States had begun to make diplomatic overtures to Myanmar, which had been unexpectedly well-received. Just a few years previously, in 2008, after a massive cyclone had devastated a significant portion of Myanmar, its leaders had overcome their deep-rooted suspicion and accepted disaster assistance from the US. When Barack Obama took over the presidency in January 2009, he and his secretary of state, Hillary Clinton, recognized the opportunity to turn that hint of thawing into a genuine diplomatic opening. Clinton visited Myanmar in 2011, the first visit by an American secretary of state in more than fifty years. President Obama joined her on a second trip, and the US set about easing some of the harsh sanctions against Myanmar while encouraging democratic reforms. Most important, the Obama administration installed a brilliant and knowledgeable expert, Derek Mitchell, as a special envoy to Myanmar, with the rank of ambassador, in 2011. Mitchell, an established Asia hand whom I had known in Washington, was officially made ambassador to Myanmar in 2012. A seasoned diplomat with expertise—the polar opposite of "the ugly American"—is critical to establishing and maintaining productive relations. Mitchell and Dr. Michael Green, my good friend and colleague at CSIS, had coauthored an important article in *Foreign Affairs* in 2008, suggesting that the US rethink its unyielding stance toward the junta.

Other nations, especially Myanmar's neighbors, soon followed suit. ASEAN, the Association of Southeast Asian Nations, which fosters economic, political, and security cooperation, extended a hand in 2014 and even offered Myanmar the chairmanship. Such gestures can help legitimize an outcast government in the eyes of the global community, bringing it back into the fold of forward-looking countries.

In 2015, Aung San Suu Kyi's party, the National League for Democracy (NLD), emerged victorious in a general election that had been closely observed by international organizations dedicated to supporting and monitoring free and transparent democratic elections. I serve on the board of one of those organizations, the International Foundation for Electoral Systems (IFES). I heard the story that the former military general who was the chair in charge of administering that election was under pressure by his own military-aligned party, Union Solidarity and Development Party (USDP), during the week-long announcement of results to somehow reduce NLD's landslide. But the eyes of the world were effectively on the Myanmar government, which had ushered in reform and the promise of democratic elections. What would the chair do? Would he alter the results for a less resounding victory for NLD and more seats for USDP to avoid humiliation—or would he let the election results stand? A couple of close colleagues and advisors pleaded with him to do the right thing and not buckle under political pressure. The general made the right decision, perhaps influenced by the extensive transparent international and media scrutiny. He was on the right side of history, and Myanmar was praised for its peaceful transition of power. The international community rewarded this hopeful development by dropping sanctions, providing new investment, and offering acceptance to this long-isolated country.

　　　　　·　·　·　·　·

Not only did Myanmar's constitution prevent Suu Kyi from becoming the formal head of state, but it also left the military in control of a guaranteed significant number of seats in the parliament and of key ministries in the government. She did assume a position that left her with enormous de facto power in the country, which she hung on to until the coup on February 1, 2021. And here's where another assumption may break down.

Aung San Suu Kyi was long the darling of the liberal West, a beacon of democracy, a martyr, wasting away under house arrest at the hands of an authoritarian regime. Once her position in the government was legitimized, she traveled to the US to meet again with President Obama, in a display of affinity and common purpose. However, Suu Kyi also met with China's Xi Jinping to celebrate their mutual friendship and acknowledge some form of shared future. Surely, the leadership in both Washington and Beijing recognized that the geopolitical game was being played under a new set of rules. The bad old days of the Cold War, when accepting support from one great power was perceived as a hostile act by the other, were long gone. Myanmar could now hedge its bets and make overtures to both the liberal democratic West and the authoritarian collectivism of China. Time would tell which relationship would reap the greatest rewards.

The US was at a disadvantage. China had stepped into the aid and development void created by decades of American disengagement. Something close to a million Chinese had migrated across the border from Yunnan or had been brought in to work on Chinese infrastructure projects, joining the ethnic Chinese already established in Myanmar. Chinese financing was underwriting much, if not all, of the tangible economic progress in Myanmar in the last twenty years. And all this despite the prior regime's reluctance to blindly do China's bidding. How likely was it that Myanmar's government, even if it had given way to more democratic tendencies, would turn its back on its largest benefactor?

I had an opportunity to visit Myanmar in the period following the installation of Aung San Suu Kyi's government as part of a project investigating data, statistics, and policy sponsored by JICA, the aid agency of the Japanese government. Japan's largest foreign-aid footprint is with its Southeast Asian neighbors. It has many of the same needs as China, such as access to natural resources, and maintains a similarly pragmatic, or agnostic, approach to the internal affairs of those countries; although Japan has a longstanding commitment to development, is sensitive about its history in the region, and is seeking to build constructive, future-looking partnerships.

Underlying our research were two key premises: first, the wealthier a country becomes, the more data it generates; and second, the more democratic a country becomes, the more accurate and truthful its data becomes, and the more responsive to democratic actors, those data need to be. The trip took us to Naypyidaw, Myanmar's eerie capital city, constructed only within the last twenty years.

There, I met with the country's chief statistician, who had been trained in Japan.

She explained to me that during the years of the military dictatorship, there was little need in government agencies for data and statistics. For the most part, they made up whatever numbers they need for their planning. Low-level bureaucrats or regional officials never wanted to displease their authorities, and so they simply lied when asked for data. I saw almost no computers in the statistical offices other than in her office, only endless stacks of paper, and learned further that there were significant deficiencies one or two management layers down, with many of the agency's employees neither completely numerate nor literate. Now, however, she was confronting the reality that in a democracy, the need for real-time data explodes and continues to grow as a country moves up the democracy and development scale. Yet, here was an educated, highly placed official who had never heard the term "big data." Liberalizing forces may have been resurgent in Myanmar, but an enormous amount of heavy lifting would be needed just to lay the basic foundation for transparent and effective governance.

The situation became even more confused by Aung San Suu Kyi's disappointing policy regarding the minority Muslim Rohingya once she became the de facto leader of the Myanmar government. Despite withering testimony describing a campaign of atrocities amounting to ethnic cleansing and even genocide on the part of the government and the Buddhist majority, Suu Kyi stood before the International Court of Justice and acknowledged only "intercommunal violence" and counterattacks against "insurgents or terrorists." She chastised the nations of the West for criticizing or interfering in internal matters of which they knew too little. The international community also looked on in shock as her government jailed a number of prominent journalists who were investigating the attacks on the Rohingya in Myanmar's Rakhine province.

Condemnation was swift. I want to say that it's easy for us to sit halfway around the world and criticize, and that the criticism was legitimate, but outsiders can never know the pressures inherent in a fragile fledgling government. Democracies rarely mature along a smooth path but proceed in fits and starts. If we in the West were to be honest with ourselves, we might recognize that democracy advocates projected their aspirations on Aung San Suu Kyi, a telegenic, sophisticated, sympathetic figure, whose harsh treatment at the hands of an authoritarian government had violated established standards of decency. But we may never have fully understood either Suu Kyi's intentions for Myanmar or the realities on the ground once she came to power. Certainly, she had to appease the generals who continued to control many key levers of government. She would have to tread softly regarding their actions against the Rohingya. Similarly, she would have had to strike just the right tone with her political followers, in Myanmar and also with China, the behemoth on her border, that had insinuated itself so deeply into Myanmar's economic future. Whether Aung San Suu Kyi had actually backed off her commitment to democratization or her statements and actions once in government were born of political necessity may never be known for sure, given her return to prison.

At the same time, the new Trump administration in Washington didn't focus on Myanmar, or other developing countries, in the same way that Obama's government had. America's priorities shifted, and it largely dropped its scrutiny. In fact, if anything, the US would have been more likely than before to tacitly support the military's resistance to Chinese influence.

As irate former supporters around the world called for Aung San Suu Kyi's Nobel Prize to be revoked, the only voice missing from the outcry was that of Xi Jinping. His nation has its own history of suppressing a Muslim minority, detaining roughly a million Uyghurs in internal camps, and most recently, had invited international condemnation for its authoritarian crackdown in Hong Kong. Suu Kyi perhaps recognized the benefit of tacit support from China and advanced discussions of new cooperative projects. Chief among these has been the China-Myanmar Economic Corridor (CMEC), which China considers vital to the economic health of its western provinces, such as Yunnan. CMEC is a potential jewel in China's Belt and Road Initiative. As proposed, it will consist of gas and oil pipelines; railroads; a series of additional dams along the Irrawaddy; and a "special economic zone" to facilitate trade, not just in Myanmar, but throughout southern Asia and beyond, as this massive undertaking will connect China to the vast Indian Ocean trading routes, especially for oil.

The coup on February 1, 2021, and the arrest of Aung San Suu Kyi threw all of that into renewed turmoil and uncertainty. She had continued to enjoy the support of the people, even as she cozied up to the Chinese and pursued policies that critics believed resembled too closely some policies of the authoritarian junta. Arguably, it was that warmth that convinced the generals that they had had enough of the experiment with democracy. Tragically, the same transparency and international support that facilitated the 2015 election that brought Suu Kyi back into government did not stop the military from rejecting the election results, using the spurious pretext of electoral fraud, and spiraling the country downward into the tragic chaos of nationwide conflict compounded by economic, humanitarian, and COVID-19-related crises. The military commander in chief, Min Aung Hlaing, will be on the wrong side of history, and the Myanmar people will never forgive him for ignoring their will and destroying the burgeoning democracy they enjoyed for only a few years prior.

And, just as China's leaders had declined to join the rest of the world in denouncing hateful policies under Suu Kyi's government, they remained relatively silent when the generals seized back control and put her once again under arrest. This is what the world needs to understand: China's only interest in the political outcome in Myanmar is that whoever is in power there will preserve internal stability while remaining friendly enough to allow China to reap the rewards on its investments. Beijing has little interest in whether Myanmar's government is democratically elected, ensures basic civil rights, or treats all its citizens equally under the law. China isn't in the business of promoting its ideology in other countries. Rather, it looks to take out of those countries whatever it deems necessary for its survival, such as energy and natural resources, to plant its flag in places that offer some economic or geopolitical advantage— employment for its workers, access to shipping and trade routes, or even military installations.

If anyone was to doubt China's prioritization of expediency in geopolitics, they only need to look to the fall of Afghanistan in the late summer of 2021. When the US abandoned the country to Taliban control, causing most of the world beyond the Middle East to turn its back, China indicated that it would be ready to step in. Though Beijing stopped short of formally recognizing the incoming Taliban regime, it did clearly state that it "respects the right of the Afghan people to independently determine their own destiny" and will develop "friendly and cooperative relations with Afghanistan." Of course, Afghanistan's desperate need for foreign investment and infrastructure development dovetails all too nicely with China's preferred mode of incursion into developing countries. Maybe Afghanistan will become the next major link in China's Belt and Road Initiative, or maybe China will become the next in a long line of great nations that have gotten sucked into the quagmire that Afghanistan has proven to be for other powerful countries.

The experience of Afghanistan after the fall of its government in 2021 echoes that of Myanmar after the coup. By early 2022, less than a year after the junta came back into power, foreign investors were fleeing. "In just one short year, the generals have undone the gains of the past decade," wrote the editors of *The Economist*. "Employment has fallen. Dollar-a-day poverty has more than doubled, engulfing nearly half the population. In cities it has tripled. The currency has plunged by 60% in the past five months. The economy is 30% smaller than was forecast before the coup and the pandemic. Electricity blackouts are widespread. Schools are, in effect shut." Energy companies from France, Australia, and the US pulled out, as have a large Indian shipping concerns and even a Chinese company.

Afghanistan, too, faced a major humanitarian crisis only months after the Taliban takeover. While tens of millions of Afghans were facing the prospect of famine, and less than a quarter of the country's health clinics were operational, the Taliban denied that any crisis existed. "The refusal of Taliban officials to publicly acknowledge the country's growing crisis is exacerbating a problem that they didn't solely create," wrote Jane Ferguson in *The New Yorker*. "One of the largest blunders of the two-decade-long U.S.-led effort in Afghanistan was a failure to build a self-sustaining economy, which has now resulted in financial free fall—unpaid workers, starving families. The country's government remains chronically aid-dependent and unable to generate significant tax revenue." Contained in that analysis are some of the fundamental goals of development that this book addresses, in summary: self-reliance enabled by broad-based economic growth, competent and inclusive governance, and the ability to generate and harness a country's own resources.

● ● ● ● ● ●

What is the right balance between fostering development for its own sake—because it's in the enlightened self-interest of countries of abundance like the US to do what it can to help lower- and middle-income countries to lift themselves up—and fostering development to advance American interests?—In the case of Myanmar, the US commitment to democratic movements was tested. Many questions were raised, and the answers remain unclear.

Both the United States and China find themselves somewhat paralyzed by indecision, with each great power able to rationalize actions for or against the competing factions in Myanmar. The road forward will be trickier for the US, however, for the simple reason that it has no consistent record or policy concerning Myanmar and can't quite articulate what it wants to see happen next. China, on the other hand, has clear and specific ambitions regarding Myanmar, is already deeply committed on a number of fronts, and is explicit in its development policy about not considering issues like democracy or human rights in its aid program. There's a big difference between America's ambivalence and China's noncommittal attitude. Beijing has begun paying some lip service to bringing more transparency and altruism to its foreign aid programs. As set out in its January 2021 white paper, titled "China's International Development Cooperation in the New Era," China's stated policy is that Chinese infrastructure projects need to dovetail with the developing strategies of "participant" countries, which those countries should control and direct. The paper speaks about aid in terms of "economic cooperation," and says the right things about the interplay of trade, investment, and development.

Franklin Roosevelt is rumored to have said of Nicaraguan dictator Anastasio Somoza, "He may be a son of a bitch, but he's our son of a bitch." That statement later encapsulated the fundamental irony at the heart of American foreign policy during the Cold War era. The United States convinced itself that it would do what it had to do in the service of stopping the communist threat to liberty and justice for all. All too often, from Latin America to Africa to Southeast Asia, we tried to protect democracy by throwing our support behind anti-democratic forces. Of course, the Cold War was beyond strange as a moment in history. Two great superpowers were competing for moral and political domination, each amassing great armies and arsenals, willing to risk the destruction of the planet in pursuit of their competing national ideals. Time after time, as the US moved to support pro-democracy efforts, Washington would eventually face a tough decision between acting on behalf of the people and risking conflict with the Soviet Union. Today's superpower competition is more about economics, resources, supply chains, and whose standards will be used. Who's to say that the stakes aren't just as high?

Myanmar stands to benefit in very practical and immediate ways from its cooperation with China. It's most likely too late for the US to make the kind of meaningful hard investments that China has already made. So what did Aung San Suu Kyi hope to gain by improving that relationship? Historically, it has meant a lot to be in the good graces of the US. Some will argue that the American seal of approval has lost some of its value, but the US is still the dominant global force for transparent democracy and human rights. The US had played a meaningful role in Myanmar's economic and political development, and a less self-interested one than China has played. For ten years, Myanmar had been on a solid upward trajectory. One could argue that if the generals had held off just a little longer, even five more years for the economy to mature, Myanmar would now be better positioned to make decisions about its future that were grounded in moral values, not just economic need.

And here exactly is where we see the potential importance of the soft-power tool kit. Let's stipulate that it's in America's interest that Myanmar develop into a functional, multi-party system with a self-sustaining economy—a "non-vassal state" making mean-ingful contributions to global and regional well-being. Imagine, for example, that a generation of Myanmar's political elite and business leaders had benefited from education and training offered by the US, including through partnerships between the US and local universi-ties and attendance by some in the United States. What if education in engineering offered by the US had made Myanmar less depen-dent on government-backed Chinese construction companies, or if economic advisors had helped the country to mobilize and allo-cate domestic resources by establishing a better internal tax base? What if the US had engaged with the Asian Development Bank, the World Bank, or the Development Finance Corporation more effectively or had worked in partnership with our Quad partner countries—Japan, India, Australia—to enable an alternative means of financing for core infrastructure and energy infrastructure so that Myanmar wouldn't have been so dependent on China? What if the US had joined the TPP, creating an attractive trade alternative? Perhaps Western aid workers in human rights and education, or support for political activists and journalists could have helped inform public opinion, even policy, when it came to the Rohingya. The tragedy is that real progress had been made, and maybe with a little more time, that progress would have been hard to undo.

Most significantly, what if the United States and its allies had worked together to provide Myanmar with vaccines, medical equipment, and personnel and were seen by the population as having helped Myanmar respond more effective to COVID-19? Granted, every country, no matter its economic status, had its hands full with the pandemic, but a gesture of cooperative outreach would have held meaning. Just as the humanitarian assistance offered after the 2008 cyclone served to break the ice and trigger a diplomatic thaw, imagine how big a game changer timely pandemic assistance might have been, not just in Myanmar but in so many other countries with limited resources.

The list of possibilities is long. The point is not that such tools and techniques would have made a country like Myanmar dependent on the US and its OECD partners instead of on China or would have left the country vulnerable to exploitation by the West. Nor is the point to look back and regret what America could have or should have done differently there. (I won't argue that we should have given a blank check to the military junta, or that we should have turned a blind eye to Aung San Suu Kyi's selling out of the Rohingya.) The point is that what emerging countries value most is the capacity for self-determination, to get out from under the yoke of obligation that larger global powers have often imposed. When handled deftly, the soft-power tool kit can build solid, productive relationships, not only between individuals but also between nations, based on shared principles, that can carry weight in moments of change and decision.

Investments in developing nations can and should take many different forms. It's not only about creating large influxes of capital or relieving shortages of goods, and it's not about finding new markets, natural resources, or bases of operations for the American private sector. It's about sharing knowledge and experience, perception and attitude, about enabling and empowering countries that are lower down on the development scale to make their own decisions about their development aspirations. There's no doubt that the overtures and inroads made between 2007 and 2015, even if they seemed small at the time, helped to enable the free and fair elections that appeared to set Myanmar on a course for reengagement with the international community.

Much of that progress may have been reversed, and new challenges have developed. With the US and China uncertain about how to proceed in Myanmar after the coup, the other enormous neighbor to the north, Russia, was more than willing to step in with investment and support, adding another volatile player to geopolitical confusion. And the US State Department, having for so long resisted expressing a position, declared in March 2022 that the atrocities and ethnic violence Myanmar's military has committed against the country's Rohingya minority constitute "genocide."

If we can take any lessons from the recent history of Myanmar, however, it's that assumptions and expectations can trip us up, as can hasty, knee-jerk responses to rapidly changing circumstances. Patience, observation, commitment, and expertise propel successful statecraft. The interest of the US and its allies isn't always best served by choosing sides in a fight for governmental control, but sometimes by finding the most effective ways to support the people of a country in need.

Chapter 2

AMERICA, GLOBALIZATION, AND ME

The Case for Conservative Internationalism

For too long, development was undervalued by our foreign- and national-security policy makers as an arm of American power; consequently, they have rarely used it as a lens to view strategic challenges. Although the U.S. government has undertaken a variety of steps over the past decade to elevate development to the same level of influence as defense and diplomacy it must do far more. It should not only increase development's impact but integrate it fully into American economic and diplomatic efforts by making it truly a pillar of U.S. national security and foreign policy.

—"Our Shared Opportunity: A Vision for Global Prosperity," CSIS

The publication in 1958 of *The Ugly American*, Eugene Burdick's and William Lederer's novel depicting the blunders of United States diplomats in Southeast Asia, sent shockwaves through the American public and its leaders in Washington, with profound and lasting ramifications for both statecraft and foreign assistance policy. The novel joined other seminal post-war books, like Aleksandr Solzhenitsyn's *The Gulag Archipelago* or Thomas Merton's *The Seven Storey Mountain*, in reshaping how Americans thought about themselves and their place in the world.

I read *The Ugly American* as a young man several decades after it was published, and it caused an epiphany. It was as if all my upbringing, education, and early career coalesced in the reading of that book into a reordered sensibility and purpose. I have written that the book spurred a massive reorganization of America's economic and diplomatic engagement with developing countries then emerging from European colonialism. Not only is it one of the most influential books on foreign policy in the last century, but it absolutely set me on my personal path. Twenty-odd years later, the authors' vision of a "small force of well-trained, well-chosen, hard-working, and dedicated professionals…[who] must be more expert in [a country's] problems" still lies at the heart of my vision for American foreign-assistance workers.

The roots of what we now call globalism, or internationalism, began to take hold in the middle of the last century, even before the end of World War II. Desiring to avoid repeating mistakes made after World War I, the major powers convened an unprecedented series of multinational meetings that laid the foundations of the "liberal world order" that continues to hold sway. The commitment to that new world order was instilled in me at a young age, in part through the story of my own grandfather, who had fought in Patton's army, helping liberate Europe and making that new world

order possible. That lesson would be reinforced in the next generation; my father's long career in international finance was preceded
by distinguished US Navy service.

The 1944 Bretton Woods Conference in New Hampshire
focused on economic cooperation. Franklin Roosevelt and his advisors believed firmly that free trade not only promoted international
prosperity, but that prosperity would foster international peace.
Mismanaged war reparations and then various steps taken to mitigate the effects of the Great Depression had contributed to tension
and hostility that ultimately led the world back into war, convincing
leaders around the world to work toward economic cooperation as a
means of achieving peace and prosperity. Out of that conference were
born the International Monetary Fund, the General Agreement on
Tariffs and Trade to deepen global trade ties and the International
Bank for Reconstruction and Development (IBRD), which, with
the addition of the International Development Association (IDA),
provides interest-free loans and grants to governments of the poorest
countries, and it has become the World Bank.

.   .   .   .   .

The paradigm of the interwar era, in which the judgment of many
nations was clouded by bitterness and the desire for some form
of revenge, was giving way to an intentional magnanimity. Also
in 1944, the Dumbarton Oaks Conference in Washington, DC,
undertook the initial groundwork for "a general international organization," which would eventually become the United Nations
after the San Francisco conference in 1945. Underlying the work
of all these meetings was the mutual understanding that cooperation among nations would be necessary to establish and maintain
universal peace. One of the stated goals at San Francisco was "to
achieve international co-operation in the solution of international
economic, social and other humanitarian problems." With Europe
and Asia still shattered by World War II, all the assembled parties
acknowledged their mutual interest in improving the lives of people
everywhere, even in former aggressor nations. The commitment to
nonmilitary assistance to support economic and social development

and promote integration into a progressively more peaceful and democratic global community was effectively formalized.

There were many inspirational figures working to achieve these collective goals. Particularly, I look to Arthur Vandenberg, the Republican senator from Michigan who authored a resolution in 1948 in support of regional defense alliances, leading to American participation in NATO the following year. Vandenberg had been a staunch isolationist in the years before the war. But after witnessing the Japanese attack on Pearl Harbor, he became a full-throated internationalist. The Vandenberg Resolution that he presented in the Senate, allowing for participation in defense alliances outside of the UN Security Council, enabled the United States to participate in the new NATO pact. Vandenberg also played a central role in assembling the legislation authorizing funding for the Marshall Plan, discussed below, and moving it through a Republican-controlled Congress.

There was also important work being done to prioritize moral imperatives in addition to defense and development needs. Fifty members of the new United Nations came together under the leadership of Eleanor Roosevelt, the chair of the UN Commission on Human Rights, to adopt the Universal Declaration of Human Rights as a formal resolution of the United Nations General Assembly in 1948. Its thirty articles declare that all citizens of all countries, regardless of color, creed, or religion, are entitled to fundamental rights. In addition to civil and political rights, such as to life, liberty, and freedom of speech and association, the UDHR specified economic and social rights, such as health and education. Many of these important guarantees have been under threat over the last seventy years, but the UDHR continues to provide a universally recognized foundation of international support for human rights and accountable government.

At the same time, the United States asserted its new identity as a global power by taking on a foreign aid challenge of unprecedented magnitude: the Marshall Plan, the enormous initiative launched in 1948 to support post-war European rebuilding and recovery. The Marshall Plan combined idealism with self-interest, as is the case with most foreign-aid efforts. The United States had learned that it was important to be magnanimous in victory, and certainly, the battered countries of Europe could not have gotten back on their feet so quickly.

US assistance was driven, at least in part, by geopolitical necessity and enlightened self-interest. With the Soviet Union backing away from the post-war commitments to peace, the tensions of the Cold War had begun to take shape. The Communist Party had just taken control of Czechoslovakia in a Soviet-backed coup, and the American government, terrified by the looming spread of communism, realized it would have to help Europe get back on its feet quickly lest, one by one, countries start falling under Soviet domination. That would take quite a bit more than anything the World Bank or IMF could make happen.

The tools of the Marshall Plan included loans to private industry, infrastructure projects, and public health initiatives, but also what might be called soft economic assistance, and a form of strategic planning, management advice, and training at all levels, in order to get various industrial sectors reintegrated into national economies. The influx of American capital and expertise represented only a very small percentage of the GDP of the recipient countries—but it certainly accelerated economic recovery and political stability, catalyzing other public and private investment, and at the same time strengthening national relationships. One of the great lessons of the post-war experience in Europe is that foreign aid doesn't work in a vacuum but only in partnership with the recipient. Aid is always a supporting actor in someone else's drama. The country in need has to have what's referred to as "country ownership"—strong leadership, intentionality, and a clear vision of its future. In retrospect, many historians have credited the success of the plan to the fact that most of the recipient countries had been so advanced before the war, with functional governments and established institutions, engaged citizens, and strong formal economies. They've also suggested that foreign aid has proved slower to succeed in less developed parts of the world, where the aid effort more often involved the need for countries to create, instead of to rebuild, institutions.

Still, the country-specific, catalytic, multi-year design of the Marshall Plan persists today as part of the DNA for American assistance programs. Development fads come and go, but the basic architecture remains. Perhaps most significant but less recognized was the long-term impact of the Marshall Plan on future geopolitics. The plan's advisors sought to get business and political leaders to think bigger, to consider their individual concerns as part of a larger national and regional enterprise, which actively advanced the integration of Western Europe, ultimately facilitating the formation of the European Union.

Beyond the effort in Western Europe, it might not have been easy to tell the difference between United States foreign aid initiatives and other strategic foreign policy moves over the next decade or so. The Cold War—the division of the world into essentially two armed camps, plus what were quaintly called "non-aligned" countries—dominated political consciousness and motivated most, if not all, initiatives between the US and any other nation. It wasn't until the early 1960s that foreign assistance took the next big step forward, spurred in part by the publication of *The Ugly American* and in part by the election of John F. Kennedy to the presidency.

Kennedy engineered the Foreign Assistance Act of 1961, which created the United States Agency for International Development, or USAID, and consolidated five previous development agencies into one. His administration also created the Peace Corps, which introduced a whole new cadre of educated young people to development work, and the United States Army Special Forces—the Green Berets. The relevance of this elite military unit to internationalism lay in the humanitarian and peacekeeping components of its mandate, which demanded knowledge of local languages and cultures. If one specific aid initiative defined JFK's ambition, it would be the Alliance for Progress, a program to foster economic cooperation and integration with Latin America. It had only been about two years since Richard Nixon, then the vice president, had been physically attacked by a mob in Venezuela. The attackers protested the United States' support for dictatorial regimes in the Western Hemisphere and our preference for addressing security over economic needs in our aid.

Kennedy intended to create real long-term economic partnerships between the US and Latin American countries, but the program could never be completely divorced from American efforts to stop the spread of Soviet-led communism. The prospect of another

Cuban-style revolution leading to some kind of domino effect so close to our shores terrified Washington. And even the best-intentioned development efforts were constantly overshadowed by events like the Cuban Missile Crisis or the disastrous Bay of Pigs invasion, which did so much damage to American credibility in the region. While the president had come to understand that the battle for the developing world would be fought on economic ground, there was some element of genuine altruism in the bones of the Alliance for Progress. Kennedy wanted to "complete the revolution of the Americas, to build a hemisphere where all men can hope for a suitable standard of living and all can live out their lives in dignity and in freedom."

It would be interesting to speculate about what might have happened if JFK had paid the same attention to Africa as he did to Latin America. Africa had been almost entirely decolonized in the post-war years, but by 1960, there were more US foreign service officers in West Germany alone than in all of Africa—a testament to the strategic concerns of the moment. The administration, including USAID, looked at the continent perhaps a little paternalistically, with JFK believing he could win over African leaders on a personal level, and that alone would protect access to valuable resources. The steady parade of Africans on state visits to the White House became almost a running joke at the time, but very little in the way of aid materialized to address living conditions, governance, economic infrastructure, or other fundamental development needs.

The aid model that arose in the Kennedy years held sway in the US for the next twenty-odd years, as the deepening Cold War played out in different parts of the world. This was the America into which I was born, a country under a cloud of constant threat and anxiety. Still, my upbringing instilled in me a kind of faith—the conviction that the liberal world order established after World War II had, in fact, succeeded in keeping the peace. Yes, there had been awful wars and revolutions, but no global conflagrations, no hideous exchanges between the two great superpowers. When people question the ongoing need or value of that order, or of the giant global institutions underlying it, I acknowledge that some updating and re-prioritizing are certainly needed, but that the peace continues to hold. The liberal world order is one of the greatest achievements in modern history. Conflict is anti-development, while development and economic integration disincentivize conflict.

From the mid-1960s, US foreign aid attention spread into Africa, Asia, and the Middle East. Regional aid efforts, often of limited duration, have, over the years, been at least partially motivated by the geopolitical imperatives of the times, most often the Cold War fear of Soviet expansion. JFK's successors, Lyndon Johnson and Richard Nixon, proved less enthusiastic in their support for his aid program, and soon, the disaster in Vietnam, where the US had earlier embarked on multiple development projects, came to symbolize not just a failure of diplomacy and military policy, but also of foreign assistance, particular assistance that was informed by strategic motivations. What had been full-throated bipartisan support for foreign aid began to weaken, leading, as the Vietnam War was drawing to its ignoble end in the early 1970s, to a set of reforms collectively called New Directions. In Congress as well as in the aid community, there was a desire to disassociate foreign aid from the military, to eliminate any suspicion that development work was bound up with intelligence activity. The focus would be on "the poorest of the poor" and on basic human needs: food, medicine, and housing, especially in rural areas, as opposed to large-scale infrastructure projects or loans to industry. Programs targeted agriculture, family planning, and education instead.

A case can be made that New Directions and subsequent changes to the aid apparatus fixed things that weren't necessarily broken. At its inception, USAID brought together several agencies, streamlining and coordinating aid efforts. As new agencies came into being in the Johnson era and subsequently, each with a specific narrow agenda, some of that cohesion was lost, and strategy became more muddled. The focus on humanitarian aid may also have crowded out valuable infrastructure projects and programs related to economic and social policy and democratic governance, the lack of which would have ramifications into the present day.

A major aid concern during the Johnson years was India, the leading non-aligned country of the Cold War era, with a population larger than all of Africa and Latin America combined. India experienced a devastating famine and was rescued from mass starvation by US assistance, even though that humanitarian effort went forward under a Cold War cloud, with the USSR also vying to supply aid, through which it could wield influence. The aid to India involved massive quantities of grain, but much more: technological assistance to enable advancements in seeds and processes, roads, irrigation, infrastructure, training, and education. The "green revolution" in India modernized large-scale agriculture and helped bend the curve of global trends in development toward both food and population control.

Attention to the human dimension of development has remained a central priority of foreign assistance for the last fifty years. The results have been significant, with demonstrable improvements around the world in basic education, literacy, public health, local infrastructure, and so on. Reflecting this perspective on aid, the United Nations Development Program launched the Human Development Index (HDI) in 1990 "to shift the focus of development economics from national income accounting to people-centered policies." The HDI measured the progress of countries in life expectancy, education, and GDP per capita. This represented an important evolution in how development is measured and understood. But like New Directions, it did not directly address the larger contexts of economic policy, governance, or rule of law that ultimately enable self-reliance.

Not all the factors that propel progress along these lines are direct or quantifiable. Achieving the kinds of progress measured by the HDI requires leadership. Aid workers seek to work in partnerships with local political leaders, who, in the best of circumstances, recognize that reducing the number of orphans in their country or eradicating malaria would translate into popular support. Supporting education and training of future leaders, whether in the US or in their own countries, has been one of the most important tools of soft power over the last fifty years, so much so that a later chapter is devoted to the topic. The US has committed an enormous amount of scholarship money for at least two cohorts of business leaders and political figures from the developing world who received advanced degrees from American universities while simultaneously supporting constructive relationships between those schools and developing country universities. Think of Barack Obama's father, who came to the University of Hawaii for a PhD in economics, or

Gebisa Ejeta, a plant geneticist and agronomist from rural Ethiopia who studied at schools there that were partnered with the University of Oklahoma before coming to the US for graduate work at Purdue. Dr. Ejeta received the 2009 World Food Prize for developing the first high-yielding hybrid sorghum plants resistant to drought and certain parasites, which enhanced food security for hundreds of millions of people in sub-Saharan Africa.

Sending trained economists, urban planners, MBAs, public-health specialists, or engineers and other experts back to their home countries to become government officials, or teachers, or entrepreneurs is enlightened self-interest on at least two levels. First, and most important, improving the quality of leadership helps move countries up on the development scale, bringing them closer to self-reliance. And second, we can at least hope that the contacts they make and the values they absorb during those years of education are Western, rather than what they might acquire while studying at, say, a university in Beijing.

During the Vietnam era, USAID had more than 10,000 employees, but the changing priorities and reduced funding through the 1970s and 1980s brought about a substantial reduction in those numbers. After Ronald Reagan took office, foreign aid again became more closely tied to strategic concerns.

The Reagan administration did take aim at a number of international priorities. On the practical development front, the Caribbean Basin Economic Recovery Act of 1983 made possible the Caribbean Basin Initiative, which provided tariff and trade benefits that allowed much freer access to US markets for countries of Central America and the Caribbean. The CBI sought to enable more economic integration in the hemisphere, enabling upward progress on the development scale.

On a much grander scale, Ronald Reagan delivered a speech to the British Parliament in 1982 in which he called for a global initiative "to foster the infrastructure of democracy—the system of a free press, unions, political parties, universities—which allows a people to choose their own way, to develop their own culture, to reconcile their own differences through peaceful means." The following year, Congress authorized the National Endowment for Democracy (NED), about half of whose funding goes to support four core organizations: the National Democratic Institute, the International Republican Institute, the labor-focused Solidarity Center, and the Center for International Private Enterprise. The other half is granted to hundreds of nonprofits and civil society groups around the world and is used to support the NED's own research and studies.

NED would be unique in that it was publicly funded through the State Department but privately managed so that it operated independently of government. One goal of the organization would be to allow democracy promotion work to operate in full public view, where it would not be mistakenly conflated with intelligence activities. NED inspired similar pro-democracy institutes in many other countries. And fifteen years later, it gave rise to a multinational Movement for Democracy to promote positive engagement among political leaders, civil society, and the private sector. When NED first started, a little more than a third of the world lived in democracies. Forty years later, that number is well over half, but the world is trending in dangerous directions, in what some are calling a "third wave of autocracy." Established democracies from the Americas to Europe and Asia are now threatened by the persistent erosion of public trust and the subsequent weakening of their institutions.

· · · · · ·

In 1989, the ground shifted again when the Berlin Wall came down, and the Soviet Union, the existence of which had been either explicitly or implicitly driving so much American development work, collapsed. The United States would, of course, have a host of new development concerns as former Soviet-bloc countries now needed to find paths to self-reliance. But suddenly, there was less perceived urgency about military spending and humanitarian aid. This would be the "peace dividend" from the end of the Cold War, with the bipartisan consensus in Congress being that those concerns would somehow be addressed by the global community. The fall of the USSR caused the US to do some reordering of its soft-power priorities, looking to step in to assist with democratic reforms, privatization, and the development of market-based economies, but also reducing funding and attention to some traditional development relationships.

The private sector, however, saw the opening of the former Soviet Union as a potential bonanza. Companies fell over each other as they rushed in to unlock new markets, form new partnerships, and get in on the ground floor of new investment opportunities. At the time, the prospect of all these countries suddenly blossoming in vibrant self-reliance perhaps blinded many people to the enormity of that challenge. Core industries and infrastructure—even as inferior as it was—had been owned and managed by the state or by Moscow and operated in noncompetitive markets with rigid price and wage controls for so long, accounting for millions of jobs and dictating societal norms. Moreover, the original Marshall Plan did not extend beyond the Berlin Wall. The Soviet Union had blocked participation by Eastern Europe, so those countries had never benefited from the capital or expertise that had flowed into Western Europe and propelled modernization and rehabilitation.

Although its direct aid capability was somewhat curtailed on a macro level, USAID sought to harness the enthusiasm of the private sector and facilitate the transition in several ways, most notably the creation, in concert with other countries, of the European Bank for Reconstruction and Development, the EBRD, and the establishment of ten "enterprise funds" for Eastern Europe and Eurasia. These institutions were intended to enable a public-private partnerships model that would help countries transition to democratic societies and market economies. They helped create financial structures and instruments where none had previously existed in areas like mortgage lending, credit financing, and investment banking.

In addition, the George H.W. Bush administration launched a new initiative in 1990, the Citizens Democracy Corps (CDC), an organization that would "support democratic change and market-oriented economic reform," according to a White House statement, by mobilizing volunteers and private-sector initiatives. Unlike the Peace Corps, which was an agency of the US government, the CDC would be self-sustaining through independent financing after a small federal grant got it off the ground. This group has morphed over the twenty-five years of its existence and merged with or absorbed other groups. It is now known as PYXERA and has established partnerships in over ninety countries between multinational corporations, national development agencies, local governments, and NGOs. This kind of working partnership would be the model for the work I would do at USAID fifteen years later.

While these efforts resulted in huge successes, especially in the Baltic states, Poland, and the Czech Republic, achieving self-reliance would prove more difficult in countries with more complicated national identities, or that saw an opportunity to revisit old regional conflicts, or that lacked basic governmental institutions after the long dependence on Moscow. A fair amount of handwringing persists, however, over the fact that the efforts to establish good governance have not kept pace with economic development. Kazakhstan, for example, boasts a vibrant, growing economy without yet establishing itself as a functioning democracy, while Russia has moved steadily away from accepted democratic practices. EBRD, for its part, built requirements for governance and democratic reforms into its grants and investments, which at first seem to yield positive results. The EBRD actually cut off Russia after Russia's invasion of Ukraine and annexation of Crimea in 2014—a tough but correct call, given that Russia had been the bank's largest lending client.

It could be argued that US missteps in the years after the fall of the Berlin Wall might have exacerbated geopolitical tensions. The situation in Russia could be likened to that in Germany after WWI. I had the unique opportunity to be in Russia in 1989, just at the time the wall came down in Berlin. I traveled across the country from Moscow and St. Petersburg to Irkutsk and Bratsk and even made it to still Soviet-dominated Mongolia and Uzbekistan. People were talking about the unlimited potential of the newly liberated countries of Eastern Europe, but nothing I saw in Russia at the time would have made anyone optimistic. The society and economy were so closed. The people were poor and, at least to my teenage American eyes, backward. Food was rationed, the infrastructure was antiquated and inadequate, there was no private enterprise, and the military was everywhere.

In the ensuing decade, the United States made both financial investments and commitments of technical assistance to help Russia make the transition into a free-market democracy. The Russian Democracy Act of 2002 allocated continued assistance based on the stated premise that "a democratic and economically stable Russian Federation is inherently less confrontational and destabilizing in its foreign policy and therefore that the promotion of democracy in Russia is in the national security interests of the United States."

Still, some argue that much more could have been done. An economy in desperate need of modernization could have benefited from something akin to the Marshall Plan to rebuild industries and institutions, encourage public-private partnerships, establish economic infrastructure, and so on. Thirty years on, the story of progress for the former member states of the Soviet Union is a mixed bag, with many notable success stories, in terms of both economics and governance. In some countries, authoritarianism has yet to release its grip, while in others, economic growth has been tempered by democratic backsliding. Many countries have become members of the European Union and some have been accepted in the OECD, but overtures from NATO have been seen as a provocation by Russia, driven by the United States, most perilously in relation to Ukraine.

With the specter of communism removed, a new set of global challenges came into focus: environmental issues, HIV/AIDS, narcotics, radicalization and terrorism, and anti-democratic movements. As it began to dawn on leaders that these challenges would never be effectively managed by individual countries acting in isolation, the old vocabulary of "multilateral alliances" and "internationalism" began to give way to "globalization."

Several factors led to the shrinking of the USAID workforce during the Clinton years. First was the administration's "reinventing government" program, in which agencies were streamlined to concentrate on the core work inherent to government—goal setting, program design, strategic planning—leaving the on-the-ground execution of those agendas to be contracted out to nongovernmental entities. Just as importantly, congressional conservatives led by North Carolina Senator Jesse Helms, the chairman of the Senate Foreign Relations Committee, believed that the "peace dividend" created by the end of the Cold War included the opportunity to dismantle the US foreign aid apparatus. By 2002, USAID direct-hire personnel had fallen by 37 percent, while the number of countries in which the agency was active nearly doubled. What arose to fill the gap was the vast network of NGOs, consultants, academics, and private contractors that we can think of as the "development-industrial complex." This new operational model for foreign aid has come in for its share of vilification. Critics complain about what they perceive as the cushy sinecures and bloated budgets of entrenched private development firms. Yet they often fail to recognize the sacrifices made by the majority of aid workers around the world, especially those who have been imprisoned, injured, or killed as a result of their work. Perhaps a more legitimate concern is that as the government contracted out more of its aid work, it risked losing control of the larger strategy and purpose, effectively contracting out the very thinking behind the aid effort. In some of the more troubled parts of the world, for instance, in Haiti, the many aid organizations can wind up working outside of any unified plan, often to the frustration of the struggling population.

The 1990s were not a good time for aid work to be so decentralized and fragmented. Arguably, voters found George Bush to be overly consumed by international affairs, enabling Clinton to win the presidency by concentrating on domestic issues. The Clinton administration faced challenges that required responses involving defense, development, and diplomacy: Somalia, Rwanda, Bosnia, and Haiti, to name a few. Aid organizations would have to step in to help rebuild societies in failed nations that had been ravaged by conflict. By the year 2000, globalization had become the most powerful force in development, meaning that traditional aid donors like the US looked more to the opening up of borders and markets, new trade alliances, foreign investment opportunities, and digital connectivity to fuel economic growth around the world. That new dynamic would bring its own problems and challenges and would spark approaches to international development that enabled and encouraged that kind of activity.

Globalization can be seen as a product of the post-Cold War world, in which a relaxation of the great East-West power struggle allowed policy makers to turn their attention to more lofty long-range ambitions. It was in this context that the 1992 UN Framework Convention on Climate Change and the 1997 Kyoto Protocol to operationalize the convention were adopted and that the United Nations established the Millennium Development Goals in 2000, to which all member nations and twenty-two international organizations committed. The impetus for the MDGs was provided by the OECD's Development Assistance Committee, which functions like the Major League Baseball commissioner of development. The DAC, chaired in the later 1990s by Ambassador James Michel, sought to promote international development goals that would attract broad support and advance a consensus on a partnership approach to locally owned development at a time of diminishing confidence in foreign assistance and dwindling development budgets. The eight MDGs, targeting developing nations, were to: reduce extreme poverty and hunger; achieve universal primary education; promote gender equality and empower women; reduce child mortality; improve maternal health; combat HIV/ AIDS, malaria, and other diseases; ensure environmental sustainability; and develop a global partnership for development. To help achieve these goals, the G8 finance ministers agreed in June 2005 to provide enough funds to international financial institutions to cancel billions of dollars in debt owed by members of the heavily indebted poor countries. The MDGs would provide an important measurement framework for development until evolving into the Sustainable Development Goals in 2015, which would set out a development agenda for 2030 applying to all countries, not just developing countries.

The terrorist attack on the United States on September 11, 2001 signaled the next and most recent fulcrum moment in aid and development. Throughout the prior decade, many leaders and policy makers had begun to operate under the assumption that globalization was inevitable and that as they developed, countries would naturally plug into a Western-led international system and move inexorably toward democratic governance. Over time, and with some assistance, that would naturally lead countries to prosperity. The 9/11 attacks, and all that happened afterward, shattered that idea for many, a disillusionment that would be repeated in the financial crisis of 2008 and later with the Russian invasions of Georgia and Ukraine.

Despite so much attention being diverted to global anti-terrorism, the immediate post-9/11 period saw an enormous uptick in aid spending, highlighted by major new initiatives. In 2004, Congress established the Millennium Challenge Corporation, a foreign aid agency that would operate independently of USAID and the State Department. The MCC was novel in a number of ways. For starters, the agency assisted only countries that met established standards and indicators of ruling justly, investing in people, and economic freedom. Eligible countries would develop and submit proposals, and once a grant was approved, that country would be responsible for managing all aspects of implementation. The program fit neatly into the good-governance and anti-corruption agenda that had taken hold as a foreign-aid priority during the George W. Bush administration. Development, however, is rarely linear, as is evidenced by the erratic progress in some of the former Soviet-bloc states. Many of the countries that once were awarded MCC compacts are no longer eligible under the applicable criteria, as in the case of El Salvador or Honduras.

That administration also committed to PEPFAR, the US President's Emergency Plan for AIDS Relief, the largest commitment by any nation to address a single disease in history until the advent of the COVID-19 pandemic. The implementation of PEPFAR was spread over multiple agencies within the US government, working with partners in fifty countries around the world. Over $85 billion has been committed to the program since its inception in 2003. Arguably, the experience of PEPFAR should have better prepared the US to play a global leadership role in combating COVID-19.

I came to USAID in the immediate aftermath of 9/11. Having spent my early working years in international finance, I felt compelled to move into policy and development work. I was fortunate to work under the leadership of Andrew Natsios, who ran the agency from 2001 to 2006 and is responsible for taking it into the future. My concentration was in the kind of multi-stakeholder public-private partnerships that would be needed given the way the world had changed. Consider that in the 1960s, 70 percent of resources flowing to the developing world were foreign aid overseas direct assistance (primarily from the United States). The remaining 30 percent would have been in the form of foreign direct investment, remittances (money sent home by workers outside their country of origin), private philanthropy, and so on. With globalization and the expansion of international trade capital markets, foreign aid became a much smaller fraction of our economic engagement with developing countries. By 2000, that balance had completely reversed, with only 20 to 30 percent of resources coming from foreign aid. And by 2020, that had fallen to 10 percent or less. Also, over recent decades, domestic resources of many developing countries have become their most important source of financing for development. These shifts should be seen as part of many positive trends in the world.

The development picture had become much more complex, with many new players, from wealthier and more capable local governments to multinational corporations looking to develop emerging markets and work with global human talent. Other factors like increased trade, foreign investment, global education, travel, and migration combined to make the new multi-stakeholder partnerships I was working on a viable next step. So, for instance, economic growth in large sections of Africa would depend on internet access, which would mean electrification, digital hardware such as black boxes, telecom cabling and wireless capacity, and trained personnel to maintain and repair all that infrastructure. USAID effectively became the Johnny Appleseed of the internet there, providing some funding for hardware and working with manufacturers to train locals on their equipment. Much of this was made possible by the Leland Initiative, which sought to increase internet connectivity in Africa by empowering local private-sector companies and governments to work with multinational companies to install, manage, and promote the systems. So, an internet provider in an African country today may be the result of a working partnership between USAID, a multinational tech company, an NGO, and a local energy supplier from the late 1990s or early 2000s.

Similarly, USAID would work with companies in certain commodities, like coffee, to establish new sources of beans, train farmers in advanced techniques, help organize and enable consortia, guarantee markets and prices, work with local governments and regulators, and manage supply chains, with the goal of ensuring economic and even social gains for all stakeholders. The success of such enterprises would require engaging not only with the private sector but also with labor rights organizations, government labs and scientists, NGOs, community leaders, public health and education, and more. The Global Development Alliance office that I directed at USAID would bring such efforts to reality, acting as a convener, catalyzer, and accelerator for change.

My colleagues and I worked hard to institutionalize this partnership approach in addition to the current emphasis in development on domestic resource management, taxes and a formal economy, and the renaissance of development finance. All of this rose to the fore during Andrew Natsios's tenure and with the support of other key figures like Secretary of State Colin Powell. Today, the World Economic Forum is founded on the multi-stakeholder solution to problems.

The Obama Administration deserves credit for emphasizing development in its National Security Strategy and in promulgating the first US Global Development Policy. But there was little in the way of new development initiatives during the Obama administration. The administration did undertake an updated version of the Alliance for Progress, called the Alliance for Prosperity, and the great-power competition was no longer a prime motivator. The stated purpose of the initiative was to address the pressing concerns of the 2010s—the conditions driving mass migration from the Northern Triangle countries of the Americas. Some processes or mechanisms came into (or came back into) fashion: budget support, which directed aid money directly into a recipient country's treasury to be allocated to specific sectors and priorities to cushion the short-term impact of economic reforms, and a move to provide aid money to local NGOs, known in the aid world as "local solutions." These were not seismic shifts, however, and in fact, not much new came out of the Obama years, which was focused more on "rebuilding at home." His administration provided adequate stewardship of existing efforts but spent more political capital on his domestic agenda.

When President Obama initiated an "Alliance for Prosperity" for Central America, inspired by the Alliance for Progress, great power competition was not a prime motivator. The stated purpose of the initiative was to address the pressing concerns of the 2010s—

the conditions driving mass migration from the Northern Triangle countries of Central America to the United States. Current events demonstrate that the challenge of migration driven by insecurity and lack of economic opportunity remains with us.

The ensuing Trump administration came in with limited appetite for global initiatives. Even so, it came forward with some of the boldest ideas since the Bush administration, including a reauthorization of the US Export-Import Bank (EXIM) and a major revamping of the Overseas Private Investment Corporation (OPIC). We'll examine those institutions, and their place in the development world, in a later chapter.

There was, however, an important shift in attitude that started to take shape perhaps around 2013 or 2014 and that became more concrete during the Trump presidency: the realization that the world was edging closer to a new bilateral power competition between the United States and China. Virtually every step by the Trump team related to international affairs was taken in response to the growing presence of China.

Forces in my political party have been vocal in recent years about their unhappiness with globalization. Even the most ardent "America First" supporters insist on other countries helping shoulder the burdens of the world's problems, acknowledging that even the United States can't go it alone. As a conservative internationalist, I don't merely accept globalization as inevitable; I embrace it as vital. I do not envision that the United States can, or even should, play the role of the world's fixer. But I do believe that we must use every tool at our disposal to help developing nations move toward self-reliance and become viable allies and partners. The history of foreign aid tells us that targeted, carefully conceived, multi-party development plans can succeed when they empower governments and populations to advance on their own terms.

Imagine an updated version of *The Ugly American*, which one could set in a fragile state like Mali, or amid the growing economic competition in Southeast Asia. In its time, the novel spurred major improvements in US policy with regard to developing countries, including foreign aid. But there remain gaps between what the United States is doing and what it could do to help shape the developing world. We must not forget the lessons and models of the past, even if some of those tools sorely need updating. After the American withdrawal from Afghanistan, for instance, the aid community had to again confront the dilemma of a country in pressing need of humanitarian aid, the provision of which could be seen as support for a profoundly undemocratic government. To my mind, the US and its allies cannot let the outrages of the Taliban allow us to turn our collective back on the people of Afghanistan. Food and medical supplies must still flow, as must targeted support for women's and girls' education and for the apparatus of a functional state with a viable banking system, even if aid organizations have to find other avenues than the Taliban government.

The EBRD still has a critically important role to play. In the thirty years of its existence, the work of this development finance institution has extended beyond Europe into Central Asia, the Middle East, and North Africa, where most of its activity is in energy, infrastructure, financial services, and manufacturing. By sustaining important markets and encouraging further economic integration with Europe and the West, the EBRD can become a force multiplier in response to the China challenge playing out via the Belt and Road Initiative. Integration can help mitigate radicalization in vulnerable societies.

The Trump administration, at first skeptical of the value of multilateral organizations, made noises about divesting the United States share in EBRD, which I thought would have been reckless, with potentially disastrous consequences in the context of a new superpower competition. I was critical of the plan, which fortunately was never set in motion. I had an even bigger battle on my hands in 2017 when Trump's proposed budget cuts called for a 30 percent decrease for diplomacy and development, which would have eliminated essential programs while gutting humanitarian aid and multilateral support. As part of the drastic cuts and reorganization the administration was asking for, the idea of merging USAID into the State Department was floated. It seemed like no one else in Washington saw that as problematic, but to me, it would be another nail in the coffin of US influence around the world. I worked to remind people of what had happened to the United States Information Agency (USIA) when it was subsumed by State. USIA had been a vitally important public diplomacy vehicle, with a large, uniquely specialized staff whose work was poorly under-stood, undervalued, and underfunded at State, effectively cutting the agency's legs out from under it. I envisioned the same fate for USAID and worked hard writing and lobbying to get that plan shelved. USAID was able to remain independent, although it was determined that the agency head would continue to report to the secretary of state.

International development has come a long way since the 1950s. But in fragile and conflict-affected areas, the US government could do a much better job of working collectively across development, diplomacy, and defense. While the United States was able to weather communism, it has had less success against geopolitical competitors like Russia and China, which reap the benefits of the post-World War II order without full willingness to participate in it. America's long-term interests are best served by ensuring the rise of like-minded partner countries around the world that can maintain the rules-based liberal world order that has kept the peace for nearly four generations.

Chapter 3

NATIONS READY FOR PRIME TIME

Not Your Grandparents' Developing World

E verybody wanted out of Afghanistan. I opposed both the timing and manner of our withdrawal. The American public stopped paying attention long ago, despite the very small amount of loss of US personnel in our final years there. And I'd bet that by the summer of 2021, the average person on the street couldn't articulate why we were still in Afghanistan, no less why we had invaded in the first place. Democrats and Republicans in Washington predictably griped about the missteps of opposition administrations and even about presidents from their own parties, an indication of the mess that our involvement in Afghanistan had become and the absence of viable political options. Donald Trump handed the mess over to Joe Biden, having signed on to a withdrawal plan that even some senior members of his own party considered to be a recipe for disaster. The Biden administration, as eager as anyone to get the US out of another "forever war," was happy to use the previous administration's commitment for cover and committed itself to following through with the plan. I agree with the assessment of many veteran South Asia hands in Washington, including former ambassador Michael McKinley, that Biden's precipitous pullout was a mistake, but that mistake wasn't made in a vacuum. Rather, it came after years of miscalculations and unfocused policy, combined with the fractious dysfunction of the government in Kabul.

While there is no shortage of presidents and policy makers at whom we can legitimately point the finger of blame, what will never be in doubt is that chaos and desperation triggered by the US departure represents a human tragedy, arguably a preventable one. I think about it the same way I think of Vietnam in 1975 and Cuba in 1958. The US had picked a side, and our side had lost. I worry that Afghanistan could end up like Ethiopia in the early 1980s where there was an internal conflict along with major drought and food insecurity: Immoral. Outrageous. As the Taliban overran the country throughout that summer, I was stunned by the complacency, the lack of emotion and compassion among my Washington cohort. Even after the fall of the country was a fait accompli, I continued to call for "humanitarian parole" to allow as many Afghans as possible into the US, regardless of their political status. I made it my business to do at least one thing every day in support of Afghanistan and its refugees.

It is also possibly one of the greatest wastes of American talent and effort in memory. When the United States established itself there in the early 2000s, Afghanistan was essentially a textbook example of a failed state. After Russia pulled its forces out in 1989, the Taliban took control over the country in the middle of a civil war in 1996. Little, if any, advancement occurred during their rule. Afghanistan had become essentially a ward of the international community, with severely limited governmental function, inadequate infrastructure, and a broken society. Worse yet, the Taliban allowed the country to be used as a training ground for terrorist organizations, most notably, of course, al-Qaeda.

Some missteps occurred almost at the start. When a grand council, a *loya jirga*, was convened at Bonn in late 2001 to pave the way for a new constitution with a commitment to the rule of law and equal rights, representatives from all competing factions with the country, including most of the powerful warlords, were included. The Taliban were not, nor was there a sufficient understanding of the true workings of more traditional elements in the society, in which faith leaders held sway. The US and its allies gravely underestimated how deeply their behavior, and the government they helped install, would be resented. At the same time, the international community failed to reckon with corruption festering in the secular political elites who were managing what passed for a government and who would be needed moving forward. Military support would be needed but would be crippled by the ongoing distraction of the parallel war in Iraq.

Since that time, countless Americans at all levels of government and in the private sector brought their expertise to bear. Trying to steer the ship at the highest level were brilliant people who were committed—for all the right reasons—to development and a peaceful settlement. These included not only McKinley but also career foreign service officers like former Deputy Chief of Mission in Afghanistan Annie Pforzheimer; Ambassador Tony Wayne, former "quarterback" for US assistance to Afghanistan; and Ambassador Rick Olson, another veteran of the office of Development and Economic Affairs in Kabul.

From my perspective, the heartbreak of Afghanistan lies in how close it came to being a success story for American assistance to people seeking political, economic, and social development. The progress we helped foster there is more significant than most Americans realize, and we cannot ignore the critical role we need to play still.

I've made Afghanistan a focus of my work for years, writing reports, articles, and papers and hosting dozens of panel discussions, roundtables, and other public events. During the Trump years, senior administration officials came to me, insisting that I continue to help keep eyes focused on the precarious situation in Afghanistan. Annie Pforzheimer, the deputy chief of mission in Kabul and then acting deputy assistant secretary of state for Afghanistan, recognizing that my work helped prevent the administration from pulling out altogether, told me to get myself over there as quickly as possible to assess the situation from the inside out.

I last visited in February of 2019, and the variety of perspectives I encountered there validated for me the soft-power strategies the US had employed since 2001 when the Bonn Agreements paved the way for a new constitution, relatively free and fair elections, education, rights for women and minorities, and a functioning finance and banking system. Even a senior cleric I spoke with, a Taliban sympathizer and no fan of the US-supported government of Ashraf Ghani, made it clear that he and his followers wanted the security forces of the US and its allies gone but hoped we would maintain a presence to continue the work on development issues. At the other end of the spectrum, the more secular elites I met at the palace, many of them bearing advanced degrees from American universities, feared any kind of US departure. "Are you going to abandon us?" they asked me again and again.

Twenty years ago, when the US invasion ended the first incarnation of Taliban rule, there were essentially no Afghan girls in school. By 2020, there were more than 3.5 million. Girls who were just entering school in the early 2000s have since entered the workforce and have held important positions across civil society, including in the elected legislature. The positive impact on Afghan culture is hard to quantify, but there are other indicators of a freer and more open society, such as the fact that by 2021, more than 60 percent of Afghans owned cell phones and more than 80 percent reported having access to them, and roughly a third of them are on social media platforms, where they can engage with each other and the world beyond their borders.

These are the kind of changes that will be hard to undo, especially when one considers that nearly two-thirds of the Afghan population is under twenty-five years of age and have spent essentially their entire lives enjoying such freedoms. I believe this is exactly what good aid and development work looks like: the empowerment of a society to realize and exercise agency and self-determination. As cataclysmic and perhaps violently repressive as a Taliban regime might be, it will need to accommodate, or at least negotiate with, all these more liberalized sectors of society if they intend to avoid further chaos or even civil war.

The United States faced some excruciating choices in the wake of the Taliban takeover, but there were hidden opportunities as well. It has become something of a trademark of US foreign policy to withhold assistance or to impose sanctions on countries whose governments carry out policies considered anathema to American ideals. And always, the question is asked: Who pays the price? In 2021, I was among the few lonely voices in Washington speaking out against our withdrawal. Knowing what was at stake for the Afghan people, and possibly the whole of the South Asian subcontinent, I argued for leaving some small contingency force in place to give the Taliban some pause, or at least make our retreat conditional, asking for certain guarantees or accommodations. There were great challenges ahead that were likely beyond the control of an inexperienced government of ideologues, especially if there was to be a sudden exodus of the educated elites that made up the civil-servant class that kept things running.

For instance, nonmilitary aid in 2019 was believed to be around 22.4 percent of Afghanistan's gross national income, or GNI. Compare that to 1.92 percent for Honduras. The Taliban will need that money to govern, to keep the country's basic infrastructure, as rudimentary as it might be, operational. Hard-liners would not be able to remain intractable in the face of such need, meaning that the US and its allies had a "carrot" with which to influence internal Afghan policy.

Moreover, Afghanistan, like many of its immediate neighbors, had struggled to become economically integrated into the larger regional and global economies. In addition to training educators and legislators, tax collectors, and government administrators over the last twenty years, international advisors and aid workers had helped Afghans improve and diversify their agricultural economy and establish "air bridges"—two-way trade relationships—with the Gulf and India. And then there was the potential of the TAPI (Turkmenistan-Afghanistan-Pakistan-India) pipeline, always seemingly in development, to move natural gas through these countries. At one time, the US facilitated talks between Afghanistan and Uzbekistan about a possible land bridge to Pakistani seaports on the Indian Ocean. If the Western alliance withdraws its money and know-how, after doing so much to develop Afghan infrastructure over the last two decades, it's no mystery which large economic power will step in to complete those projects.

Afghanistan today differs profoundly from when the Taliban first governed at the end of the last century. China, with whom it shares a small swath of border, was not the force it is today, neither regionally nor globally, always alert to new lands to exploit either as part of its Belt and Road Initiative or for the extractable resources, although tension with Pakistan remains ongoing, tied both to border disputes and ethnic or tribal conflict. I have long argued that foreign assistance stands adjacent to foreign policy, and Afghanistan is likely to test that assertion. Will the changes brought about through soft-power strategies make a return to pre-2001 conditions impossible? The Taliban has made some initial "concessions" regarding the basic education of girls, declaring that it will be allowed, although limited by stricter religious rules, and women would remain part of the workforce. At the time of this writing, women are being pushed out of public life and education for girls beyond a young age is being heavily restricted. Hopefully, these policies will be reversed. The new government will find that restricting the newly established economic integration of Afghanistan with its neighbors will reverse the progress that the population is coming to expect. It's a different world, one in which survival may literally depend on multinational partnerships and cooperation.

If we keep Afghanistan in our sights but widen our view, we can see almost breathtaking changes in the developing world, particularly since the end of the Cold War era that provided that backdrop for the last great upheaval in that country. Take a look at Colombia as one impressive example. When the Russians and the mujahadeen were fighting at the end of the last century, Colombia topped everyone's list of bad actors in the Americas. Most of the world believed its government and economy to be controlled entirely by drug cartels, the only constants being violence and lawlessness. If that wasn't literally true, a number of analyses, some classified, seemed to point to Colombia becoming a failed state. But in the fall of 2021, Colombia was among the first nations to step up and offer sanctuary to thousands of Afghan refugees, regardless of diplomatic status, until their passage to the United States could be cleared.

Each low- or middle-income country follows its unique development path, but they tend to fall into two distinct camps—those that today have maturing economies and stabilizing governmental institutions and stand poised to become relevant players in the international community, and the fragile, or failing states that seem paralyzed and unable to make progress through the stages of development that Walt Rostow identified during the Kennedy years. Our understanding of the development process has, of course, evolved since Rostow laid out his formulaic model, and it's now understood as a complex and fluid process that rarely proceeds in a straight line or in the same way from one country to the next. The more countries that break through (or "take off," as Rostow used to say), the more potential partners there are for the United States and its allies to address global challenges. The success stories during my own lifetime and career are many: Dozens of nations are richer, freer, healthier, and more self-sufficient than in my parents' time. Once dormant economies, including Bangladesh and Indonesia, are quietly establishing themselves. Yet thirty to forty states, such as Honduras and Haiti, seem unable to break the cycle of poverty and corruption that drives people to abandon their homes in search of safety and sustenance. The resulting exodus of populations imperils the future of the countries left behind while increasing the pressure on the economic and social structures of the countries that absorb them, in many cases giving rise to nationalist and authoritarian governments that are anathema both to the global order and the democratic values that the US has long sought to promote.

Many nations find themselves stuck somewhere in between or moving in the wrong direction. Afghanistan is arguably the most recent and most egregious example, with twenty years' worth of economic, social, and governmental progress set to be stymied or reversed by a reactionary regime. Venezuela, too, saw its comfortable rise derailed by a dysfunctional and unaccountable government. Global swing states, including India and Brazil, stand ready to become booming economic engines yet are wrestling with extreme poverty, challenges to responsible governance, and environmental and health catastrophes.

How does a nation like Colombia alter its course? There is, inevitably, some interplay of foreign assistance and internally driven efforts. Ultimately, the goal of development efforts is to help enable a country's people, in their unique conditions, to achieve and to realize the future they have envisioned for themselves. In the case of Colombia, foreign aid played a direct and decisive role, and the country has been a particular focus of mine since my time at USAID. I've visited multiple times and have hosted ambassadors, the interior minister, and even the president on critical visits to Washington.

As recently as the 1990s, Colombia bore the weight of an atrocious "country brand," having struggled with low-level internal conflict for decades. Even the most upper-crust Colombians trying to do business in the world had to contend with the assumption that their capital was drug money. As discussed previously, analyses in the late '90s outlined Colombia's precarious conditions, and the country seemed conceivably on its way to becoming an ungovernable criminal state plagued by violent internal conflict. Colombia was losing population from all levels of society. Those elites who hadn't emigrated or escaped to second homes in the US and elsewhere found workarounds that may have offered some security but kept them isolated, both socially and economically. The government, under President Andres Pastrana, knew it needed help but also needed to be seen as solving its own problems. With the support of a population fed up with endless drug wars (even the FARC, ostensibly a politically motivated guerrilla insurgency, used narcotics as its primary means of financing), Pastrana's government was willing to step up and take responsibility but needed the goodwill and practical support of a country like the US.

In 2000, after being approached by President Andres Pastrana, whose able ambassador had been personally knocking on doors in Congress and lobbying, President Bill Clinton approved an agreement known as "Plan Colombia" through which the two nations would partner in the effort to stem the narcotics trade, quiet the internal insurgency, and set Colombia on a new path forward. The far-reaching goals of the accord—"securing an increase in U.S. aid for counter-narcotics projects, sustainable economic development, the protection of human rights, humanitarian aid, stimulating private investment, and joining other donors and international financial institutions to promote Colombia's economic growth"— encapsulate a necessarily multi-tiered approach to meaningful and successful foreign assistance. The US provided considerable military support, to be sure, with which Colombia was able to put enough pressure on the FARC to change the dynamic of negotiations. That wouldn't have been enough to get the country moving forward, however. Soft power initiatives aimed at improving governance and financial mechanisms and infrastructure, along with the government's willingness to address the issues that had been root causes of the conflict, helped to restore the national pride that drew the elites back, which meant tax income and domestic investment, critical elements of "domestic resource mobilization"—the process by which a country self-generates the money needed to sustain itself.

For example, one initiative that arose out of Plan Colombia had USAID partnering with the Alliance for Restorative Justice and a number of Colombian organizations to find ways to reintegrate former guerrilla fighters into a broken civil society. Drawing on restorative justice models from places like South Africa and Northern Ireland, assistance was provided to ease combatants back into peaceful and productive lives in their communities, rather than fall back into the high-crime gang culture that had pervaded Colombia's large cities. Colombia needed these young men back in the mainstream workforce if a new formal economy was to take hold.

The city of Medellin, once synonymous with drug cartels, exemplifies the kind of urban renewal projects transforming Colombia. The influence of American soft power was evident in the leadership of former mayor, Sergio Fajardo, who earned a PhD in mathematics at the University of Wisconsin and who campaigned on a promise of allowing the citizenry to participate in some of the biggest public-spending decisions. Fajardo believed in the idea of "the most beautiful for the most poor" and oversaw the creation of green spaces and a futuristic Metrocable system of gondola lines that gave residents of the poor communities on the outskirts of the city access to Medellin's newest schools, libraries and museums, commerce, and new economic opportunities.

It may be hard to imagine a new metro system having such a dramatic impact on the experience of inequality, but infrastructure matters. But one Medellin local explained to a journalist from *The Telegraph* in 2018, "The metro was the beginning of all the good stuff. It was like a bridge to a different world. We suddenly realized that things could change. It was the beginning of a revolution in Medellin. It was the first positive thing that had happened in this city for decades. It gave us confidence. People got out of their barrios, their neighborhoods. They went to work in different places from where they lived. The metro became a vast bridge, joining disparate parts of the city. People mixed. They looked outward. It may be just a metro—but it changed the psychology of the city."

The Colombian economy is now revitalized, and travel and tourism had been booming until the 2020 pandemic. In Medellin, which has been called the "Colombian Miracle," the homicide rate today is about one-twentieth of what it was in the 1990s, and poverty has been reduced by nearly two-thirds. With these economic steps forward have come improvements in education, health care, and other services vital to a thriving society.

.   .   .   .   .

By the time of the Trump administration, Colombia was ready to be acknowledged as a new kind of player on the world stage. What its leaders wanted was an invitation to join the Organization for Economic Cooperation and Development, or the OECD. The thirty-eight member nations of the OECD represent the "grown-ups table" of the international community, and membership signals stability and self-sufficiency. It means that a country has, in effect, "arrived." Rather than coming to the rest of the world with its hand out in need, it is positioned to contribute and be of value. When the Trump White House needed a knowledgeable Republican to attend a high-level conference in Colombia, they approached me, presumably because of my long-standing interest in the Americas.

At the conference, Colombian officials asked for my help in engineering the OECD invitation, which I agreed would be very important. On my return to Washington, I wrote a series of timely articles that shot around Capitol Hill and the White House, as well as the State Department and the Office of the US Trade Representative. I know that happened, because when Colombia was eventually admitted to the OECD, I received a call from their ambassador, extending thanks on behalf of the Colombian president.

This is what it looks like when a country becomes a meaningful, burden-sharing partner: Even before offering to take in Afghan refugees, Colombia had sent troops to Afghanistan and Iraq as part of the multinational force, and it hosted two million Venezuelans fleeing the economic crisis there, granting them normal work status, as if issuing the equivalent of American green cards, as Venezuela had done for Colombia decades earlier.

*   *   *   *   *

Latin America had taken center stage during what I look on as the heyday of American foreign aid, starting in about 1961 with John F. Kennedy's Alliance for Progress, through which he hoped to "complete the revolution of the Americas, to build a hemisphere where all men can hope for a suitable standard of living and all can live out their lives in dignity and in freedom." We can wish that all our neighbors to the south could follow a path like Colombia's, but that has not been the case. Venezuela, for example, has taken a sudden turn in the opposite direction. Once a relatively stable, economically integrated, and increasingly affluent country, twenty-plus years of corrupt, authoritarian, and socialist rule under Hugo Chavez and then Nicolás Maduro have generated millions of refugees fleeing desperate economic conditions. Brazil, a great country on the verge of becoming a global presence, has also faced several dilemmas. For instance, the last few decades have seen the transformation of Brazil's *cerrado*, its vast central savanna, into one of the largest centers of agricultural exports in the world. But the development of the Amazon, driven by Brazil's need for security, agriculture, and industrialization, has drawn international criticism of the future of the Amazon. In Central America, Panama and Costa Rica have both climbed steadily up the development curve, while Nicaragua, run by a dictatorship, and the three countries comprising the Northern Triangle—El Salvador, Guatemala, and Honduras—suffer from security, political, and economic challenges exacerbated by our consumption of illicit narcotics, which use these countries as transit points. We will address those in more detail later in the chapter.

Arguably the most puzzling and frustrating Latin American country, at least from the development perspective, is Mexico. Until very recently, great masses of legal and illegal migrants made their way toward the United States. For the fifteen years before the pandemic, more people were crossing *to* Mexico *from* the United States than vice versa. While Mexico is still a country of origin, it is increasingly a country of transit and destination for Central American migrants.

A variety of factors have contributed to this declining migration flow. One theory is that as the Mexican economy grows stronger, there is less urgency to seek opportunities elsewhere. Michael Clemens, an economist at the Center for Global Development, posited, in a 2018 paper on foreign aid as a deterrent to emigration, that emigration decreases when countries reach a certain level of wealth, around $8,000 GDP per capita. Note that this finding is critical to understanding the twenty-first-century crisis of global migration, arguably the most significant destabilizing factor in the developing world. Mexico surpassed this level of GDP per capita in 2005, which corresponds to the beginning of major decreases in migration by Mexicans. Other economic factors include increased trade and employment. For example, NAFTA (signed in 1994) has had a positive, long-term impact on Mexico's development, global exports, and foreign direct investment. (NAFTA has become a convenient scapegoat for job loss in the US manufacturing sector, most of which should be ascribed to other factors such as automation.) Furthermore, the recession of 2007–2009 led to a decrease in jobs in construction and other sectors in the United States where illegal immigrants tended to work, which diminished incentives to migrate illegally. Demographic and social factors have also played a role in decreased migration, such as lower birth rates and perceived hostility north of the border toward Mexicans. Additionally, crossing into the United States has become increasingly difficult (due to increased security and border enforcement) and dangerous (due to human trafficking and organized crime).

Curiously, Mexico seems to represent two ends of the development spectrum. The northern part of the country, abutting the US, has been on an amazing upward trajectory, becoming more affluent and cosmopolitan. But further to the south, in Oaxaca or Chiapas, where the country abuts the Northern Triangle countries, the situation has deteriorated, with more poverty, more insecurity, and weaker governance.

.   .   .   .   .

Bangladesh is another success story. Readers of a certain age will recall the Concert for Bangladesh, organized in 1971 by former Beatle George Harrison and Indian sitar virtuoso Ravi Shankar. The media at the time was awash in horrific pictures of devastation in the wake of warfare, genocide, and famine from Bangladesh, also called East Pakistan after a failed war of independence. The concert raised millions of relief dollars at the time, but as so often happens, the crisis in Bangladesh faded from public consciousness.

The United States' complicated historical relationship with Bangladesh was, for many years, refracted through harsh Cold War considerations. Decisions made by the US were perceived as having denied food aid to the newly independent Bangladesh for geopolitical reasons, exacerbating famine conditions rather than relieving them. The negative impact on the relationship, and on how Bangladeshis thought about agriculture and development, was profound. But the US later rebuilt the relationship, establishing a very constructive partnership over thirty years, supporting market-oriented food systems. At the same time, the US worked on family planning in partnership with religious leaders and village elders.

The long-term result has been remarkable. The economy of the country that a senior official on Henry Kissinger's team called a "basket case" fifty years ago has evolved steadily. The GDP of Bangladesh has surpassed that of its onetime antagonist Pakistan, and some predict it could outpace Singapore and Malaysia within the decade. Bangladeshi Prime Minister Sheikh Hasina was quoted in

2021 suggesting that "by 2031, Bangladesh would be an upper-middle-income country and by 2041, it would be a high-income and prosperous country." While Bangladesh has some ways to go before achieving those ambitious goals, health and education metrics have soared while infant mortality has plummeted. Indoor plumbing is now widespread, and childhood vaccination rates are extremely high due to joint efforts by NGOs and the Bangladeshi government.

The progress demonstrates the potential of foreign aid when working in conjunction with local innovation and capable leadership over a sustained period of time. But at the same time, it sheds light on some pitfalls and limitations. The country falls short of being a functioning democracy, getting a ranking as a "hybrid regime" per the *Economist Intelligence Unit*'s Democracy Index, the same level as India under Modi. India was invited to President Biden's summit of Democracy, while Bangladesh was not. If India merits inclusion, why not Bangladesh? Although the Bangladeshi prime minister who made those bold predictions is a woman, which in and of itself could be considered progressive in South Asia, her government has long been locked in a bitter struggle with the opposition party (also led by a woman). And that struggle has edged the country in the direction of one-party rule that clamps down on opposition politicians and unsympathetic journalists.

As we examine in more detail in later chapters, emerging economies rely on empowered local actors and strengthened local capacity and institutions. Two community-based institutions, in particular, played a huge role in jump-starting local businesses and getting the economy moving forward. The first, BRAC, established in 1972 by Sir Fazle Hasan Abed as the Bangladesh Rehabilitation Assistance Committee, set out rebuilding homes and fishing boats destroyed in the war and then later began building medical centers. Soon, BRAC was involved in projects across the country related to agriculture, fishing, literacy, crafts cooperatives, vocational training, and much more. Fifty years later, BRAC, now Building Resources Across Communities, had spread far beyond Bangladesh and was believed to be the largest NGO in the world, working in partnership with such organizations as the Bill and Melinda Gates Foundation and the Omidyar Network. The second, Grameen Bank, began making microloans in 1974 and continued to grow until it was formalized by law as an independent bank in 1983. So significant was its impact over the ensuing years that founder Muhammad Yunus received a Nobel Peace Prize in 2006.

There are any number of lessons to be gleaned from the rising fortunes of Bangladesh. Perhaps most importantly, while the American investment—in terms of manpower, expertise, and financing—was substantial, the real blueprint for change, and the mechanisms through which much of that change was affected, came from the people of Bangladesh. Rather than imposing a model from the outside, assistance played a supporting role in someone else's drama. Given its incredible progress, the world should be optimistic that Bangladesh will continue on a positive trajectory. At the same time, Bangladesh has a number of challenges, including governance and growing inequality.

Finally, it has been fifty years. Progress on this scale takes time, and development demands both patience and commitment. One of the great frustrations at USAID, from its inception, is the need for annual budget approval, often making long-term projects and investments problematic. In my reimagining of foreign aid, both individuals and nations need to be in it for the long haul.

* * * * *

Leaders need only to look a little further east for some of the best examples of countries that have worked their way up the development scale, often with invaluable outside assistance. Historically, the rapid ascension of the four "Asian Tigers"— South Korea, Taiwan, Singapore, and Hong Kong—has been lauded as one of the great economic success stories. As recently as 1960, the continent of Asia was poorer as a whole than Africa and was still reeling from the devastation of World War II and the Korean War. There was no Asian equivalent of the Marshall Plan that had helped rebuild Europe, although the US poured millions of aid dollars into the reconstruction of Japan, motivated at least in part by the desire to build an economically vibrant democracy as a bulwark against the spread of Soviet influence. Japan's economic recovery was so successful that by the second half of the 1990s, it had gone from being a recipient of aid to being the second-largest economy in the world and, at one point, the largest aid donor nation in the world. Elsewhere in Asia, American intervention had some obvious disastrous results, but in the case of the Asian Tigers, our aid helped create important members of the global community.

Taiwan, for example, represented one of the most prominent (and successful) programs in the early days of USAID. No one would want to argue that our motives during the perilous Cold War years were always altruistic, and indeed Taiwan and South Korea both had great significance in the geopolitics of the era. Nonetheless, American assistance effectively supported the Taiwanese ambition to quickly become an economic powerhouse. In his history of USAID, *The Enduring Struggle*, John Norris points out that US aid dollars constituted roughly half of public investment in Taiwan in the 1950s and '60s. This major investment contributed greatly to a modernized industrial base and new infrastructure. USAID advisors helped drive land and tax reform, shape fiscal policy, and train a new professional class to manage the transition from a limited agrarian society to a booming industrial economy. The transition nearly tripled the country's gross national product in a fifteen-year period.

USAID did not, however, push to enact democratic reforms. As it so often did in the post-war years, the US opted to work with a military regime in order to expeditiously meet its objectives. But Norris turns to another author to explain why the lessons of Taiwan's success must inform assistance efforts in the future: "Michael Pillsbury makes the case that the US success in Taiwan can be attributed to high-level ownership in both Washington and Taipei, and the important role of Western-trained technical experts in influential roles. But more than anything, Taiwan would seem to demonstrate that successful development isn't formulaic. The policy prescriptions were sound, but they were successful only because they reflected an adroit understanding of how to push reform through an inherently political process. Chiang Kai-shek viewed economic development as a strategic imperative, the United States made long-term investments in people and not just infrastructure, and both AID and the government were willing to work through hard choices as they occurred."

Other vibrant economies are emerging across Asia and Central Asia. Kazakhstan, which, until the unrest in 2022 triggered an incursion of Russian troops, rarely figured prominently in geopolitical discussions, has fostered a growing entrepreneurial class. In the late 1990s, the nonprofit Kazakhstan Loan Fund began providing microloans to entrepreneurs in a single Kazakh city. By 2006, the fund had transformed into KazMicroFinance, with eight branches and additional rural outlets, fueling innovation and independence for a wide variety of local enterprises and focusing especially on female business owners. In 2019, an infusion of $50 million from the International Finance Corporation, a sister organization of the World Bank, accelerated job creation and helped combat poverty by enabling diversification in Kazakhstan's economy, which had been so dependent on natural resources, including oil, gas, and other minerals. Kazakhstan is still a work in progress, of course, and political issues, both internal and regional, could sidetrack its growth, but its recent history nonetheless illustrates that innovation, entrepreneurship, and diversification are all critical stepping-stones in any country's progress toward a self-sustaining formal economy that functions through all strata of society.

Despite the stunning rise of China and the roaring of the Asian Tigers, a combination of demographics, uncertain governance, complex political allegiances, and environmental threats make the future of the region somewhat precarious. While droughts imperil other parts of the world, Southeast Asia (especially in many island nations in the Pacific) must confront rising sea levels. Development efforts include training and financing for farmers and fisheries. Investments in updated water treatment and waste management systems are transforming agriculture in Laos and elsewhere. Consultation on the development of telecommunications and financial infrastructure will enable Singapore's growth as a financial hub as China takes control of Hong Kong. And through new lines of open trade, Vietnam has rebuilt itself into a thriving center of tourism, textiles, and manufacturing.

.   .   .   .   .

The inescapable reality is that parts of the developing world simply aren't developing. Roughly thirty states—from Haiti and Honduras and South Sudan to war-torn countries like Syria, Yemen, and Afghanistan—comprise the "bottom billion" (in economic terms) of the world's population and seem likely to remain troubled for the next forty or fifty years.

What makes progress possible in some parts of the world while problems appear intractable in others? In the most troubled countries, multiple global trends—the surging youth population, urbanization, environmental challenges, corruption, and broken institutions—come together in a catastrophic perfect storm. In Africa and Southeast Asia especially, people are crowding into cities. While cities have the potential to be great economic engines, without proper planning and leadership, the services and infrastructure can quickly become overwhelmed, and they can become incubators of crime, extremism, and public health crises.

Some in the US wonder why this should be their concern, but problems like these become everybody's problems. When a youthful population has little access to education or employment, the only remaining options are crime, radicalization, or, ultimately, migration. Remember Michael Clemens's assertion of a need to achieve a per capita gross domestic product of around $8,000 to stop this kind of exodus. In countries at the bottom of the development scale, that level of income will be unforeseeable for a long time. For example, in Cambodia and Nicaragua, and even in resurgent Bangladesh, it's still less than $2,000. In Haiti and the majority of African nations, it's under $1,000. Those countries continue to produce migrants.

Few issues in the developing world have sucked up as much oxygen in American politics as the steady stream of migrants coming north from Central America, particularly the Northern Triangle countries: El Salvador, Honduras, and Guatemala, which have been another major focus of my work. These three troubled nations have experienced overwhelming economic, political, and security challenges in recent decades. A combination of domestic troubles, including governmental corruption, anemic economic growth, high rates of violence, and few jobs in the formal economy, have had international repercussions. When 75,000 unaccompanied minors—children—showed up at the US border in the summer of 2014, it became the most visible and controversial episode in the ongoing migration crisis at the US-Mexican border. At the time, I was struck, and not in a good way, by the fact that 100 percent of the media coverage was about the kids at the border and exactly none of the attention focused on what was driving them there in the first place.

I wanted to know more. In 2015, I hosted President Hernandez of Honduras at CSIS, who expressed his belief that the US needed something along the lines of a Plan Colombia for Central America. There weren't a lot of people in Washington who wanted to take up that hot potato, but I did, and so did the head of the Inter-American Development Bank at the time, Luis Alberto Moreno. When I stood up at a security conference in Halifax and spoke about the need for a Plan Colombia for the whole of the Northern Triangle, I was quickly approached by one of the luminaries in attendance, General John F. Kelly, who later served as chief of staff to Donald Trump until the two fell out. Kelly asked me to participate in a meeting on these issues that he was organizing in Miami. At that time, Kelly was the four-star general in charge of the Southern Command and was a man who had immense moral authority in my eyes. Of course, I would attend.

In Miami, I marveled at the convening power that Kelly had, arguably more even than that of the State Department or USAID, in the hemisphere. I suspect that he, too, was frustrated that he was able to bring key ministers and business leaders from so many nations to the table when State and USAID should have taken up this task. I was also struck by the depth of interest in and respect the attendees exhibited for IADB's Moreno, which helped motivate me to launch a study about what was driving people to flee Central America. I secured a grant and traveled to all three countries, interviewing more than a hundred people, from government ministers and business executives to local politicians and community leaders, priests, gang leaders, and aid workers from around the world. That research became the basis for a report I issued at the end of 2016 that laid out a series of priorities. First, we needed sustained and concentrated attention on the Northern Triangle, rather than dealing with the region only when there's some crisis or flare-up. Second, there had to be strengthened governmental capacity in each state. Third, we needed a commitment from all the relevant stakeholders, including the population at large, especially the elites in each country, whose taxes and skills would be necessary to reinvigorate societies. In conclusion, any plan would have to address corruption and the more remote parts of each country in which there was, euphemistically put, "limited state presence."

After that, I became active in supporting the Obama administration's Alliance for Prosperity, meeting with officials and representatives across the government, organizing roundtables and conferences, and writing papers and articles. This major initiative of the Obama administration to address the root causes of the Northern Triangle problems won bipartisan support. Congress approved a substantial amount of money to fund this undertaking. Unfortunately, once Obama left office, the Alliance for Prosperity lost its momentum. The incoming Trump administration seemed unable to focus on anything beyond the drug trade and the border crisis, exhibiting, at best, a conflicted approach to development in the region, with significant cuts in foreign aid and inadequate proposals to address the root causes of both those problems.

Nonetheless, the United States remains a major partner for these three countries, with strong bipartisan support for even larger appropriations in subsequent years. While the United States has always played a powerful role in this region, the coverage in Washington tends to be erratic in its grasp of greater underlying issues. The region is still portrayed as having insoluble problems with little in the way of progress.

There is neither a "magic bullet" nor an "out of the box" solution to the problems of the Northern Triangle. Most of the solutions are relatively straightforward but politically hard and involve a mixture of economic, development, political, and security reforms. The problems of the region are, in fact, solvable. But they require sustained attention from the United States, political will in the NCTA countries, including cooperation rather than obstruction from elites in these societies, and ultimately strong and inclusive economic growth to go with strengthened governance.

Mass migration from the Northern Triangle to the United States will decline only as: 1) GNP per capita approaches $8,000, which is slightly over double the current level; 2) transnational crime, drug trafficking, and gang violence and activity are significantly reduced; and 3) the social contract is developed and solidified, meaning people can have confidence that jobs, education, health, infrastructure, and a voice in the political process are reliably delivered. One development in Washington at the end of 2020 let in a ray of hope for this troubled corner of the Americas: the passage of the United States-Northern Triangle Enhanced Engagement Act, which followed on a series of other anti-corruption initiatives. The act mobilizes multiple departments and agencies of the government to develop long-range plans intended to advance economic prosperity; combat corruption; strengthen democratic governance; improve civilian security in El Salvador, Guatemala, and Honduras; and curb irregular migration from the region. One piece of the legislation deals specifically with corruption, calling for individuals or entities suspected of significant corruption to be placed on certain State Department lists, bringing targeted sanctions into play. Of course, there is some danger that a situation could inadvertently arise where the corrupt individual's presence on the list jeopardizes a portion of the country's assistance. A cut in aid would also exacerbate the problematic conditions in the region, undermining the Biden administration's long-term objectives there, and also as the situation relates to US-China competition. A loss of aid could push Guatemala and Honduras, two countries that recognize Taiwan, inadvertently closer to China. For example, during the COVID-19 pandemic, China sent generous quantities of vaccines to El Salvador, which had recognized China as opposed to Taiwan, while withholding them from Guatemala and Honduras.

The western hemisphere is home to another tragically failing state, Haiti. The Caribbean nation suffered under autocratic, corrupt, and incompetent rule for much of the twentieth century and has been battered by a series of natural disasters, including hurricanes, floods, tropical storms, and earthquakes. Public-health crises are practically routine. At times, Haiti's disparate crises pile on top of each other in a perfect storm of devastation. In 2016, just when it seemed cholera had finally been brought under control on the island, Hurricane Matthew devastated Haiti's infrastructure. The newly contaminated water supply brought about a sudden surge in cholera cases, starting a new cycle of misery. The year 2021 brought another earthquake, a direct hit from Tropical Storm Grace, and if all that wasn't enough, the assassination of the sitting president.

I went to Haiti in 2015 and visited the US ambassador there, Pam White, to understand how the country was rebuilding after the earthquake. I had been to other post-colonial Francophone cities, like Dakar in Senegal or Abidjan in Cote d'Ivoire, and I had found them to be markedly more functional and congenial than Haiti's Port au Prince. I couldn't quite understand what would account for that difference. When I asked a different former US ambassador to Haiti, who had served two years as ambassador to Haiti in the Bush years, he talked about the broken and ineffective governing class there. Throughout his time there, he said, he never heard any Haitian politician use the phrase, "This will be good for the Haitian people." The problem, simply put, was governance. It's hard to quantify the foreign assistance money and the generations of aid personnel who have flowed in and out of Haiti. But without effective governance or leadership, progress seemed impossible.

This is of paramount importance to development work. Haiti has come to be known in development circles as the "Republic of NGOs" because of its ongoing dependence on outside intervention and aid. And that's not a good thing. The well-intentioned assistance can come to dominate and actually stymie a struggling nation's ability to build its own necessary infrastructure and institutions. Ricardo Seitenfus, the former OAS senior representative to Haiti, declared: "There is a malevolent or a perverse relationship between the strength of the NGOs and the weakness of the Haitian state. Certain NGOs exist only because of the Haitian calamity." In one glaring example, the bottled water distributed by NGOs during one crisis actually displaced water that was widely available from Haitian companies.

Another Haitian academic hit upon the need for carefully planned and sustained assistance. "The NGOs go from project to project without taking the time to develop a strategy for us to respond to our own needs and develop self-sufficient organizations.

At the end of their projects, everything vanishes and we're back where we started."

Despite the deluge of aid and assistance, Haiti's 11 million people continue to live with the lowest scores in the western hemisphere on the UN Human Development Index, which ranks countries according to measurements of education, life expectancy, and per capita income. The central problem of governance mirrors the situation in so many other failing nations. There is no significant middle class to speak of and very limited wealth. Those Haitians who would occupy the upper tier have left for the US or elsewhere, largely abandoning the Haitian political and economic spheres to a shifting cast of self-interested politicians. The Haitian political system has not produced leaders capable of bringing about meaningful change, and foreign assistance so far has resulted in the country being kept on life support pending an improved capacity for self-governance. Until that time, the USAID, the Inter-American Development Bank, the Canadian government, and various aid agencies will be on the hook to provide basic services which ought to be administered by the Haitian government.

. . . . . .

Fragile states persist across the globe, from Iraq, Yemen, and now Afghanistan in the Middle East to South Sudan and Ethiopia in East Africa to Mali and Chad in West Africa, to Myanmar and Cambodia in Southeast Asia to Guatemala and Honduras in Central America. But all the top slots on any list of the most impoverished and imperiled countries in the world are filled by African nations, not just sub-Saharan countries, but many in North Africa too—Sudan, Somalia, and Libya.

Environmental devastation and the surge in the youth demographic are global challenges but are significantly magnified in sub-Saharan Africa, where the population will likely double by 2050. The enduring paradox is the persistent failure of so many of its nations to thrive despite the immense richness of its natural resources and its enormous potential labor force. Drought, flooding, and desertification have resulted in shrunken grazing lands and agriculture, driving more and more people into urban areas now bursting with expanding populations. Where opportunity is scarce, radicalism and revolution thrive, compounding the existing issues of inadequate governance and corruption. Additionally, ongoing conflicts over old colonial borders show how Africa's fraught history remains a burden.

And yet, there is something happening in Africa. In 2010, Steven Radelet, then at the Center for Global Development, published *Emerging Africa: How 17 Countries are Leading the Way*. Radelet argued that contrary to popular perception, many African nations had seen dramatic economic growth, poverty reduction, and improved governance and accountability since the 1990s. What's especially notable about Radelet's observation is that during a period in which China had invested so much in hard infrastructure in Africa—roads and rails, dams and power plants, seaports and mineral extraction—he ascribes the improving conditions to five soft-power factors: more democratic and accountable governments; stronger economic policies that empower business, entrepreneurship, and trade; reimagined relationships with the international community that resulted in debt relief; the spread of new technologies; and the education of a new generation of leaders in politics, business, and the social sphere. The US and its allies may never be able to compete with China on the infrastructure front, but they can certainly continue to enable meaningful progress in these other all-important areas.

I visited Ghana in 2002 and was taken with the calm and stability. I knew that USAID had done much to foster health and education, and Ghana had kept HIV somewhat at bay compared to other countries in Africa. I also knew that Ghana had the advantages of a functioning democratic government, the absence of conflict with neighbors, and an attractive, ecologically diverse landscape. But perhaps most importantly, people there were receptive to outside assistance but determined to make their own success in their own way. I look to Patrick Awuah, a Ghanaian who returned home after studying and working in the United States and started Ashesi University, a private university in Ghana based on the liberal-arts model of Swarthmore.

Awuah understands that Africa's destiny must be controlled by Africans. "Today, there is a significant push for other regions to engage with Africa. China is looking to engage with Africa. The West is looking to engage with Africa. We need to make sure that whatever change happens in Africa is African-led and not led from somewhere else. To do that, we need to be educating people on our side of the table who can engage in those conversations and make sure that the best interests of African citizens are front and center. We need to get to a place where the educational system here matches anywhere in the world."

Mo Ibrahim, the visionary engineer and entrepreneur who built the communications network that allowed Africa to leapfrog past outdated copper-wire telephone technology, enabling the spread of cell phones across the continent, echoes the idea that most meaningful and effective change must come from within. "I'm an African. I'm not afraid of Africa," Ibrahim told CNN in 2019. "I believe there's a big gap between the perception and the reality of Africa. Whenever there's a big gap between perception and reality, there's a wonderful business opportunity." The advent of cell phones meant much more than the ease of communication. The phones enabled online education and banking, the dissemination of critical public health information, and updated commerce and employment.

Steven Radelet says, "While emerging Africa holds the keys to its future, the international community can play an important supporting role. Donors can make aid more effective by letting the emerging countries take the lead in establishing priorities and implementing programs, and they can make larger and more enduring commitments."

Africa remains a place of harsh contrasts, rich in natural resources and majestic beauty, with numerous countries on the rise, but also with many wracked by conflict, poverty, and corruption. Once a continent in critical need of development aid, Africa is now looking for infrastructure, investments, trade, innovation, and private sector growth. While some wealthier nations are turning to commercial, diplomatic, and development tools to create win-win situations in Africa, China is ready to invest a lot of capital and has been steadily establishing its presence. As we will examine more closely in the next chapter, Africa has what China needs, not just in terms of food, energy, and extractable resources, but as a source of income for its workers and companies and as a vast new market for its manufacturing sector. In fact, China has had a surprisingly long relationship with many African nations, dating even back to the days of Mao Zedong, who capitalized on a "solidarity" among post-colonial nations trying to find their way.

It's necessary to recognize that Beijing views Africa not only through the lens of economics but also for its geopolitical importance. In Djibouti, for example, a new Chinese-built seaport stands adjacent to a Chinese naval base, an important piece of China's ambition to establish a "string of pearls" linking its Pacific coast to Europe and the Mediterranean through the Indian Ocean. No one should underestimate what's at stake for China on this complicated continent.

For the United States and its global allies, foreign aid has a critical supporting role to play. Two signature US initiatives. First was Power Africa, launched in 2013 under President Obama, with the goal of bringing clean and affordable electricity to the nearly two-thirds of the African population that lacked it. Power Africa brought together several agencies, including USAID, the US Export-Import Bank where I sat on the Sub-Saharan Advisory Committee, and the Overseas Private Investment Corporation (OPIC) (now, reformed and with greater capacities, called the Development Finance Corporation), while tapping the private sector for investment and expertise. Providing access to power would be the first step to modernization and economic development.

Five years later, in December 2018, the Trump administration announced Prosper Africa, a plan which I helped author, to open markets for American businesses, grow Africa's middle class, promote youth employment opportunities, improve the business climate, increase two-way trade, and enable the US to compete with China and other countries with business interests in Africa. It was my contention that the US was still saddled with an outdated perception of Africa as a continent in despair, and our relationship was still based on traditional foreign assistance, like health and food-security programs. The time had come to recognize that African markets represent some of the greatest opportunities for private-sector growth in the developing world. Prosper Africa, through which the US government could coordinate and stream-line disparate projects in multiple departments and agencies, can be an ideal manifestation of enlightened self-interest. Expanding trade and empowering new markets while establishing cultural and governmental ties that advance American principles will boost emerging nations while serving our own economic interests.

·   ·   ·   ·   ·

Nothing shines as harsh a light on the vulnerability of the poorest countries as a pandemic. Few of the poorest nations have well-funded or reliable health-care systems or thriving formal econo-mies. Citizens have little or no savings, and governments don't have the resources or the infrastructure to offer meaningful assistance. It's only been ten years since an outbreak of cholera sickened 10 percent of the population of Haiti, and there, as in so many other failed or failing states, the COVID-19 crisis represents a humani-tarian disaster.

There's been no shortage of handwringing about the yawning divide between the richer and poorer countries when it came to the response to the pandemic. The wealthier nations found cover in the idea of "putting your own oxygen mask on first." But even that couldn't account for the disparity in vaccinations between North America and Europe on the one hand and Africa, Latin America, and Asia on the other. International vaccination organizations like COVAX and GAVI were scrambling for supplies while stockpiles of vaccines remained unused in the United States elsewhere. And yet the health-care systems of many of those wealthier nations were so overburdened that was little left with which to shore up the delivery of pandemic relief elsewhere. And now, as supply has become a lesser constraint, developing countries are facing the same challenge as the United States and Europe confronted in convincing their citizens that the vaccines now available to them are safe and effective, and that widespread vaccination is essential for the restoration of public health and the economy.

In an economically integrated world, a threat to the prosperity of one nation ripples out, affecting its neighbors, allies, and trading partners. All one has to do to confirm that is to recall the pressures on global supply chains in 2020 and 2021. The COVID-19 pandemic is a disruption in progress, reminding everyone that there are no walls high enough to protect from global challenges, including pandemics, environmental challenges, global migration and displaced populations, shifting demographics, and political radicalization.

Chapter 4

THE SLEEPING GIANT ROARS TO LIFE

The Birth of a New Global Power

I'm not saying China's an enemy of the United States of America. I'm just simply saying that if we do not handle the emergence of the People's Republic well, it will be catastrophic for the world.

—General Michael Hayden, former director of the CIA and the National Security Agency
(*The Guardian, 3/9/2016*)

I n the first half of 2021, Jack Ma was nowhere to be seen. The Chinese tech mogul, among the wealthiest and most influential tech entrepreneurs in China, if not the world, and an enthusiastic self-promoter and ubiquitous media personality, had dropped out of the public eye. Imagine if Jeff Bezos or Elon Musk or Richard Branson suddenly disappeared from one day to the next. Maybe we would speculate that he had retreated to some remote palatial hideaway for rest and relaxation or that he was off secretly planning the launch of some brilliant new venture or even hiding from the media in the wake of a tawdry scandal. But nobody would assume, as most people did about Jack Ma, that he was the unwilling guest of his own government, either imprisoned or under house arrest, after giving a speech that subtly criticized China's system of financial regulation.

Ma was "missing" for three months before turning up on a golf course, and afterward, he maintained a much lower profile. In July of 2021, a Chinese court sentenced another tycoon, an agricultural billionaire named Sun Dawu, to eighteen years in prison for "provoking trouble," among other crimes, after a dispute between his workers and a state-owned farm got out of control. The stories of Jack Ma and men like him—cautionary tales, to be sure—encapsulate both the promise of China's economic transformation and perils inherent in a system subject to centralized government control.

I am not a China scholar, but no one can work in international development policy without learning a thing or two about the great behemoth of the East. In retrospect, many of the major aid and development initiatives I was involved with (from the outside) during the Trump administration were motivated, either directly or indirectly, by the challenges posed by China's skyrocketing growth as an economic power and a global influencer. All the initiatives during the Trump administration that I played a role in: my work shaping the "Prosper Africa" partnership plan, supporting the BUILD Act (Better Utilization of Investment Leading to Development), which created the new United States International Development Finance Corporation (DFC), arose out of recognition of the ground we were losing to China. Reviving the moribund EXIM Bank and supporting the Trump administration's capital increase for the World Bank, two other initiatives where I played a role, were in response to the Chinese investment money flowing into the developing world.

Let's look at how China achieved this elevated position, what that tells us about what they need moving forward, and what it will mean for the US and its partners. Before falling out of favor, Jack Ma had been the poster child for China's entrepreneurial class, made possible by the economic reforms—the "opening up to the west"—instituted in the late 1970s under Deng Xiaoping and gaining momentum over the next twenty or thirty years. Deng came into power in 1978, two years after the fall of the "Gang of Four," the notorious cadre of Communist Party leaders who held sway during the final years of Mao Zedong's life. The Cultural Revolution they oversaw had laid waste to China's economy and left the cultural and social life of the country shattered. In 1980, per capita GDP was less than $200—below even that of, say, Haiti, Nicaragua, or Angola at the time. (Recall from the previous chapter Michael Clemens's assertion that a minimum threshold per capita GDP of $8,000 deters emigration from most struggling countries.) A significant portion of the population lived and worked in agricultural collectives or worked in state-owned factories in hastily constructed government towns. Foreign trade was limited at best, not only because of China's isolation, but because there were hardly any production surpluses beyond what was needed for its own population. Industry and technology were desperately outdated, and access to capital was essentially nonexistent.

Recognizing the need to lift the country out of the poverty and the chaos resulting from the Cultural Revolution, Deng Xiaoping pursued a program he called "socialism with Chinese characteristics." Jump-starting the country's devastated economy would require a sudden and substantial influx of foreign investment, technology, and expertise as well as business savvy. Deng looked to the example set by the "Asian Tiger" nations neighboring China—Hong Kong, Singapore, South Korea, and Taiwan—which had ridden a wave of intensive industrialization to rapid economic growth. These countries had also become major financial hubs, which China made use of to facilitate its entry into the global trade and financial system before establishing its own financial center in Shanghai. By the early 1980s, China had taken the significant step of joining major institutions like the World Bank and the International Monetary Fund, further advancing that ambition. As its own financial resources grew over the coming decades, China would begin to flex its economic muscle by taking central roles in the major regional development banks.

The government established a number of "special economic zones"—delineated geographic areas where regulations would be relaxed to allow for some free-market activity. The idea was to create a business environment that would be attractive to foreign investment by easing taxes, tariffs, and duties and offering access to the exploding Chinese workforce, which, at the time, was streaming into the cities and hungry for work. Almost any wages under any working conditions would constitute an improvement over the impoverished peasant lives they were leaving behind. Beginning in 1979 in just four cities, these little islands of opportunity became economic hotbeds, drawing, at first, business from Taiwan and Japan, and Chinese nationals working outside the country, but then European and North American corporations as well. It was like a shot of adrenaline for the Chinese economy. Soon, another fourteen cities were so designated, and by the late 1980s, more cities and regions came online along its borders, its coast, and the Yangtze River. Initially, the special economic zones facilitated exports of China's growing manufacturing surplus but evolved over time so that the presence and influence of outside corporations sparked innovation and brought new technology into the country.

Elsewhere, carefully regulated forms of entrepreneurship, private enterprise, and ventures joining the public and private sectors were encouraged, thereby seeding the growth of a "socialist market economy." New companies, some started with government capital and others with overseas investment, formed the foundation of a burgeoning manufacturing sector. As the vast number of jobs created drew many from the poorly educated rural population into urban centers, China moved aggressively to upgrade its own infrastructure—from transportation to education—and began planning gleaming new cities to accommodate the twenty-first-century workforce that Beijing envisioned.

China succeeded spectacularly in its quest to make itself over into the workshop of the world. It's important to remember that

Chinese leaders were single-minded in their pursuit of a complete transformation of the country. General Michael Hayden, who served as director of the CIA and knows something about the quest for global stature, said bluntly that China's goal was "absolute growth at any price" and "absolute stability at any price." Western companies, used to being sensitive to stringent laws and regulations in OECD countries, recognized that there was little or no OSHA in China, little or no EPA seeking environmental impact statements, and no worker-rights activists or demanding trade unions. Baby boomers will remember how the phrase "made in Japan" was once synonymous with low-cost, low-quality mass-produced goods, but how in the space of hardly more than a single generation, Japanese manufacturing morphed into a global standard for technical precision, efficiency, dedication, and productivity. From the small beginnings in the 1980s and '90s, China has been moving swiftly along that same trajectory. For most of the twenty-first century, while still shipping great quantities of shoddy, knock-off goods, often with little respect for globally accepted standards for product safety, worker rights, or intellectual property claims, the country has quickly established itself as a reliable manufacturer of some of the most in-demand electronic and digital equipment. China now sells more manufactured goods than any other nation in the world, and not just low-cost consumer goods, but steel and cement; cars, ships, and planes; textiles and clothing; and heavy equipment. China's star is rising in the critical next-generation industries, like robotics, artificial intelligence, and pharmaceuticals.

By 2020, modernization and economic expansion had raised the per capita GDP in China to more than $10,000, and a new, mostly urban, consumer middle class had been born. Consumption created demand, which, in turn, created more jobs and then more demand in an upward spiral of growth. International trade grew as overseas producers dove into the enormous Chinese market at the same time as Chinese companies began selling into markets around the world. China's lifting of hundreds of millions of its people out of poverty so quickly surely qualifies as a modern miracle. As recently as the year 2000, the US was the number one trading partner for about 120 countries, compared to less than half that number for which China claimed that position. By 2021, that situation had completely reversed, with China taking the lead as the largest trading partner for about 135 countries. Those relationships confer enormous clout and influence on the government in Beijing.

At first, the Central Bank of China invested safely, putting most of the nation's newfound wealth into United States treasury bills. Over time, however, China began diversifying and taking calculated risks. It began lending money to Chinese companies or underwriting hard infrastructure projects that employed those companies, creating a cascade of short-term and long-term economic benefits. Many of the country's newly minted entrepreneurs who had taken advantage of those opportunities became wildly successful and enormously wealthy, which was unprecedented for private citizens in China. Those who, like Jack Ma, captured the attention of the media and the public found themselves in competition with the central government for respect, admiration, and credit. For some, like Ma, that competition would be their ultimate undoing.

The leadership in Beijing never got used to the idea of relinquishing central control and planning of the economy. The one constant in the country's development has been Beijing's rejection of the rules of engagement—its insistence on doing things its own way and on its own terms. Interconnectedness proved to have its advantages, but interdependence was never going to be thought of as one of them. Xi Jinping has made "self-reliance" a key component of his ambition for China. With an inadvertently ironic nod toward the Western management principle of vertical integration, in which a corporation sought to incorporate and profit from subsidiary industries necessary to its business, like energy or transportation or the supply of raw materials, China set about building a global network to sustain the core industries in its economy. The most far-reaching of these efforts is the Belt and Road Initiative (BRI), initiated in 2014 by Xi Jinping. BRI was envisioned as a modern incarnation of the fabled Silk Road, the ancient network of trade routes that linked the Western world to the Middle East and Asia. The twenty-first-century version called for the construction of roads, railways, bridges, tunnels, airports, and seaports in an overland chain extending across Southeast Asia, South Asia, and Central Asia to Europe as well as a series of ports—the "string of pearls," in the parlance of Chinese planners—forming a dotted line connecting the coast of China with Southeast and South Asia, the South Pacific, the Middle East, and Eastern Africa.

The stated aims of the Belt and Road Initiative reveal only part of the story. This massive undertaking reflected not only economic policy but, in ways both subtle and profound, foreign policy and even some elements of domestic planning. While filling an infrastructure gap in the Chinese economic system, BRI has also greatly expanded China's geopolitical influence and will offer relief from some internal challenges on the country's horizon. To begin with, the surging prosperity and the new buying power of the population vastly increased demand for food, energy, and goods. This growing demand, combined with exploding export business, began to outstrip the country's once-formidable natural resources.

China wants electrical power from Myanmar. From Africa, it wants copper, cobalt, manganese, and other ores; Chinese companies now have interests in mines across a wide swath of mineral-rich Central and West Africa. From Russia and Central Asia, it takes oil and gas and other mineral resources. Where it doesn't have direct ownership, China can exert influence and control in any number of ways, such as putting in its own experts and administrators, negotiating favorable long-term contracts, providing financing or infrastructure, and other business practices that may or may not conform to globally accepted standards.

Chinese construction companies have built dams, ports, railways, power stations, and roads from Sudan to Angola, Zambia, and Djibouti. However, as in other parts of the world, China's incursion in Africa has been a double-edged sword. In Uganda, a country desperately trying to accommodate an influx of millions of refugees from strife-torn neighboring countries, almost all the new infrastructure is built by China, while China has become one of the country's largest trading partners. But only three years after construction was complete on the Chinese-built Karuma and Isimba hydroelectric plant, the engineering is suspect, as cracks are starting to show. A highway in Uganda, also built by Chinese companies, was over budget and years behind schedule at the time of this writing.

In Asia, there are rail and pipeline projects in Malaysia and Indonesia, and rail and factories in Thailand, among other countries. Among other projects underway in South Asia is the massive China-Pakistan Economic Corridor, similar to what's planned for Myanmar. Today, China depends on massive amounts of iron-ore imports, much of it from Australia, and as we've seen, Beijing doesn't like being dependent on anyone for anything. Wherever it can, it seeks ways to minimize the cost of sticking a straw into other countries for the resources that will fuel its growth.

In the Americas, an Argentine-Chinese hydroelectric complex is in progress, and Peru, where Chinese companies already control billions of dollars in mining, signed a memorandum of understanding in 2019, committing itself to join with the Belt and Road Initiative.

China has become the world's largest user of the Panama Canal, where most observers fear a mushrooming Chinese investment in the surrounding countries has gone a long way toward enriching local officials while leaving those countries deeply in debt, thus cementing Chinese influence in Latin America.

The resulting relationships with other countries proved to be utterly unique in the global community: China has managed to establish a presence of one kind or another in every corner of the world while remaining insular, guarded, and remote, even within those countries. Richard Carey, former OECD Director for Development Cooperation, sees parallels between China's "development" engagement with other countries and those of Japan in the late 1990s, when Japan became such an important aid donor. A significant amount of Japanese development investment was in the form of "tied aid," meaning aid that was conditioned on Japan getting something in return, for example, an agreement from the recipient country to spend that aid money on goods or services from the donor country. Not surprisingly, many countries publicly frown on this practice and have officially abandoned it (even if from time to time many countries continue to practice tied aid). But Japan persisted, and China appears to have learned from Japan's playbook.

The impact of Chinese infrastructure projects on the countries in which they were situated didn't seem to be a primary concern of the Chinese planners and developers. Myanmar is a case in point.

The enormous infrastructure projects planned and financed have never been intended to boost Myanmar's economy or improve the lives of its citizens. The proposed system of hydroelectric dams would alter the flow of the Irrawaddy, threatening farming and fisheries. The work would be done by Chinese companies using Chinese financing and use labor brought in from China, so little or none of the money generated by the massive construction project would get to local governments or corporations or into the hands of individuals. Most of it would find its way back to China. As we've seen, upward of 90 percent of the power generated by these plants would be redirected over the border into China.

China is motivated by what's good for China. Growth and stability. Its interest in the hydroelectric infrastructure in Myanmar arises out of China's own need for electricity. Beijing seems uninterested in exporting ideology, building alliances, or creating cultural bonds. As control of the Myanmar government swung from one end of the political spectrum to the other, and then back again, China proceeded to do business with whichever regime held power, regardless of ideology or foreign policy. Similarly, China accepted that the cost of doing business in Sri Lanka would be to support the political campaigns of the president and the family members who shared power in order to secure the contracts for the white-elephant port in Hambantota, another key link in the chain of BRI outposts that would keep China supplied. When that project inevitably started to lose money, adding to Sri Lanka's already crushing debt burden, the Chinese renegotiated the terms of the deal with the subsequent administration and won for themselves greater control of the land and facilities. Likewise, in the Balkan country of Montenegro, a billion-dollar expressway—a "highway to nowhere"—was commissioned by a former prime minister in what the current administration suspects was a deal born of megalomania and corruption. Again, Chinese banks, construction companies, and imported workers all took money out of the deal, but Montenegro was left with a huge unpayable debt to Beijing at a time when the country would have preferred to strengthen ties with the West. A massive freight hub on the Kazakh-Chinese border, the Khorgos Gateway, has also raised some red flags, with a significant number of empty shipping containers reportedly passing through it and ongoing Chinese subsidies boosting its performance metrics.

This isn't to say that these incursions have always worked out badly for the lower- and middle-income countries in which China planted its economic flag. Argentina and Brazil, for example, are both reaping the benefits of the demand for meat from China's increasingly middle-class population. The meat of choice in China is pork, and those two countries sell the great majority of their soy— soybean meal is used as pig feed—to the Chinese. (The dispute that landed Chinese billionaire Sun Dawu in prison had to do with pig farming, his primary business.) Beef has also become an important trade commodity; China is now the largest single export market for Uruguayan beef.

The welfare of other nations is not a priority for Beijing. The Belt and Road Initiative is perhaps best seen as a vehicle by which Beijing can rewire the world's economy and reorient it toward China. If the countries along its length grow strong and self-reliant and eventually can share the burdens of future global challenges, it would be a happy but unintended consequence. The goal is to keep the engine of Chinese growth humming and provide for a billion and a half citizens. It's important to understand that China's economic relationship with the developing world essentially follows an extractive, neo-colonial paradigm, using the weapons of trade, finance, and construction. We can't deny that the United States has, in its past, made mistakes. We have been imperfect, and many historical forays into economic development reflected self-interest and callousness. But I would argue that American intentions were fundamentally broader, better, and carried the weight of the rule of law and good governance.

. . . . . .

In addition to the rapidly growing need for raw materials and energy, China faces a looming demographic time bomb. The birth rate has been declining for years—it is currently just under 1.7 births per woman, meaning below what would be needed to replace the current population—in part because of Beijing's one-child policy and established preference for boy babies over girls. The working population will shrink while having to support a larger population of aging and retired workers. This is already having a measurable effect on productivity, as consumption wanes and overseas companies find other sources of labor. China needs to keep its workers gainfully employed and put off the time when they become economic burdens of the state. This is another critical reason that, after working so hard for so long to close itself off from the global community, the Chinese leadership began to seek new modes of economic engagement beyond its borders in the early 2000s. The construction that China finances, either directly or indirectly, is rarely, if ever, performed by local companies. Rather, Beijing makes capital available to Chinese firms, some of which are joint public-private ventures and which invariably bring in Chinese workers. The government is lending money to its own corporations, some of which will end up in the pockets of Chinese workers and some of which will come back into the national treasury.

It is the nature of the underlying proposition offered to people by the Chinese one-party system with a centrally controlled economy: The state will look after everyone and everything. It will provide jobs, housing, security, health care, education. The state will worry about it all so that you don't have to. It's a big promise, and it may not be so easy to fulfill. What China asks of its people in return is to relinquish control, to accept that they have no say in government or policy. Don't ask questions, don't deviate from accepted norms, and don't even think about dissenting. That bargain has held, and the transformation of China over the last forty years is unparalleled in modern history, but is it sustainable? Cracks are beginning to show, and many predict that the recent decline in China's spectacular growth rate is likely to be a continuing trend.

The aging population represents one of the three immediate and interrelated threats to China's continued growth. The demographic challenge is accompanied by threats of debt and what could be described as a deceptive business model—the "three Ds."

China's widely discussed "debt bomb" not only could derail its own progress but could have far-reaching global consequences now that China has become the world's second-largest economy. In the early 2000s, the country was sitting on a mountain of cash, amassed as its unique economic model matured. Much of that money was reinvested into domestic and overseas construction and infrastructure, state-owned enterprises, and private companies. More money went into financial institutions, most notably the Asian Infrastructure Investment Bank (AIIB), a Chinese-led alternative to the Asian Development Bank, the World Bank, and other multilateral institutions where China has less clout. In fact, it was China's behavior related to institutions like these that woke up the Trump administration to the magnitude of the threat to US interests it could pose. When the AIIB first came into existence during the Obama presidency, the US and Japan were the only major countries that chose not to participate, while scores of nations—from smaller developing countries to established economic powers—rushed to join. The Obama administration was vague about the reasons for its reluctance, but at least one person in the administration had begun to see the writing on the wall. Michael Froman, then head of the National Economic Council in the Obama administration, took a trip to Africa and was reportedly shocked by the scale of China's involvement in the power sector in Africa. That realization, along with the lack of electricity as a key constraint to growth, helped catalyze what became the US government's Power Africa initiative, led by USAID. Power Africa seeks to bring all US government agencies together to support US private investment that will help bring electricity to the estimated two-thirds of the African population who have none.

Still, when Trump came into power, responding to China using our soft-power tools wasn't initially at the top of his priority list. He quickly took aim at some of the development-related US institutions and programs that struck him as misguided or superfluous. Among those were the Overseas Private Investment Corporation (OPIC) and the Export-Import Bank of the United States (EXIM), both of which have been of fundamental importance to US support for development. In other words, these were critically influential soft-power tools of this country. Chapter 10 puts the efforts to keep these entities vibrant into the context of upgrading the US development apparatus for the future.

Something else seemed to have happened in 2017 that hardened the views of the Trump administration toward China. I don't know what caused this shift, but most of the senior officials at the time suddenly seemed to realize that the US couldn't close its eyes to the machinations by its only legitimate rival on the world stage. From that moment on, the only time the Trump White House took an internationalist position on some issue, it was clearly out of fear of China. The only question that would move the administration to act in such matters was, "Are you prepared to cede that space to China?"

China had already begun to borrow heavily, floating a great amount of bond debt in the wake of the financial crisis of 2008 and 2009. When the rest of the world was stagnating or contracting, China pushed forward with housing and infrastructure, creating jobs and keeping the wheels turning. As we've seen, the Belt and Road Initiative would also help sustain the forward momentum. All of these efforts drove more borrowing so that by 2018, China was carrying more than $30 trillion in public and private debt, with a record-high number of corporate debt defaults. Xi Jinping wants to characterize this as a natural and unremarkable offshoot of the economic boom and has proposed a host of belt-tightening measures to alleviate the pressure, including cutting back on loans to state-owned enterprises and reducing public expenditures, which can't be good news for a society dependent on the largesse of the central government. Others outside of China view it as a dire threat to the global economy.

Behind shiny new facades of some of China's sprawling new cities, the signs of debt stress are showing. To be sure, many of China's cities are enviable monuments to success and, in some cases, excess. Shenzhen, for example, a city of nearly thirteen million inhabitants, linking the mainland to Hong Kong, has a majestic futuristic skyline that rivals New York. The city is not only a thriving commercial and financial hub but a manufacturing boomtown, described as the electronics factory to the world. At least five Chinese cities boast even larger populations, including Beijing, Shanghai, and Guangzhou, but even in those immense metropolises, real-estate prices have started to level off.

Moving into the interior of the country, you'll find dozens of cities with a different story to tell. Construction began in 2009 on Kangbashi, a planned community adjacent to the once-thriving coal city of Ordos in Inner Mongolia. By 2012, row upon row of high-rise apartment towers had sprung up, along with an enormous central square, an ultra-modern museum and library, and an imposing sports stadium. The government built roads and other infrastructure to supply the city with water, gas, and power. Having instituted a program designed to relocate much of the rural population to urban centers, planners envisioned a million new residents streaming into Ordos. And indeed, some pioneers did come early, which convinced many real-estate developers of the rosy future. Towers and complexes continued to go up, even as other new construction remained vacant. A decade later, however, more apartments may be empty than occupied. Residents report deserted streets, undersupplied stores, and an absence of neighbors. According to reporting in *The Wall Street Journal*, even some of the sold apartments may be unoccupied, having been bought for future use by families or as investments.

The longer that Kangbashi and Ordos and other new Chinese cities remain overbuilt "ghost towns," the more onerous the interest payments on all that debt will become. In a sense, that pressure mimics, on a small scale, the pressure facing China as its national debt and the debts incurred by large Chinese companies, both private and state-owned, continue to balloon. Ironically, while the ghost-town phenomenon is symptomatic of the looming economic challenges, it could also turn out to be the kind of situation that actually accelerates the slow-down in growth.

Real estate plays an outsized role in the economy of contemporary China. The constant development and construction in urban centers, often backed at least in part by government financing, has generated fantastic wealth for individuals and corporations. Those companies have then expanded into virtually every other sector of the economy, buying interests in manufacturing, entertainment and technology companies, and even agriculture. Real-estate speculation has driven up the cost of new homes, making new home buyers anxious to get into new developments as early as possible, so it's become common practice to sell apartments before the buildings are even completed. This expectation helped fuel the rush to put up new apartment blocks in places like Ordos well before there was sufficient population to warrant it. At the same time, real estate has become the largest repository of individual savings in China.

The problems of Evergrande, one of the country's largest developers, now with holdings across a broad spectrum of industries, revealed the fragility of the real-estate boom. The company faced unsustainable debt, unable to complete projects under construction, even when units had already been sold. Such massive companies in China are often described as "gray rhinos," companies "so large and so entangled in the country's financial system that the government has an interest in their survival. A failure on the scale of Evergrande would ripple across the economy, and spell financial ruin for ordinary households." If a company like Evergrande is crushed by its debt, the impact will be felt by thousands of individuals and municipalities. The failure of multiple companies, in real estate or any other sector, will reverberate across Chinese society.

The final of my three Ds refers to China's deceptive business model. For years, China rightfully held itself out as the cheapest and most convenient manufacturer, largely due to the enormous amount of surplus labor generated by the transition out of a rural economy. For twenty or more years, workers were happy enough to have jobs, that the low wages and total commitment demanded by employers were worth it. Over time, though, China became the victim of its own success, at least as far as the labor force was concerned. The new industrial cities offered that housed the workers offered better schools for their children and unprecedented educational opportunities for young adults while also exposing them to the goods and services available to people with higher and more stable incomes.

Younger workers were hungry for the jobs of the future and surrounded by images of financial success, while the great majority of older workers often lacked the skills and training to keep up with the changing demands of the workplace. Still, wages rose, and many companies pulled their manufacturing business out of China, seeking even cheaper labor elsewhere. As Scott Rozelle and Natalie Hell point out in their book, *Invisible China*, the disconnect between the uneducated, aging rural transplants that typified the bulk of the labor force for so long and the technology-driven future poses a major economic roadblock both within China and in countries whose economic health is linked with China's.

Rozelle and Hell speculate that China will get caught in what economists call the "middle income trap." That is, the country's past success was built on an unskilled labor force and relied to a large degree on the export of low-cost goods. However, that formula has a limited life. A significant percentage of the workforce is never going to become part of a vibrant creative class capable of driving innovation that will be necessary for China to compete with the most developed nations. China has not made itself attractive to creatives. You don't see ambitious entrepreneurs looking to move to Beijing or Shanghai in the way they flock to New York or London or Silicon Valley.

While the birth rate continues to decline and the workforce shrinks, China is challenged to find new ways to boost productivity. New technology and automation will likely be the only answer, which is going to necessitate either heavy investment—at a time when the existing debt load represents a financial cliff—or new kinds of multinational partnerships to facilitate the transfer of expertise.

But China has developed a reputation for appropriating foreign expertise by whatever means necessary, freely helping itself to other people's intellectual property. While some business successes have come from genuine innovation, many Chinese companies rely on some copycat version of Western innovation. Time and again, China has figured out how to beat Western companies at their own game. But so far, few Chinese businesses have excelled at reinventing the game.

The point here is not to criticize China for unfair practices but to recognize that throughout history, innovation has been the most dependable driver of economic growth and progress. What new industries or inventions or practices will China come up with that will be transformative and uniquely theirs? And how will they prepare their workers and pay the costs of the needed innovation?

The rosy picture of economic stability that China presents to the world is undermined by several other factors, including the fragility of global supply chains, as highlighted by the COVID-19 pandemic, and the threat to trade and cooperation arising out of increasingly strained political relations between China and the major Western economic powers. The chatter about the US or other countries decoupling from business relationships in China or reshoring industries gets louder by the day, even though many experts believe such steps could cause as much pain in the West as they would in China.

. . . . .

For those of us in the development community, it's hard to not be very impressed by the magnitude of China's achievement. In the span of two generations, China has realized for itself, with virtually no external assistance, exactly what we envision as the development arc for every lower- and middle-income country. Fifty years ago, conditions in China were equal to or worse than those in countries considered most in need of foreign aid. Living standards in mainland China were abysmal, and opportunity was all but nonexistent for most people. Many countries in similarly dire straits were, and still are, dependent on external assistance. They are targeted by donors, UN commissions, and NGOs. But China saw none of that. Every step forward was planned and executed internally, becoming a machine of growth capable of feeding on its own success. In many ways, that is the ultimate goal of development: to enable a country to move itself out of a state of dependence and into a position of stability, prosperity, and individual well-being.

The example China has set is also its greatest unstated promise to many LICs. Chinese companies are eager to build dams and ports and factories in poor countries, filling development gaps left by the West, and surely some of that dynamism will rub off. But there is inherent deception in that promise. China is not seeking to share its secrets or its industrial capacity. It does not seek to establish a network of partners or alliances. It is not trying to foster multilateral cooperation. But if China is doing business in another country and brought about some semblance of positive change, if it has seemed to fill in the gaps in development left by the West, we can be sure those countries will look toward China in the future.

But with China now involved with roughly 5 percent of the world's infrastructure, the West has to do better. Many developing countries cannot identify viable options other than China for development partnerships. If you're the government in Uganda or Sri Lanka or Montenegro or Myanmar, you may not have the luxury of choosing between Chinese or Western financing for construction for your airport or expressway or rail hub or gas pipeline. Your choice may very well be between a burdensome Chinese loan and no financing, or between a shoddily built dam and no dam at all. The West has to renew its vigilance regarding the influence that China is building through these projects and investments and mobilize its collective resources—regional development banks, private capital, European and Asian partners, and all the tools of aid and development—to enable better alternatives. The answer will not lie in underbidding Chinese companies for the right to build the next port or railway somewhere but in enabling infrastructure alternatives along with building local capacity for the long haul, and our "offer" has to include the promise of greater self-reliance and agency.

In 2005, Deputy Secretary of State Robert Zoellick gave a speech to the National Committee on US-China relations in which he called upon China to become a "responsible stakeholder" in the "international system that has enabled its success." At the time, that seemed eminently possible. There was barely a hint of Cold War mentality in the relationship between the two nations. China didn't seek to replace democracy or capitalism with its ideology, as the Soviet Union had. China was already deeply and inextricably enmeshed in the global economy. Zoellick believed in the possibility of cooperation but understood what a meaningful partnership would require. "We have many common interests with China," he acknowledged. "But relationships built only on a coincidence of interests have shallow roots. Relationships built on shared interests and shared values are deep and lasting."

As Zoellick saw it, leaders in Beijing had shown an inclination to reform, and he envisioned that spirit filtering into Chinese civil society, eventually leading to a gradual move toward greater political freedom, even elections of some kind. He asserted that such liberalization would be necessary because "in the absence of freedom, unhealthy societies will breed deadly cancers."

But China moved in precisely the opposite direction over the ensuing fifteen years, becoming ever more authoritarian. Xi Jinping, named president in 2013, managed to abolish the two-term limit in 2018, making him, conceivably, president for life. Under his watch, the central government has tightened controls over many aspects of society and economic life. Tycoons like Jack Ma, who arguably got too big for his britches, have paid the price. Jack Ma's biggest sin may simply have been that his business concentrated on the consumer-facing piece of the tech sector. Beginning in 2021, Beijing cracked down on that entire sector, once thought to be essential to a future-oriented economy. New regulatory guidelines, and the government-mandated derailment of a number of large tech IPOs, including one of Ma's companies, have all but wiped out the fortunes of a number of tech tycoons. Meanwhile, tech companies that focus on hardware and infrastructure, like Huawei, have flourished, as have companies in the energy sector, such as the battery manufacturers supplying China's booming industry in electric cars and buses.

But such treatment has not been reserved for high-profile individuals. Foreign corporations have been stung as well. For example, the Swedish clothing retailer H&M ran afoul of Beijing after declining to purchase cotton from Xinjiang province and found its Chinese trade shut down virtually overnight.

Robert Zoellick's dream of shared values leading to greater cooperation grew ever more remote. With the passage of the sweeping national-security law in Hong Kong in the summer of 2020, Beijing effectively reneged on its promise of "one country, two systems" and crushed the growing pro-democracy movement there. China also has unfinished political business in Taiwan, which has become an economic success story independent of controls from the mainland. Having seen what became of Hong Kong, Taiwan worries about China's intentions, while the West frets about the possibility of intervention. Internally, China's treatment of the minority Uyghur population in its northwest has drawn accusations of crimes against humanity, including genocide. And yet, all condemnation from the international community has been met with stony silence, and the political and moral gulf between China and the West has continued to widen.

Most tellingly, China has been essentially absent when it comes to the most significant global challenges of our era. In the summer of 2021, a scientific report commissioned by the United Nations reported that global warming was already having catastrophic and likely irreversible effects on climate. As the US and other leading and industrial nations rushed to accelerate their reductions to carbon emissions, China responded coolly that it had already agreed to the targets in the Paris Accords and saw no reason to take further action. China, already the world's largest producer of greenhouse gases, was already on a course to increase fossil-fuel emissions before a planned cut-back in 2030. Even as Beijing pays lip service to reducing carbon emissions, new coal-fired power plants and factories continue to come online.

The UN report was met with the greatest alarm by the smaller nations of the developing world—the countries that are most vulnerable to the impact of climate change but have the least ability to do anything about it. If China will not take steps to defend against climate change for its own sake, how can the LICs, or any other country, for that matter, look to China for relief?

China also showed its true colors in during the COVID-19 pandemic, beginning in 2020. Here was a global health crisis that claimed millions of lives and crippled the economies of countries large and small. The virus originated in China, where the secrecy, obfuscation, and lack of early controls accelerated the spread of the disease around the world. China shut down the virus at home by shutting down lives in a way that only an authoritarian central government can do. Chinese-made vaccines were distributed internationally, primarily in Asia, but many experts questioned the efficacy of those vaccines. A number of nations reverted later to Western vaccines, even when they were in limited supply.

The long-term goal of foreign assistance and development is to bring more countries into the ranks of mature nations capable of productive partnerships so that they can contribute their share of what I call "the condo fees of global leadership" and share the burden of problems like climate change and public health in a concerted manner. China has yet to deliver in any meaningful way on either of those fronts, but it hasn't turned its back on the international community. Pronouncements from Beijing in 2021 and 2022 offered promise regarding cooperation on the environment and on global development. The goal is to avoid exacerbating the us-or-them posture that is currently taking shape and to build a new, more constructive relationship. It serves no country's interests to provoke trade wars or culture wars or any other kind of war. Still, it is imperative that we understand that nature abhors a vacuum. Beijing will rush in to fill any void not addressed by the United States and its allies—from vaccines to digital connectivity, from education to energy. China is extremely capable and focused and can make offers to developing countries that are hard to refuse. The goal of American soft power, as detailed in the second half of this book, is to enable better alternatives to those offers, alternatives grounded in the premise that prosperity and self-sufficiency develop hand-in-hand with freedom. The global challenges ahead will require global solutions, and the goal of our soft power is to help countries become part of those solutions.

PART II
THE TOOL KIT

Chapter 5

FREEDOM AND PROSPERITY

A Positive Theory of Change

W hat does positive change look like in the world of development? A number of metrics are available that show a
country's progress up the development ladder. Perhaps
the per capita GDP has reached a certain threshold number, or
the percentage of its GDP that comes from foreign aid has dwin-
dled or even vanished. Perhaps human security and well-being
have increased over time. Maybe a country that was once a major
aid recipient has transformed into a valued trading partner or a
once-struggling nation has achieved membership in the OECD.
Simply stated, development success means that a country has moved
from being a burden on the international community to sharing
the burden of global challenges while its people benefit from the
changing conditions. The theory of change that I outline in this
chapter and explicate in more detail in the chapters that follow
boils down to a few basic principles: the most significant driver

of progress is broad-based economic growth, internally driven but perhaps catalyzed by outside actors. That growth can only take hold in a social and political environment imbued with fairness and the rule of law, and strengthened by high-quality education and capable institutions.

In the 1960s, Walt Rostow, the advisor to John F. Kennedy who influenced the Foreign Assistance Act, posited a model based on stages of economic development, beginning with a traditional, agricultural society with limited technology, through what he famously called "take-off," with a manufacturing sector, physical infrastructure, and the emergence of an elite social class. Ultimately, a mature economy would comprise self-sustaining social, political, and economic institutions and be fully integrated into larger regional and global markets and systems. Development theory has evolved considerably since the 1960s when Rostow's model provided the framework for American overseas assistance. That model is now seen as dated and overly simplistic, insufficient to describe the complexities of individual developing cultures and economies or to account for the iterative, non-linear character of development. A country might have arrived at the moment of "take-off" but is still fragile and easily derailed on its drive to maturity. It could get stalled at any stage, like those countries that find themselves stuck in what aid workers call the "middle-income trap," in which an insufficiently skilled labor force or an undiversified economy limits continued growth.

Other economic theorists have offered different models and perspectives. Douglass C. North and his colleagues talk about the difference between *limited access* and *open access* social orders. All fragile countries are characterized by a limited access order, in which the resources and institutions necessary to create income and wealth are available to a finite cadre of elites who control production, trade, and government; and thus, they maintain power over the rest of the population. In a 2007 World Bank report, "Limited Access Orders and the Developing World," North and his coauthors noted, "LAOs encompass a wide variety of societies—the Roman republic and empire, Mesopotamia in the third millennia BCE, Britain under the Tudors, and modern Nigeria, Bolivia, and Russia. The limited access order is a general strategy for organizing society, not a specific set of political, economic, or religious institutions. Some are vicious authoritarian regimes (Uganda under Idi Amin) while others have elections (Argentina); some are failed states (Central African Republic) while others exhibit long-term stability (Mexico); still others have been socialist states (the former Soviet Union). All share the basic principle of manipulating the economy to produce rents, stability, and prevent violence." By contrast, open access orders are just what the name implies. Elites, and social stratification, still exist in OAOs, but they are by definition inclusive, in that anyone in such a society can, by law, access the sources of income generation. It follows naturally that OAOs thrive in the long term only in functioning democracies, whereas LAOs are generally characterized by autocracy, plutocracy, and oligarchy.

The economist Paul Collier talks about the "bottom billion" that inhabit the world's poorest countries, all of which are what North would call fragile limited access orders, as opposed to basic or mature LAOs that are further along on the development scale. Collier describes four basic traps that developing nations fall into: the conflict trap (debilitating wars); the natural resource trap, which can involve limiting access to wealth-generating resources or building an economy dependent on finite resources; the landlocked country with bad neighbors trap; and the bad governance in a small country trap.

Another great thinker on the subject of fragility is Daron Acemoglu, who, along with James Robinson, wrote *Why Nations Fail*. Acemoglu and Robinson see things through the lens of political and economic *institutions*—the rules and mechanisms within a society—which they see as ultimately more important to a country's success than geography or access to resources or ongoing conflict. They describe two types of institutions: *extractive*—those that exclude large segments of society from political and economic opportunity—and *inclusive*, which allow access for the widest possible strata of society. Inclusive institutions depend on a clear and consistent set of rules, that is to say, good governance and the rule of law.

These great economists and social theorists parse fragility and development in their unique fashion, but certain core principles run through them all. The transition from a limited access to an open access order, or from extractive to inclusive institutions, can only occur in the presence of social and political empowerment and transparency. Open market economies and liberal democratic political institutions need each other.

Fragility, in the context of development, is complex and unique to each country. It's rarely productive to think in binary terms about a country being fragile or not, but to understand fragility as a spectrum, along which a country's position is usually fluid, moving in different directions according to different metrics. There is no single, fixed definition of fragility, according to Ambassador James Michel, who served in the State Department and at USAID, and as chair of the highly influential Development Assistance Committee of the OECD, but it is commonly characterized by:

- Poor governance

- Limited institutional capability

- Low social cohesion

- Diminished societal resistance

- Low levels of human and economic development

- Violence

- Absence of respect for the rule of law.

One step in the right direction was the Global Fragility Act, signed into law in 2019. The act is intended to reduce violent conflict around the world, not by sending in the military as we have so often done, but by stabilizing and improving conditions that give rise to conflict in troubled areas. This new mandate calls for the formation of ten-year development plans aimed at least five selected vulnerable countries or regions. These plans are to involve the State Department and USAID, as well as all other relevant departments of the government, such as Defense or Treasury. For years, I've argued that the US needs targeted development plans—along the lines of the very successful Plan Colombia—for multiple countries, and I look at the Global Fragility Act as the first big step in that direction. On April 1, 2022, the White House announced that the initial priority countries and region for implementation of the Act would be Haiti, Libya, Mozambique, and Papua New Guinea—along with the region of coastal West Africa, which includes Benin, Côte d'Ivoire, Ghana, Guinea, and Togo.

Today, we see a variety of more subtle but equally significant indicators of progress up the development curve beyond increased wealth. The status of women improves as they gain access to education and the job market; birth rates decline while life expectancy rises; health needs move from basic hygiene and sanitation to wellness and prevention; education moves beyond improving literacy rates to advance training that keeps up with global technology. Countries now think in terms of power grids and digital infrastructure, as well as trade alliances and investment partnerships.

Rostow put forth his theories in the context of the groundbreaking Foreign Assistance Act of 1961. But international assistance is not the same as development, a complex, iterative process which involves domestically driven economic, social, and political progress and improvements in the quality of life. Direct assistance can never be more than a supporting player in another country's narrative. The OECD's Development Assistance Committee, in promoting a partnership model for development cooperation for the twenty-first century, emphasized that "the efforts of countries and societies to help themselves have been the main ingredients in their success." Each society is responsible for its own development. This is why committed local leadership is of such paramount importance. Neither buckets of aid money nor legions of advisors can stand in for political and civic leaders in a developing nation who have a vision of their own future and are able to communicate it to and win the support of the populace. Former USAID administrator Andrew Natsios described the massive aid effort in South Korea after the Korean War. American diplomats and aid workers insinuated themselves into all levels of the government, even sitting in on cabinet meetings, pushing the country's development in the direction they believed best, which had primarily to do with agriculture. But the South Korean leadership had a somewhat different vision, one of rising industrial strength. The president appreciated the counsel and assistance and worked closely with the outside advisors while steering the country as he thought best. The collaboration worked ideally. "Without him, we would have failed," said Natsios. "But without us, *he* would have failed."

Of course, there have been what can be called "autocratic success stories," countries that experienced broad-based economic growth under the stewardship of authoritarian governments or governments still transitioning toward full democracy. Singapore is a case in point, as is Vietnam, which remains a socialist republic under the Communist Party but continues to improve its economy through trade, tourism, and global integration. Communist Laos, next door, is as close as any country to being classified as a vassal state of China. Rather than write off countries like these as potential partners and important actors within the global community, OECD nations should recognize the opportunity to build relationships and influence through soft power.

Economic growth has accelerated, both globally and particularly across a wide range of developing countries. In his preface to the landmark 2008 report from the World Bank's Commission on Growth and Development (*The Growth Report*), economist Michael Spence wrote, "The number of people living in high-growth environments or in countries with OECD per capita income levels has increased in the past 30 years by a factor of four, from 1 billion to about 4 billion." It's interesting to note that Spence refers to the past thirty years, which constitute a kind of golden age of development. The Cold War had ended, and no one had yet begun to even imagine a new bilateral competition with China. Aid work was at least partially freed from those geopolitical constraints. Those years saw not just economic progress around the world but improvements in health and literacy, the status of women, democracy, and connectivity. It was in this period, in 2000, that the Millennium Development Goals (MDG) were established at the United Nations and then expanded and updated in 2015 as the Sustainable Development Goals[1], which continue to provide a philosophical and ethical compass for aid and development, both public and private.

At first blush, the economic statistics cited by Spence seem promising, but an increase in GDP on its own can't guarantee the success of a country's development. *The Growth Report*, the conclusions of which provide much of the theoretical foundation for my work, first at USAID and then at CSIS, acknowledges that no two country narratives are alike, but found certain key factors common to all success stories. A maturing nation will have:

1. fully exploited the world economy;

2. maintained macroeconomic stability;

3. mustered high rates of saving and investment;

4. allowed markets to allocate resources;

5. enabled and prioritized committed, credible, and capable governments.

Of these factors, I believe that functional and transparent government comes first, the mechanics of which I deal with in depth in Chapter 7. Numerous studies have confirmed the link between good governance, particularly democratic governance, and a reduction in global poverty. Entrepreneurs and investors are

---

1   Sustainable Development Goals: 1. No poverty. 2. Zero hunger. 3. Good health and well-being. 4. Quality education. 5. Gender equality. 6. Clean water and sanitation. 7. Affordable and clean energy. 8. Decent work and economic growth. 9. Industry, innovation, and infrastructure. 10. Reduced inequalities. 11. Sustainable cities and communities. 12. Responsible consumption and production. 13. Climate action. 14. Life below water. 15. Life on land. 16. Peace, justice, and strong institutions. 17. Partnerships for the goals.

unlikely to commit resources to an environment that lacks stability, reliability, and predictability. The same characteristics will also offer a national workforce a sense of security in the future, which would limit migration to countries with better employment prospects. Good governance, in this case, means not only general effectiveness but also a commitment to the rule of law and to regulatory policies that encourage business and investment and minimize the barriers to entry into a formal economy. James Michel argues that the rule of law is as critical to good governance as democratization. Kofi Annan defined the rule of law this way in 2004:

> The rule of law...refers to a principle of gover-
> nance in which all persons, institutions, and enti-
> ties, public and private, including the State itself,
> are accountable to laws that are publicly promul-
> gated, equally enforced, and independently adjudi-
> cated, and which are consistent with international
> human rights norms and standards. It requires, as
> well, measures to ensure adherence to the princi-
> ples of supremacy of law, equality before the law,
> accountability to the law, fairness in the application
> of the law, separation of powers, participation in
> decision-making, legal certainty, avoidance of arbi-
> trariness and procedural and legal transparency.

There exists today a Rule of Law Index, compiled by the World Justice Project, that makes evaluations based on the key principles of accountability, just laws, open government, and accessible and impartial dispute resolution. If I'm to start a business, I want to be clear about the rules under which it will operate, to know that everybody—competitors, vendors, customers, and so on—will be playing by the same rules and that a change in regime or administration isn't going to mean a change in the rules. I want to know that contracts have meaning and are enforceable; that taxes, tariffs, or fees won't spike suddenly or capriciously; that ownership rights can't be revoked; or that a coup or political revolution won't mean a government takeover of my industry. And the workers in my business will need to know that their livelihoods are not subject to the needs of an opaque or corrupt ruling class or that systemic inequality or an oppressive judicial system or hierarchical social system might hinder their personal advancement. Fundamentally, workers, owners, and managers need the assurance that opposing political movements within a country are committed to the same fundamental economic model.

One great setback to private-sector growth in development was the discontinuation in 2021 of the World Bank's Doing Business project, which was as close to a quantitative measurement of the rule of law as we're likely to see. The Doing Business project provided objective measures of business regulations and their enforcement for almost 200 countries, cities, and regions within countries, using indicators including starting a business, dealing with construction permits, getting electricity or credit, ease of paying taxes, enforcing contracts, trading across borders, or contracting with the government. The average American citizen may never have heard of the Doing Business project, but the annual report was front-page news all over the world. Countries have a vested interest in seeing their rankings improve. As such, the report drove reforms that facilitate entrepreneurism and economic growth. The program was paused and then stopped completely because of suspected irregularities in the data used for some countries and the questionable behavior of some World Bank officials. With the end of the Doing Business project, there is no reliable measurement of how the rule of law affects the business environment from country to country. Ideally, the Doing Business project would be reinstated. But if that is not possible or likely, we need to find an alternative. If a vitally important program such as the Doing Business project needs cleaning up, clean it up, but to dispense with it entirely is a shortsighted decision, a clear case of throwing the baby out with the bathwater.

Other success factors also derive from good governance. For example, if we accept that a high rate of broad-based growth in an individual country's economy is only made possible by integration with an open global economy, then it stands to reason that the country's trading partners and investors will want full faith and confidence in its long-term stability. They don't want to worry about shipping channels shutting down because of persistent regional conflicts or local business partners facing government persecution.

Within the developing country, industries need access to the vast export market, while the drivers of a growing economy must be able to tap into the global network for creativity, knowledge, and expertise. Growth needs foreign investment, at least at the outset, as well as access to foreign education. It's more efficient to learn and build on existing knowledge than to re-invent the wheel. As *The Growth Report* puts it, "Sustainable, high growth is catch-up growth. And the global economy is the essential resource."

As we'll examine in Chapter 8, higher education remains one of the most effective tools of soft power. But it has diminished as a component of aid, largely because its value to US interests may not be apparent for years or decades into the future, while the time horizons for budgeting and measuring the impact of aid projects have gotten shorter and shorter. During the Cold War, the US was supporting roughly 20,000 foreign students each year for American undergraduate and graduate degrees. When the New Directions focus on basic human needs became the main driver of US development strategy, basic early education replaced higher education as a priority, and the number of scholarships offered has been slashed to a few thousand. By contrast, China, having replicated this proven technique, lavishes scholarships on close to ten times that number, sometimes even offering classes in English, the lingua franca of international business and diplomacy.

American colleges and universities are still the gold standard around the world, and there is proven value in providing access to education for future leaders of the developing world. In the last century, the US offered scholarships to thousands of South Korean nationals as part of the effort to rebuild that war-ravaged country. Aid veterans point out that those young people returned home and effectively led South Korea for the next thirty years, which is in part why the country is not only a staunch strategic ally but also one of the top ten trading partners with investments in the US that have created millions of jobs. In the aid community, this is the very definition of "graduation," although that term is now falling out of use. USAID closed its mission in South Korea in 1980, and the country became a member of OECD in 1996, the second Asian country after Japan. In 2009, Korea became a member of the OECD's Development Assistance Committee, made up of donor countries.

Most importantly, good governance, functional, accountable institutions, and an empowered civil society enable self-reliance. A stable, welcoming economy invites innovation and investment that makes possible the next most important success factor in growth: the establishment of a viable formal economy via the private sector. Economic growth driven by private-sector initiatives is the subject of Chapter 9. Government should not be responsible for job creation, as it was in the former Soviet bloc, and as it still often is in China. However, government must be a facilitator, enabling the private sector to flourish. The best social program in the world is a job. Jobs in a formal economy pay regular wages, are at least in theory regulated for worker health and safety, generate taxes, and may even offer savings vehicles for workers, who thereby channel more money into the financial markets and the economy. A formal economy is the first step in domestic resource mobilization (DRM), the process by which a country generates and spends money to provide for its population. Aid has long ceased to be the biggest wallet when it comes to financing development. The role of foreign assistance moving forward is to catalyze local capacity and a thriving private sector. That, in turn, creates jobs, which, in concert with a stable government, leads to public trust and an implicit social contract between the government and the people that allows for the collection of taxes and saving and investment. DRM makes possible a country's progress toward self-reliance, and indeed the ultimate goal of all aid programs is to see the recipient reduce its need until it eventually graduates.

With the ability to fund its own treasury, a government can plan and build for the long term, directing public investment into health, education, hard infrastructure, and vital supply chains and addressing larger challenges, like environmental stewardship. Ninety percent of the financing for that kind of infrastructure development generally comes from taxes and other forms of domestic resource mobilization. (A 2018 report from the organization Development Initiatives, "Investments to End Poverty," makes a compelling case for the importance of DRM.)

A formal economy's reliance on good governance goes beyond well-intentioned top-level leadership. It involves building and maintaining institutions, from banking systems and financial markets to regulatory agencies and administrative ministries, to regional and municipal public institutions, all of which require an educated civil-servant class. Such institutions contribute to domestic resource mobilization but also manage and regulate it. In the real world, of course, the larger and more complex government structure becomes, particularly as money starts to flow more abundantly in an economy, the greater the opportunities for corruption on a large scale. In a weak, informal economy, getting things done often involves favoritism, bribes, payoffs, and various quid pro quo arrangements. Public funds, and often foreign aid money, often gets diverted before getting to the intended destination. These habits don't die easily in a growing economy and an expanding bureaucracy and can cripple progress. So anti-corruption safeguards and strengthening local capacity for institutional integrity have become an essential part of aid efforts to foster good governance.

In a 2021 Global Development Forum, Andrew Natsios made the point that as important as modernized infrastructure can be to a country's development, that infrastructure can't be maintained without functioning institutions, and this is exactly why American soft power is so important. As mentioned earlier, there has been a perception created that when China builds a dam or bridge or port or rail terminal in a developing country, their engagement with and long-term concern for that country is minimal. There is an impression that countries see the Chinese firms as bringing in their own engineers and construction workers to ease their labor surplus at home. Experienced aid workers report that often, the recipient nation—like many in Africa—feels some measure of resentment mixed in with the hopes for the new project. Whether or not that perception is always based in reality, it has been widespread enough that China has taken steps to change the way it talks about overseas infrastructure projects. A developing nation wants assistance and advancement, not dependency. They want a country to share the expertise and resources that would allow them to build on their own, with their own labor force, in a way that meets local customs and standards.

If the US and other OECD nations see aid as an essential tool of statecraft and a way to forge relationships and nurture strategic partners, this would not be the way to go about it. Western aid programs are designed to include elements that foster civil society; further democracy, human rights, and the rule of law; and build functioning institutions that enable economic growth, public health, and education at all levels. It's significant that the piece that China has chosen to emulate is the provision of scholarships for advanced degrees. Even if experts have questioned the value of those degrees, it's clear that Beijing understands the potential impact of offering higher education, and it's disconcerting to think that they seem to be beating us at the game that we invented.

The impact of soft-power influence on the elites of the developing world is not to be discounted. Fragile or failing states often experience a "brain drain"—the best and brightest, frustrated by lack of opportunity, or for some cultural reason excluded from important or powerful positions in their home country, seek their fortunes elsewhere. Of those that find a way to study abroad, too many choose to remain there rather than putting their training and knowledge work back home. Failing nations also tend to bleed wealth. The families with money to invest are reluctant to do so in an unstable economy or in the context of a corrupt government or in a country that is experiencing a mass exodus of its workforce.

The development community spends a lot of time analyzing the impact of global migration on the countries that absorb these refugees, but not enough is said on the damage done to the countries that they've left behind. Without the monied and educated classes, who will create and manage businesses? Who will fuel financial markets, which, in turn, can capitalize new businesses? Development banks and the private sector can't take up the slack, especially if nobody is seeking funding. Without new business and innovation, without a maximized workforce paying taxes in a formal economy, there's little opportunity for the domestic resource mobilization that allows a country to take hold of its own development.

We've already seen how this played out in parts of Latin America, where the elites sought to escape the stigma of narcotics, insurrection, and governmental corruption. Now we see newly wealthy Chinese leaving the mainland, Hong Kong, and Taiwan, or at least creating options for themselves overseas, although Beijing began cracking down on some of that activity in 2020.

Foreign aid only goes so far in reversing this kind of downward spiral. Aid dollars can't rescue a failing economy or put new political or business leaders in place. What it can do is plant the seeds of change—but only if the leaders in that fragile country have a vision, a plan to execute that vision, and the ability to communicate in a way that convinces elites to bring their skills and wealth home and potential refugees to give growth a chance.

*   *   *   *   *

It's easy to put forth various theories of change and grand strategies for development, but the real world has a way of disrupting the best-laid plans. The most obvious, consistent disruptors are wars and natural disasters, but the greatest disruptor that this generation has seen is the COVID-19 pandemic. The global health crisis that began in 2020 has forced us to adjust our thinking about the world. It has triggered setbacks for multiple developing countries with shaky or unstable informal economies and for countries that depend heavily on income from travel and tourism or from a single primary commodity. Never has the critical importance of a diversified economy been felt more acutely.

The COVID-19 disruption occurred at a moment when aid donors with finite resources had begun to consider reprioritizing their efforts in the direction of fostering better government and broader institutional development beyond short-term technocratic fixes. That would mean reducing the attention paid to basic human needs unless a recipient nation is in crisis or experiencing an emergency. Evidence suggests that good governance, particularly democratic governance, leads to better development outcomes and economic growth. This transition will be difficult to negotiate at a moment when public health consumes so much attention in the aid community.

The COVID-19 crisis shined a harsh, glaring light on global inequality. Wealthier, more advanced countries made noble proclamations about vaccine distribution and providing medical expertise to less developed countries. But little of that played out in reality, even when the flow of goods and services to the global north was hampered by the crippled economies of those struggling countries. It seemed that never was there a better opportunity to harness global interconnectivity and cooperation for the sake of the public good. But darker forces seized the moment, sowing doubt and spreading disinformation that only exacerbated the threat to public health.

On the one hand, the pandemic showcased the value and importance of digital communications. The years 2020 and 2021 saw more e-commerce, e-learning, and e-government, more digital banking, money transfer, and investing than ever before. On the other hand, however, that activity brought the digital divide between rich and poor countries into stark relief. Partnerships bringing the private and public sectors together are going to be needed. So much remains to be done to bring digital technology in the global south up to speed. Without closing this new digital divide, development is likely to stall.

. . . . .

Disruptors remind us that neither diplomacy nor development proceed in a linear, predictable fashion. International actors need to remain flexible, adjusting to the evolving imperatives of each particular moment and each particular local context. Nonetheless, certain key assumptions have held true for the last seventy-five years and will continue to serve as a broadly agreed framework. A comprehensive paper from CSIS in 2013, "Our Shared Opportunity: A Vision for Global Development," laid out a description of those basic elements:

- Private-sector-led, broad-based economic growth is the transformational force in development.

- Business investment, when done responsibly, can foster growth that creates jobs for many citizens and lifts community living standards.

- A transparent, accountable, and capable public sector creates conditions that enable private investment that drives development and ensures the resulting benefits are widely spread.

The report went on to declare that "engagement in all countries should work to build long-term economic partnerships by promoting: a healthy and educated workforce of men and women; legal and judicial processes that protect local and international companies; and institutions that will provide service and transparency to citizens, businesses, and organizations." The authors of the report reiterated that developing countries don't want to be told what to do; they want to be dealt with as trading partners and economic peers, not as charity cases. Development efforts must embrace this shared opportunity, with the private sector as a full and willing partner.

Much of the very meaningful development progress of the last thirty years is today stalled or imperiled. Another important paper to come out of CSIS, "Reforming and Reorganizing U.S. Foreign Assistance," was put together by a bipartisan task force chaired by Senators Jeanne Shaheen of New Hampshire and Todd Young of Indiana. The conclusions reached by the report supported the need for a revitalized US presence in the developing world in the form of a strengthened USAID and other mechanisms through which the US can provide soft-power efforts that support broader national security strategy. The task force called for rethinking the personnel and procurement systems while cutting away redundancies and streamlining reporting. But it strongly endorsed the ongoing independence of USAID as a critical component of national security strategy, at a time when the Trump administration was considering folding it into State. The report reminded people why foreign assistance matters, citing such milestone successes as stemming the spread of the Ebola crisis, humanitarian responses from the Indian Ocean tsunami to earthquakes and hurricanes from Pakistan to Haiti, and the use of development finance instruments that enabled public-private partnerships around the world.

In the second half of this book, I will detail soft-power solutions: ways in which we can update and refocus the tools, practices, and personnel of foreign aid to enable as many countries as possible to become and remain self-reliant partners in global development cooperation rather than aid recipients. The development community has struggled to find the right vocabulary to describe a country's arrival at this advanced state. For years, it was called "graduation," which is both a bit paternalistic and inadequate. Even when we started talking about the "journey to self-reliance" during the Trump years, it didn't quite capture the significance. But what I mean when I talk about this process is that a country has become a net contributor to the global good and is an aspirational free-market democracy.

The structure set out in the Global Fragility Act of 2019 holds the promise of a coherent and coordinated framework that can be productively applied in a far wider range of countries than those experiencing conflict and fragility. That flexible structure for international cooperation can be used broadly to improve development planning and to strengthen and streamline global organizations and the development finance infrastructure, restructure and retrain foreign service staff, recommit to education, entrepreneurship and innovation, and customize aid to specific local cultures and priorities. Perhaps most important, it can help restore the preeminence of free-market democratic principles and the liberal world order.

Chapter 6:

JOINING THE BIG LEAGUES

International Institutions

I n 2020, I organized a conference at CSIS on the future leadership of the Organization for Economic Cooperation and Development (OECD). I bet that a good percentage of Washington professionals, while they may have heard discussions involving OECD, couldn't tell you exactly what the organization does. The election of a new secretary-general wouldn't take place until March 2021, but here we were, more than a year before, examining options and planning strategy. That's the level of importance ascribed to the OECD by internationalists in all fields of economic and development cooperation.

Founded in 1961, the Organization for Economic Cooperation and Development is one of the vitally important international organizations underlying the liberal world order, but it's not especially familiar to many people. This elite club of free-market economies, which also functions as one of the world's premier standard-setting institutions, has only thirty-eight member nations. Within the OECD are committees, directorates, working groups, and networks, focusing on issues such as economics, entrepreneurship, tax policy and administration, the environment, science and technology, trade and agriculture, education, labor and social affairs, public governance, statistics, and, of course, development.

Rising nations openly covet membership, which signals a kind of arrival or acceptance as a mature and significant country. For example, the Latin American countries of Chile, Colombia, and Costa Rica have become members in recent years. Brazil has a working relationship with the OECD and is applying for membership, but it has not yet completed the process. Brazil knows that the OECD stamp of approval would boost the confidence of potential foreign investors and validate its graduation to the status of a developed country. Even as the competition for new leadership of the organization was ongoing, I published arguments in favor of Brazil's candidacy, knowing that the country, under the leadership of Jair Bolsonaro, who generates controversy among some of the OECD member states, would have to make policy adjustments before its membership could be approved. For Brazil, I argued, OECD accession should be seen as a strong incentive to institute much-needed reforms and align the country more closely with global standards.

At that time, the OECD secretary-general, Angel Gurria of Mexico, had been in office for fifteen years. I believed that the next leader would set the organization's influential path in the multilateral ecosystem for at least five years, during which time he or she would face critical decisions affecting international approaches to tax systems, digital transformation, trade, foreign aid, education, corruption and public integrity, climate change, and access to critical natural resources. As various names were bandied about at the conference, it became clear to me that it would be to the United States' advantage to have someone from Australia or New Zealand in the top position. Conversations with a senior Australian official produced a name, Mathias Cormann, who soon emerged as a candidate.

The selection of leaders of major multinational organizations is a complex process involving non-public consultations, and it is always fraught with politics. All the other candidates came from

Europe—Sweden, Switzerland, and Greece—and I sensed that a strong candidate from the Asia-Pacific region, especially one from a country with economic and geopolitical priorities that aligned with those of the US, would strengthen the organization and help cement its ongoing influence at a delicate moment of global power competition. Cormann was focused on anti-corruption, as well as global standards in digital technology, and supported the idea of expanding OECD membership. Additionally, the accession of an Australian candidate would further signal to China the relevance of the OECD to Asia. My colleagues and I supported Cormann's candidacy with articles and reports that made their way through the Biden White House. After he was elected, I was invited to meet with the new secretary-general.

When we refer to "multilateral organizations" or "the international community," what comes immediately to mind for most people outside government are institutions like the United Nations or NATO, maybe the European Union. In fact, the multilateral system that supports the liberal world order comprises a network of literally hundreds of specialized organizations. They operate largely out of the public eye but are known to tiny communities of cognoscenti, in addition to the policy wonks and technocrats that staff them. The work they do literally keeps the planet running. These multilateral institutions set the rules that facilitate productive and efficient interactions between countries. They store the data and write the checks; they confer legitimacy, validation, and approval; and they serve as vehicles of collective action. They spread and protect democratic values, protect commercial and political interests, help fight hunger and poverty and environmental degradation, promote financial stability, combat terrorism, and so much more. And yet they are rarely top of mind, often even to people in government. It's very easy for politicians to take these organizations for granted, to become complacent and inadvertently neglectful. I make my living trying to influence policy in this arena and still have trouble keeping the alphabet soup of acronyms clear in my head.

While some international organizations date from the nineteenth century, the invaluable multilateral system that today supports global governance was built largely in the years following World War II with heavy American initiative and influence. The system continues to function best with continuing American attention. But the United States let down its guard to some extent, beginning in the optimistic years after the end of the Cold War. In the absence of a global competitor, the US redirected its foreign policy and development priorities. As a result, the US has been losing its historical influence in multilateral organizations, in particular its influence in the selection of outstanding leaders in senior positions. Leadership excellence doesn't always require an American at the helm. But it does often depend on US engagement and coordination with like-minded countries. Reversing the trend of waning American influence must be the highest priority of any strategy for global engagement.

The OECD is one of twenty or so major institutions that occupy what I call the commanding heights of the multilateral system and which facilitate global action across a variety of critical areas, particularly development and standard-setting. Other groups might get more headlines, like the World Bank, the International Monetary Fund, the World Health Organization, or the major regional multilateral development banks (MDBs) like the African, Asian, and Inter-American Development Banks. Institutions, including the International Labor Organization, UN's Development Program, the Food and Agriculture Organization, World Food Program, UNICEF, and dozens of others, coordinate vital services across the globe. Still others have a narrower mandate but also play important roles in the world's affairs, such as the International Telecommunications Union and the World Intellectual Property Organization.

As the geopolitical environment grows more complicated, multilateral development institutions are important forums for consensus-building and decision-making. Their work can improve human conditions, deter conflict, and promote peace and security. The United States has been at the center of the multilateral system since its inception nearly eight decades ago and continues to be a vital advocate for universal liberal values in these institutions. Historically, the United States has been the single greatest financial supporter of international organizations. However, US influence in the multilateral system over the past thirty years has gradually decreased as developing countries increase their influence and footholds.

The increased presence and influence of developing nations in the multilateral bodies can be a double-edged sword. More countries contributing money, manpower, and expertise to the institutions means a broader base for consensus and less of the onus falling on the United States and a handful of other wealthy nations. However, the benefits only accrue if those newly arrived burden-sharers are prepared to help maintain the operating system that the United States has promoted over the years—one based on principles of democracy, human rights, humanitarian concern, and the rule of law.

If new major players don't share those principles, their increased presence becomes problematic. China's growing role in the United Nations and its network of specialized agencies and bodies—UNICEF, ILO, WHO, UNHCR, and so on—threatens the international order that the US has led. In addition to serving as the host country for the UN since its inception in 1945, the United States has remained the biggest single financial contributor and has provided the largest number of employees in the UN system. China, however, has moved quickly and strategically to raise its profile and influence at the UN in recent years, overtaking Japan to become the second-largest funder, increasing its staff presence and the number of military personnel participating in UN peacekeeping missions.

At the time of this writing, China heads three of the fifteen UN specialized agencies, while the United States leads just one. China has also placed young talent at lower staff levels across these organizations, doubling the number of Chinese nationals over the last decade. According to reporting in *Foreign Policy*, "In an effort to boost Chinese representation at the U.N. and other international organizations, Chinese universities have promoted foreign language classes and offered courses and scholarships for students interested in studying international organizations." In addition, "the China Scholarship Council, which provides government-funded scholarships to students studying abroad, underscored its interest in expanding its support for Chinese nationals in U.N. bodies, stating in a paper that it had formed partnerships with nine U.N. agencies to employ interns and entry-level staffers."

The hard numbers may be lower than those of other member states overall, but remember that China has only been focusing on this mission for ten years. During that period, US representation among national delegations and the presence of qualified Americans in staff positions in the multilateral system at large have declined. Despite being the largest funder of international organizations, the United Nations has classified the United States in 2020 as one of thirty-five "Underrepresented Member States." As these trends continue, there is a genuine risk that these institutions may come to be aligned with more authoritarian norms and interests.

The multilateral system with active American leadership is, in my estimation, our best hope for broad-based growth and stability, as it can make possible the combination of private-sector investment, public-private partnerships, and responsible governance that leads to prosperity. Perhaps, at some point, China will have to rein in its spending. But for the foreseeable future, the US won't be able to compete financially with China's massive foreign investment in hard infrastructure around the world via its Belt and Road and other initiatives. The fact that China has become such a major source of development funding in Asia, Africa, and Latin America is likely to add to the weight it carries in multilateral institutions.

For the United States to continue in its global leadership role, it needs to rebuild its influence in multilateral organizations and work with allies and like-minded partners. Based on the selection of priority organizations, the US can craft a multiagency strategic approach on where and how the US wants to engage in addressing anticipated turnover in the leadership of the hundreds of multilateral institutions in the world. Conversely, if the US government remains passive on this front, it risks further ceding its influence and credibility in the multilateral system, as well as undermining the influence of its traditional network of alliances.

Leadership in the major international organizations is divided up through a series of informal understandings I call the "global spoils system." The United States and its European allies arrived at this system at the end of World War II while launching the Bretton Woods institutions—the World Bank and IMF. In this system, it is understood that an American will be president of the World Bank and that the IMF will have a European managing director. This "gentlemen's agreement" came into being when a senior US Treasury Department official, and a key architect of the system, Harry

Dexter White, was widely expected to become the first managing director of the IMF—until he was accused in 1948 of having acted as a Soviet agent. A European ended up being selected for the top job at the IMF, and that has since become standard practice. A similar understanding ensures that someone from Japan has led the Asian Development Bank since its inception in 1966. Informal arrangements among the United States, Europe, Japan, and other countries about who should lead these global institutions ensured such institutions remained committed to their founding ideals while also divvying up some of the most important posts to reflect the practical politics of the moment. While not perfect, the global spoils system has largely succeeded at promoting a world based on liberal values and keeping most nations, including the United States, in the multilateral system.

The gentlemen's agreements that comprise this global system have taken some heat in recent years. The World Bank, for example, is arguably the leading institution in the fight against global poverty. As the developing world generally become richer, there has been a push to see representatives of some emerging nations step up and take leadership roles in the institutions that helped to drive their progress. This was one of the reasons that the Trump administration's 2019 nomination of David Malpass to take over the presidency of the bank from Jim Kim triggered controversy. Malpass drew fire from Democrats in Washington and many World Bank member nations for his public questioning not only of the bank's operation but of the very idea of multilateralism, which, he said, "has gone substantially too far—to the point where it is hurting U.S. and global growth."

Pundits and politicos published columns and op-eds denouncing Malpass's candidacy, proclaiming it one more instance of then-President Trump "trashing" established norms and appointing people to run departments and institutions of government that they claimed to disdain. My concern was that with China actively insinuating itself into the multilateral system, it was precisely the wrong time to relinquish US leadership of something as important as the World Bank. I published my own columns in enthusiastic support of Malpass, and I was the only voice inside the Beltway making that argument. I had confidence that Malpass believed in the bank's mission and that he wasn't wrong to want to overhaul its bloated bureaucracy and impose tighter controls on how money was disbursed within recipient countries. I also thought his concerns about China having become one of the largest recipients of the bank's loans were well-founded. My intent was to clear away the brush of Washington infighting and ensure the ongoing health of the multilateral system. Malpass was unanimously approved as the World Bank president in April 2019.

The global spoils system experienced another "disturbance in the force" that required seeing past partisan politics when Donald Trump put forth the name of Mauricio Claver-Carone, an American of Cuban descent, to lead the Inter-American Development Bank. The IDB, the leading source of development funding in Latin America, has always had a president from one of its member countries in the region. The American stake in the bank is enough to give it de facto veto power, so Trump's nomination of Claver-Carone was essentially an appointment. Member nations were highly aggrieved by the high-handed appointment but had been unable to coalesce around an alternative candidate of their own choosing. Democrats in Washington were also outraged by what they considered Claver-Carone's hardline position on Cuba and opposed his confirmation. Claver-Carone may be a problematic choice for many, but I believe withholding financial and political support for IDB because one is unhappy with Claver-Carone's appointment would be a mistake. In essence, it would be arguing that the institution and its mission are smaller than the person leading it. He was quick to call for a capital increase for IDB, which should be something to be considered under the right conditions as the region copes with a dizzying array of problems, including the COVID-19 pandemic and the resulting economic wreckage, shifts in global trade patterns, mass migration, bad governance, and meeting the reliable and clean energy needs of the future.

Again, seen through the lens of bilateral competition with China, this was not the time to leave this institution in disarray. China is a member of the IDB and has its own agenda in Central and South America. It is already either the top trading partner or in the second position for dozens of countries in the hemisphere. Congress has been supportive about providing political and financial support for the IDB, but not enough as of this printing to force the Biden administration to enact a capital increase. Withholding support for a capital increase for the IDB over the next several years is a mistake given the challenges in the region.

During the first year of the Biden administration, confirmations were languishing for many ambassadors and officials holding ambassadorial rank nominated by President Biden to represent the United States in multilateral organizations. Like other senior positions in the Biden administration, these appointments had been sidetracked for an extended period by political rancor in Washington. In addition to the IDB, affected organizations include the Asian Development Bank (ADB), the World Bank, the Organization of American States (OAS), the International Civil Aviation Organization (ICAO), and the US representative to the United Nations in Geneva. My colleagues in the Republican Party may have had real concerns about some of the Biden administration's policies, but my belief was that if the US intends to take the bilateral competition with China seriously, legislators on both sides of the aisle had to prioritize the importance of continuity and stability in these organizations over what are minor political wins and losses. I wrote a strongly worded op-ed on the subject in the fall of 2021, which I have been told helped push a number of Biden nominees to confirmation. By the spring of 2022, most of these confirmations had gone through.

Since this power-sharing system largely reflects geopolitical realities, it has been replicated in many of the world's multilateral organizations. In some organizations, it takes the form of reserved seats for certain countries or regions; in others, there is an informal understanding that more influential countries will have greater representation and rotations; and in still others, the vote shareholdings reflect the size of the contributions made by different nation-states.

Historically, votes and influence in the major multilateral institutions have been tied directly to the percentage of shares owned by a given country. For instance, the United States owned 40 percent of the shares in the IMF at the time of the fund's inception. That percentage has been diluted to about 17 percent to make room both for allies and for newly developing countries that, as they have grown richer, have demanded a larger role on the international stage. In 2009, the US needed to pay in an additional $300 million to maintain its status at the IMF—the only country with a large enough position to have unilateral veto power. Similarly, I was persuaded by Lael Brainard, at the time the undersecretary of the Treasury for International Affairs and now vice-chair of the Federal Reserve, to testify in Congress on behalf of a capital increase for the World Bank, again to ensure the continued influence of the US in that institution.

.   .   .   .   .

At the IMF especially, the allotment of shares has become a bone of contention for developing countries. In November 2010, the Obama administration negotiated a package of IMF reforms at the G-20 summit in Seoul. The centerpiece of these reforms was an effort to increase the representation of emerging and developing countries within the IMF by shifting 6 percent of the IMF quota share to these countries. This shift would increase their voting shares as well as their financial commitments to the IMF. The reforms would also shift funds to different accounts, making more money available for emergencies involving those emerging nations. At the time, many Republican lawmakers in Washington were suspicious of quota reform, seeing it as a potential gift to the likes of Russia and China, whose percentages would increase. But in response, conservative internationalist Senator Lindsey Graham argued that the IMF "can provide stability at a time we need it. From the long view, the IMF is a strategic tool for United States foreign policy. We would be shortsighted to not embrace this reform." I wrote extensively in support of quota reform at IMF, particularly in 2014, when by making IMF quota reform part of an aid package being negotiated on behalf of embattled Ukraine, it was possible to make bailout money immediately available with no additional cost to US taxpayers.

How does the IMF or the World Bank become an ally for advancing foreign policy objectives? By working through these institutions, the US and like-minded nations can maintain influential relationships with more than a hundred countries that have geostrategic significance. Ukraine is a case in point. Infusions from IMF loans have buttressed the Ukraine economy for years, even though the country hasn't always fully complied with the conditions of the loans. Ukraine has not been a great partner or burden sharer, but allowing that economy to collapse would perhaps mean opening the door for Russian expansionism.

Perhaps an even more telling example is Pakistan. The US has poured billions of dollars of direct aid over many years, as has the IMF, but Pakistan still struggles. Some external factors, such as fluctuating oil prices, have hurt Pakistan's economy. Yet most of the problems are homegrown, arising from weak economic policies and very low levels of domestic resource mobilization, among other factors. Pakistan's partnering with China's Belt and Road Initiative—the China-Pakistan Economic Corridor—has contributed significantly to its debt burden, and its system is ill-equipped to pay back that debt. Of course, this has created a serious problem for the West for several reasons: Pakistan's geographic position in one of the world's most volatile regions, where it has significant influence, and because of it is a nuclear power. Who can say what would happen to that arsenal were the economy and government to collapse?

A bilateral bailout from China would not address the systemic policy and governance problems underlying Pakistan's mounting debt. Moreover, if China offered a bailout in the form of renegotiating the debt it held, it could lead to the kind of debt-trap diplomacy employed in debtor developing countries. A US bailout to Pakistan would never get through Congress; aid has even been curtailed recently due to Pakistan's inaction when it came to expelling Taliban insurgents within their borders. The only reasonable way to shore up Pakistan in this delicate situation is through the IMF. Also, the IMF would negotiate loan terms based on its judgment, as an independent multilateral entity, of what Pakistan needs to do to be a responsible borrower. But many in Washington, especially on the Republican side, oppose that, arguing that insofar as Pakistan's debt is held by China, a bailout now would effectively constitute a gift to Chinese banks. But again, Pakistan's situation must now be viewed through the lens of bilateral power competition. I summed up the situation in an essay for CSIS. "The IMF's focus is not projecting power and influence; rather, it seeks to help struggling nations get back on their feet. The same cannot be said for China." The unspoken fear about Pakistan, the fifth most populous country in the world with one of the world's largest youth bulges, is that a collapsed Pakistan might suffer significant political upheaval and that an "irresponsible" government might decide to more actively export nuclear weapons and nuclear know-how.

The consequences of inaction can be significant. Around the time of the Iraq war, when IMF approved a bailout package for Turkey, an inconsistent ally but with strategic value in the region, it also chose not to make much-needed money available to Argentina. Without support from the IMF, the democratically elected de la Rua government of Argentina collapsed, leading to twenty years of anti-American sentiment, much more fragile governance, and the failure of the Free Trade of the Americas Agreement. As of 2021, China had become Argentina's leading trading partner. It is building and financing an $8 billion nuclear power plant there and has installed "scientific observation" bases, including a "deep space" station, meaning that Beijing had established a military foothold in Argentina. (China's space program is run by the People's Liberation Army (PLA), as opposed to NASA, which is a civilian agency.)

There are many countries that have not proven to be great allies or burden-sharers but that still deserve attention from the multilateral system. Allowing those countries to fall out of that system would be perilous.

China has always owned a very small percentage of shares in IMF until it seemed an agreement was reached during the Obama administration to slightly increase China's share. All the member countries agreed, except for the United States. This important agreement was hung up for six years while Obama and Congress argued about how to proceed. Such delays were not entirely uncommon; members of multilateral institutions had become somewhat used to waiting while deals like this worked their way through the dysfunctional American political system. With a couple of trillion dollars' worth of cash in its central bank, China saw no reason to wait patiently while the US dithered. The Chinese decided simply to set up their own bank in 2016, based in Beijing, which became the Asian Infrastructure Investment Bank, or AIIB. This institution is not to be confused with ADB, the Asian Development Bank, a venerable and important regional development bank in operation since 1966. As the name suggests, this new institution focuses on infrastructure in Asia. AIIB has attracted 103 member nations, including many US allies, since opening its doors in 2016. Compare that to the Asian Development Bank, which has sixty-eight members after more than fifty years in operation. It would be wise to assume that AIIB will find its footing and become an attractive source of financing and know-how, further cementing its influence in the region.

As countries move up the development curve and take more control over their own growth, old-fashioned donor-recipient relationships become less useful and relevant than major power or transportation projects that can drive economic progress. Not only did such projects dovetail nicely with the kind of "aid" China is wont to export, but such big infrastructure projects had become ever more difficult to get through the traditional multilateral development banks because of hesitancy around environmental and indigenous community concerns.

It shouldn't have surprised anyone that, with its booming economy and rising stature on the international stage, China would grow tired of the slowness and infighting, as well as the frustrating rules and limitations imposed on projects by these financial institutions, and that they would prefer a development bank in which they played the central role. At AIIB, China would have nearly a third of the shares, would appoint a Chinese president (in fact, a senior Chinese technocrat from the Asian Development Bank), and recruit staff from around the world. That turned out to be easier said than done. For starters, Beijing is not the most attractive or welcoming city in the world, especially compared to headquarters sites and related accommodation provided for employees of other multilateral organizations and their families. Second, candidates for employment at AIIB believed that some of the Chinese employees were political commissars placed there to keep an eye on things; foreign workers would have to get used to being observed—spied on—as they went about their personal and professional lives. If that sounds too much like how visitors described Moscow during the Cold War, talk to a former US government colleague of mine who worked in China and confirmed through the airlines that the same Chinese man was seated next to him on every flight back to the US.

Not only did those simple concerns make it difficult for AIIB to attract the best people, but the work of the bank has been unexciting. Whereas the Manila-based Asian Development Bank has offices in forty-eight countries, researching and launching multiple development projects, AIIB has only the one office in Beijing. And rather than originating projects, it generally piggybacks onto projects coming out of the World Bank or ADB. The lesson is that while China, through the establishment of AIIB, is taking a shot at becoming a player in the multilateral community and even offering an alternative to the Bretton Woods institutions, it has fallen short, at least for the time being.

AIIB's immediate impact in development may be underwhelming, but the United States and its allies need to understand its potential and must take all necessary steps to ensure that the World Bank, IMF, and the major regional development banks remain vigorous and fully engaged. If these organizations find themselves with diminished resources, or if the influence wielded by the US decreases, there is no doubt that China, through AIIB, through its bilateral aid and export credit agencies, or through increased influence in the Bretton Woods institutions themselves, will fill the vacuum, further weakening the authority inherent in the established world order. I like to ask my more conservative colleagues in Washington—those often less convinced of the importance of these institutions, "Are you comfortable letting China set the global rules?" A good part of my support for David Malpass at the World Bank was the looming challenge of China in the multilateral system.

Beijing has proven to be very shrewd about its role in the world of multilateral institutions. AIIB is not the only alternative to the established development banks in which China has gotten involved. In 2014, China joined with Brazil, Russia, India, and South Africa in launching the New Development Bank, more commonly known as the BRICS Bank, after its five founding member nations. These five countries are all important emerging economies. For perspective, they account for more than 25 percent of the world's land and more than 40 percent of its population. Each of these resource-rich countries seems poised at the threshold but, for individual reasons, has struggled to get unstuck from middle-income status. I would argue that they've all been held back, at least in part, by problems with unstable or restrictive governance, which has in turn stymied foreign investment and delayed their complete entry into international trade. And, of course, Russia has done substantial and lasting damage to its economy as a result of its naked aggression against the territory and political sovereignty of neighboring Ukraine. (The following chapter explores the rationale, and the options, for enabling good governance in the developing world.)

Like AIIB, the New Development Bank focuses on infrastructure projects and aspires to be an alternative to IMF and the regional development banks for developing countries. For China, and for Russia as well, one would assume, it represents another way to flex economic muscle and spread influence. Although the first president was Indian and the next from Brazil, the bank is permanently headquartered in Shanghai. Also, like AIIB, the early performance of the bank has been less dynamic than its founders anticipated. In fact, for the first six years of its existence, no other nations joined the bank until Bangladesh, Uruguay, and the United Arab Emirates became members in 2021.

An institution like the BRICS Bank represents something of a conundrum for the United States and its global allies. On the one hand, establishing a new, independent development bank that operates outside the traditional Bretton Woods and regional institutions means these countries are acting on their own behalf and for the benefit of other rising economies. In theory, that means easing the burden of the older economic powers in North America, Europe, and Asia. At the same time, however, if developing countries are going to the BRICS Bank or AIIB for financing, that reduces their independence and diminishes opportunities for them to advance liberal democratic values and principles, the world order on which we've come to depend will be in greater jeopardy.

Many have advocated for United States membership in AIIB and the New Development Bank as a way to monitor and wield influence from the inside. I do not support the US joining either of these new institutions, as that would divert resources and attention from the current multilateral development institutions. Rather, I would want to see the traditional institutions step up their game with proper funding, more focused and coordinated strategies, with collaborative support and leadership from the United States.

In addition to the World Bank, IMF, and the Asian Development Bank, the major players in the multilateral development bank system include the Inter-American Development Bank (IDB), where Donald Trump broke with tradition by installing an American president in 2020, the African Development Bank, and the European Bank for Reconstruction and Development. Smaller subregional development banks target specific areas like the Caribbean or West Africa. While no American sits at the head of any of these major regional institutions (other than the IDB), the United States holds between 10 and 30 percent of the shares in each of them except for the African Development Bank, which translates into meaningful influence. It is in the interests of the US to ensure the continued value of these development banks.

Additionally, I believe that the MDBs can have a greater positive impact on development outcomes by working together in a more coordinated way, something they have not done well enough in the past. MDBs can be better about establishing common standards and benchmarks, harmonizing procurement practices, and working collaboratively to solve global challenges. There is no reason for different financial institutions working in the same countries can't be working on coordinated strategic plans on similar planning schedules, especially since many of the officials and board members have seats in multiple institutions. Global public goods, or "collective action problems," represent an area of opportunity for MDBs to work together.

. . . . .

After the MDBs comes an array of international organizations that influence processes and activities that many take for granted—but they shouldn't. These are the global standard-setting bodies, regulating everything from the food we eat to the technology that carries our phone calls, and they enable our internet usage and digital communications. We might assume that standards are objectively quantifiable. But it must be remembered that every decision and every policy concerning standards involves some kind of value judgment, which is precisely why the United States must maintain an effective presence in all these bodies. We want to set standards in an environment where transparency is presumed and the Universal Declaration of Human Rights reigns, and not one where the prevailing influence comes from regimes that routinely flout the rule of law, disrespect individual autonomy and rights, and inconsistently support private enterprise.

In 2019, in a move that sent shockwaves through Washington's diplomatic and development communities, a senior Chinese official won election as the head of the Food and Agriculture Organization (FAO), a UN agency that oversees agricultural and food safety and security around the world. At the time, the State Department under the Trump administration had begun making it known that countering the threat of Chinese influence was a top priority. In the case of agencies like the FAO, that became the job of the State Department, namely the Bureau for International Organization Affairs. Despite being very vocal about preventing China from securing this position, the US was unable to move quickly and mobilize other member countries behind the United States' favored candidate, ultimately clearing the path for China.

In the end, China's candidate routed all others, winning 108 out 191, while the candidate favored by the United States managed only 12. It isn't that the Chinese official wasn't qualified—just the opposite. In fact, most observers believed that if a similarly seasoned official from any other country had gotten the post, it wouldn't so much as raised an eyebrow. However, this election served as a wake-up call: the FAO potentially represented the tip of the iceberg. As the journal *Foreign Policy* summed it up, "This marked an international triumph for China, showcasing its growing political and economic might and its newfound ability to seed top jobs at international institutions with handpicked candidates." The article went on to report allegations that China had offered economic incentives to countries to withdraw their own candidates while bullying other countries into supporting Beijing's candidate. It also took the US government to task for allowing itself to be "outfoxed and outgunned" by Beijing in this important election.

The point is not that under Chinese leadership the FAO will suddenly start relaxing its standards and endangering the global food supply. This isn't like lead paint on our Christmas toys. However, the FAO is influential. For instance, its leader and the UN Secretary General will jointly name the next head of a subsidiary agency, the UN's World Food Program, which concerns itself with food insecurity and famine. The current World Food Program head and all of his predecessors dating back to 1992 are from the United States. It's not food, per se, that concerns the US and its allies; it's the clout and influence, and the exposure of American inattention and ineptitude, especially in an area like agriculture, which is so fundamentally important to developing countries.

Less than a year later, a similar situation arose at another critical agency, the World Intellectual Property Organization, or WIPO, where the stakes were potentially much higher than at the FAO. The US still had a sour taste in its mouth after the fiasco at the FAO and had also seen the leadership of the International Civil Aviation Organization go to China in 2015. The ICAO regulates control of airspace, among other responsibilities; and with a Chinese official in the top spot, swiftly moved to expel Taiwan from the organization. When WIPO first showed up on my radar, I had no idea what it was. And so, I set out to educate myself about the organization and learned what an important function it serves. WIPO acts as the Major League Baseball commissioner of patents, trade secrets, and intellectual property. When one registers a patent in the United States, that patent is also sent to WIPO in Geneva. I concluded that a Chinese director general of WIPO could have been the equivalent of a fox guarding the henhouse. At the time, I wrote that the decision made by WIPO's leader would have "massive implications for the future of the Fourth Industrial Revolution, where countries are vying for technological supremacy. Given China's history of IP theft, a Chinese director general storing the world's patents in Beijing would be disastrous." Having published a major paper explaining the organization's operation, a kind of "WIPO for dummies" that caught the attention of administration staffers and members of the congressional leadership, I convened a meeting of White House staffers, interested private sector parties, and others to try to get a consensus around a candidate to run WIPO.

Having learned their lesson, key players in the Trump administration were willing to act early and aggressively, which ultimately prevented China from taking over yet another critical agency. A number of factors contributed to the success of this effort, all of which should inform our future strategy regarding staffing at multilateral institutions. First, we understood the stakes very early in the process, as opposed to the situation at FAO and other organizations. Second, we had the right point person in Ambassador Andrew Bremberg, who had recently become the US Representative to the UN Office in Geneva. Third, members of Congress were engaged and mobilized, signing on to a bipartisan letter to the White House. Fourth, our diplomats overseas were actively engaged in rallying the support, particularly from those countries that rely on the integrity of intellectual property. Fifth, the countries involved, including the US, were able to form a consensus around a candidate, in this case, someone from Singapore, which satisfied various regional concerns and obligations.

Another perhaps even more critical directorship will be contested in late 2022 at another specialized UN agency, the International Telecommunications Union. The ITU is the "NFL of the internet" responsible for setting standards and norms for all information and communication technologies. In 2012, the US government banned the use by US companies of networking equipment from Chinese telecoms giant Huawei because of its close ties to the Beijing government and fears around its products being used to gather data and intelligence. That ban was extended to 2021, while other countries around the world, including Canada, the UK, and Australia, have forbidden the use of Huawei equipment, especially in new 5G networks. And yet, an official from China, Houlin Zhao, has been secretary-general of ITU since 2014.

My colleague at CSIS, Kristen Cordell, laid out the worrisome specifics of that stewardship. "Houlin is known for highly favorable comments and decisions supporting Chinese companies and is responsible for a Memorandum of Understanding between China's Belt and Road Initiative (BRI) and the ITU. China sends the largest delegation to the ITU's various study groups and is also represented, through their membership, by Huawei and other Chinese state-owned enterprises. Working through these study groups with the support of high-level ITU leadership, Huawei has introduced more than 2,000 new standard proposals on topics including 5G, cybersecurity, and artificial intelligence. China's most notable standard proposal is for a new 'Internet Protocol,' which has the potential to fundamentally reshape the internet by imposing a centralized, highly controllable Chinese model throughout the world."

More than a year and a half before the selection of a new secretary-general, no less a figure than Secretary of State Antony Blinken announced support of an American, Doreen Bogdan-Martin, to take over from the Chinese official who has held the top position since 2014. (The involvement of a senior cabinet-level official indicates the significance and relevance of this agency.) Bogdan-Martin is already highly placed at ITU as director of one of its key divisions and would slide easily into the head role. Bogdan-Martin is also an example of why we need a "US farm team" of talented people placed in career roles in multilateral organizations who can grow their careers in this system. We need many more people like Doreen Bogdan-Martin to meet the challenges of the future. The public support that a candidate receives from his or her home government is instrumental in the selection process, as was learned from Australia's vocal backing of Mathias Cormann at OECD. And what we learned during the process at WIPO was that an early start gives time to line up like-minded allies and work in concert with them on behalf of a candidate who promotes the ideals of the established order.

Standard-setting has been the province of the world's industrialized democracies, governing everything from pesticides, facial recognition, and electric cars to copyrights, train tracks, batteries, and digital payments. But experts see a growing struggle between the US and China to dominate global standards and fear that such a bilateral competition could lead to a bifurcated world in which two sets of manufacturing and technological rules and standards exist—good for no one. There are many such organizations in the world today, including the International Maritime Organization; the World Meteorological Organization; the International Air Transport Association; the Air-conditioning, Heating and Refrigeration Institute; and the International Postal Union; to name just a few. Each of them, at one time or another, will demand the attention of the US government. Although that government has been learning from its past mistakes and focusing somewhat better on key positions as they open up, it is ill-equipped to succeed across the board. Most Western allies have dedicated departments or agencies within their governments for the oversight of such multilateral institutions, but the US does not. It's always left to some small cadre of individuals to champion these causes, which are not usually top of the mind in Washington. This will have to change.

Having reached what feels like a critical moment in the emerging competition between the United States and China, it's necessary to reach a bipartisan consensus on priorities and strategies related to multilateral institutions. The relative power of the US has diminished since the unipolar moment thirty years ago after the collapse of the Soviet Union. The multilateral system hasn't suddenly grown in importance; it's always been relevant. But with the rise of China, it is necessary to pay closer attention. The US needs to flex different muscles in the international community and view the maintenance of this system through the lens of great-power competition.

Many of my Republican colleagues have loved to dismiss these institutions as costly and ineffective, an undeserved handout to the developing world, and even to our established allies. No doubt, the multilateral institutions can be more efficient financially and more productive. But decreasing American input to them diminishes this country's influence in the international community and opens the door a little wider for nations that hunger for influence but aren't aligned with the values of market democracies. Rather than throwing the baby out with the bathwater, the US must turn its attention to improving the performance and impact of all multilateral organizations.

The research carried out by our group at CSIS reveals a series of important action steps related to these institutions. We've already identified existing challenges, such as the lack of a centralized component of government devoted to monitoring the leadership openings in multilateral organizations. To ensure future effectiveness, we offered the following recommendations:

1. Establish a Multilateral Policy Council within the National Security Council. Such a group would ensure a

whole-of-government approach by coordinating policy
with all relevant departments and advisory councils.

2. The Multilateral Policy Council would conduct a Multilateral Aid Review. This review would assess the effectiveness of the multilateral institutions that the United States
supports. If aligned against the objectives of a forthcoming
National Security Strategy (NSS), the MAR could evaluate
the gaps that exist in multilateral engagement.

3. Produce a whole-of-government implementation plan for
multilateral engagement. The plan would engage relevant
agencies in specific actions, including tracking multilateral
aid, tracking and filling leadership and senior positions in
multilateral institutions, enhancing interagency communication, and improving US representation at the staff level.

4. Coordinate policy and planning with allies and like-minded
partners. The United States should be building partnerships
and alliances in each multilateral institution and maximize
influence in those organizations in which it doesn't hold
a leadership position or significant shareholding positions.
The US should be working with the G7 countries and the
Quad countries to pool resources for recruitment, training,
and placement.

5. Ensure placement of qualified US personnel at all levels of
these institutions. Not only does the United States need to
pay closer attention to its staffing footprint in multilateral
institutions and encourage young and qualified Americans
to pursue careers in international organizations, but it also
needs to revise the hiring, training, and available career
paths for foreign service and other civil service personnel.
We will address this particular piece of the puzzle in greater
detail later in the book.

The disruption caused by the pandemic helped clarify critical short-term priorities for the multilateral system. First and foremost, these institutions can help stop the economic bleeding caused by COVID-19. This would involve efforts to shore up banking systems and social safety nets within individual countries and enable the immediate distribution of vaccines and health care. They can finish the job of restoring international trade to pre-pandemic levels and shoring up industries hit hard by the crisis. Second, but related, multilateral institutions can help enable trade and supply-chain shifts triggered by the pandemic, engaging countries and regions apart from China. This might mean focusing on energy and transportation infrastructure—electricity, ports, airports, and providing bureaucratic technical assistance in areas like customs. Third, now that the world has come to rely so much more on digital communication, the international community can ensure that this space is not ceded to Chinese manufacturers like Huawei that are intimately entwined with the government in Beijing. Engineering a change of leadership at the International Telecommunications Union is the first major step in that effort.

The rise of the Asia Infrastructure and Investment Bank as an alternative to the World Bank, IMF, and other multilateral development banks highlights the fourth necessary action step— enabling high-quality, environmentally friendly infrastructure in the developing world. One key to success in all these steps will be to use ODA (official development assistance) and DFI (development finance institutions) resources not as the cure, but to catalyze foreign direct investment and domestic investment, and to help build partnerships with the private sector.

Finally, just like the United States' foreign service, multinational institutions will need to prepare for working in more difficult country environments. The good news is that many countries in the developing world have grown richer and more capable, with more avenues to progress available to them. However, that means the aid community has to focus on the countries left behind, the several dozen fragile or failing states that remain in critical condition and require thoughtful and focused intervention.

Chapter 7

PLAYING BY THE RULES

Enabling Good Governance

Good governance and the rule of law at the national and international levels are essential for sustained economic growth, sustainable development and the eradication of poverty and hunger.

—World Summit Outcome, resolution adopted by the UN General Assembly, 2005

Good governance and inclusive economic growth represent the two most vital foundations of development. The United Nations 2030 Agenda for Sustainable Development describes a world in which "democracy, good governance and the rule of law as well as an enabling environment at national and international levels, are essential for sustainable development, including sustained and inclusive economic growth, social development, environmental protection and the eradication of poverty and hunger."

A symbiotic relationship between governance and economic growth is undeniable, although governance is a complex and multi-faceted concept. The World Bank defines governance as "the traditions and institutions by which authority in a country is exercised." Going a bit deeper, the United Nations Development Program says it is "the exercise of economic, political, and administrative authority to manage a country's affairs at all levels. It comprises mechanisms, processes, and institutions through which citizens and groups articulate their interests, exercise their legal rights, meet their obligations, and mediate their differences." Good governance, the World Bank adds, is "…epitomized by predictable, open and enlightened policy making; a bureaucracy imbued with a professional ethos; an executive arm of government accountable for its actions; and a strong civil society participating in public affairs; and all behaving under the rule of law."

It is worth pausing to reiterate what is meant by the "rule of law." The World Justice Project posits four universal principles underlying the rule of law: *Accountability*; *Just Law* that is applied evenly and publicly; *Open Government*, referring to the processes by which law is adopted, administered, and enforced; and *Accessible and Impartial Justice*.

In the development community, we talk about governance, corruption, and democracy, three separate but interdependent and overlapping phenomena, coexisting in a unique balance within each society. Good governance—functional political institutions, standardized and professionalized bureaucracy, transparent processes, and a strong civil society—can reduce the opportunities for corruption on some levels and can foster adherence to democratic values. At the same time, research has established that good governance is more achievable and sustainable in the context of liberal democracy. Economies can improve, and governments can become more efficient in the absence of liberal democracy—look at Singapore, for example, which has been characterized as an "electoral autocracy"—but development, even in well-managed autocracies, often stagnates. In the words of a USAID-sponsored report, "Where democracy is less liberal, governance is poorer—more corrupt, wasteful, incompetent, and unresponsive. Entrenched poverty obstructs economic development, opens the door to recurrent crises, inhibits the effective use of international assistance, and can even lead to state failure. Failed states tend to breed other societal ills, such as crime, radicalization, uncontrolled migration, or exacerbate health crises. This is evident in the increasing concentration of the world's poor in fragile state environments. Liberal democracy can be a major building block of good governance, which, in turn, fosters and sustains broad-based development."

Let's start by looking at corruption. In 1996, Jim Wolfensohn, then president of the World Bank, famously said in a public address at the Bank's annual meeting, "Let's not mince words: We need to deal with the cancer of corruption." The costs of corruption are high, estimated by the World Economic Forum to be in the neighborhood $2 trillion a year globally, larger than the GDP of all but a handful of countries. As I wrote in a paper with my colleague Christopher Metzger, "Corruption constrains economic growth and prevents countries from becoming self-reliant. Low-income countries with weak governing institutions and poor rule of law are most susceptible to corruption, resulting in the loss of billions of dollars, which could be invested in basic services for citizens, such as education, health care, and infrastructure."

Corruption acts as a disincentive to foreign investment that can catalyze growth, as well as to internal investment. The moneyed elites in a fragile country rife with corruption will most likely park much of their wealth elsewhere rather than pump it back into the economy at home, either via the financial markets or through entrepreneurism or consumption. As a result, domestic resource mobilization (DRM) in such countries remains too low. Those in a position to pay taxes will resist doing so on the grounds that the government is too corrupt or ineffective to live up to its end of the social contract. The vicious circle is that governments deprived of needed tax revenues struggle to carry out their basic responsibilities competently. We know that DRM is critical to moving up on the development scale. It's widely accepted that income from taxes needs to account for 20 percent of GDP for a country to have a chance at self-sufficiency. In Guatemala, the figure has long been

12 percent or less, and in many countries of sub-Saharan Africa, it hovers at 10 percent or below.

Global anticorruption efforts have resulted in the creation of numerous useful indicators and indices that track and quantify corruption, such as Transparency International's Corruption Perception Index, the World Bank's World Governance and (until recently) its Doing Business Indicators, the OECD's Public Integrity Indicators, the European Research Center for Anti-Corruption and State Building's interrelated indices of public integrity, transparency, and corruption risk, and the Institute of Economics and Peace's Global Peace Index. In addition, the United Nations and the OECD have obtained broad adherence to global multilateral treaties, supported by a series of regional treaties in which the signatories agree to refrain from and respond to corruption. Sadly, the recent discontinuation of the Doing Business indicators weakens those efforts as corruption hampers foreign direct investment that is so critical to economic development.

The reengagement on this front by the Biden-Harris administration has been encouraging. Anticorruption work undertaken on the multilateral level in the last fifty years has benefited greatly from American leadership in partnership with other countries. Biden has been correct to return anti-corruption to its position among our top policy imperatives, as the issue becomes more relevant and pressing in the context of great-power competition.

The strategy paper for the administration's anti-corruption initiative clearly lays out the existential threat posed by corruption, not only to development but to all aspects of global stability:

> When government officials abuse public power for private gain, they do more than simply appropriate illicit wealth. Corruption robs citizens of equal access to vital services, denying the right to quality healthcare, public safety, and education. It degrades the business environment, subverts economic opportunity, and exacerbates inequality. It often contributes to human rights violations and abuses and can drive migration. As a fundamental threat to the rule of law, corruption hollows out institu-

tions, corrodes public trust, and fuels popular cynicism toward effective, accountable governance.

It cannot be emphasized strongly enough that these threats created by corruption—as well as by poor governance and anti-democratic activity—extend beyond the lower- and middle-income countries of the developing world. The weakening of those societies, the exacerbation of factors that destabilize nations and lead to migration or radicalization or foment conflict, has a direct effect on the United States' economy and on the lives of Americans. The exhaustive strategy laid out in the White House's initiative mobilizes and coordinates multiple agencies and departments in a detailed series of action steps that break down along five "strategic pillars:"

- Modernizing, coordinating, and resourcing US government efforts

- Curbing illicit finance

- Holding corrupt actors accountable

- Preserving and strengthening the multilateral anti-corruption architecture

- Improving diplomatic engagement and leveraging foreign assistance resources to advance policy objectives

Note the explicit acknowledgment that this cannot be a unilateral effort on the part of the United States, but rather will require collective action that engages with governments, multilateral organizations, and civil society. At CSIS, we've elaborated on these action steps, specifying that we need to help developing countries strengthen public procurement processes, leverage technology to reduce corruption within government processes, incorporate corruption efforts across development programs, and link corruption programs to national security discussions. Additionally, since private-sector growth is most directly hamstrung by corruption, it is necessary for companies in that private sector to take initiative in directly combating it.

Corruption manifests itself in a variety of ways. The routine functions of government, such as tax assessment and collection, court proceedings, permitting and licensing, often operate at the municipal or provincial level and can offer easy opportunities for corruption, which is generally defined as the abuse of entrusted authority for private gain (USAID Anti-Corruption Strategy, 2005). Small-scale, transactional corruption—the friend down at city hall who can expedite a building inspection—is referred to as "petty corruption" to differentiate it from the more deeply entrenched "grand corruption" that has become a part of the larger cultural fabric and bestows privileges on select groups of people over others. Think of petty corruption as a crime of opportunity rather than as a crime of premeditation.

Larry Cooley, who had for years run the development company MSI, differentiates between "corrupt" and what he calls "corrupting," where the former involves violations of law and the latter refers to situations or customs that, while technically legal, provide incentives to exploit public institutions for private gain, often due to the lack of guardrails to protect against impulsive sidestepping of the rules. Campaign finance rules are a clear case in point, but so are opaque procedures that allow someone to jump to the head of the line at the Motor Vehicles Office. Cooley emphasizes that by standardizing or automating governmental procedures or otherwise enabling alternatives to existing practices, real inroads can made against petty corruption, and that can lead to more fundamental changes in society at large and governance in particular, even in settings where grand corruption is endemic.

*   *   *   *   *

Those guardrails in governmental systems represent the intersection between good governance and corruption. USAID—through its Center for Democracy, Human Rights, and Governance and its country missions—has exercised soft power to promote the building of stronger and more open political institutions in fledgling democracies. For instance, USAID has launched a five-year Grand Challenge as an overarching umbrella for engaging a diverse range of stakeholders to combat transnational corruption. The Grand Challenge is intended "to crowdsource, fund, co-create, and scale forward-thinking solutions from partners across the globe to identify, expose, and disrupt transnational corruption."

In addition, politicians and aides have been invited to visit and observe legislatures in the US or elsewhere to study procedures like setting up reference services and information systems, drafting and negotiating bills, and the conduct of legislative hearings. Countries that have not had functional digital platforms, budgeting offices, or tax assessment and collection systems have received technical assistance to set up those entities and train personnel to manage them. In some cases, automated scheduling in a troubled court system has reduced opportunities for cronyism or favoritism. Standard fee structures in medical clinics have reduced demands for under-the-table fees for service. Also, modernization and computerization in treasuries, public utilities, and licensing agencies have reduced illegal payouts of government funds and illicit extractive operations. In this way, countries with limited experience in the mechanics of democracy have been empowered through technical assistance from USAID and counterpart agencies in other countries, NGOs, and multilateral organizations. It's important to note that while such technocratic fixes play a vital role, lasting change can't happen without a receptive environment on the ground, often involving shifts in power imbalances necessary to make reforms politically viable.

The working assumption behind such practical technocratic projects is that if the everyday functions of governments become more rule-driven and transparent, people in the society will begin to expect a level of fairness in public procedures, which engenders an expectation of greater integrity at other levels of government and society. Programs like this will not, by themselves, transform a society, but they can act like the initial seed money in a new business venture, setting an example and validating the venture in order to generate further investment. The goal in development is not to impose a system or structure from the outside but to empower local actors, while borrowing and adapting from others, to build systems appropriate to their culture and circumstances. Taking ownership of that progress can then foster the development of other home-grown practices.

In this regard, the OECD has encouraged attention to the broader social and political context in which corruption thrives. In 2017, it adopted a formal recommendation on public integrity that focuses on three underlying elements:

- Having a system in place to reduce opportunities for corrupt behavior;

- Changing a culture to make corruption unacceptable socially; and

- Making people accountable for their actions.

Since then, it has worked with countries around the world on public integrity reviews designed to foster reforms and build trust.

At times, the term "governance" has been used in development circles as a kind of code word for combating corruption, in the belief that authorities in a fragile state would more likely welcome an outside intervention in the form of an aid project that "fosters good governance" than one that "establishes anti-corruption measures." The power elites in a struggling nation can endorse improved governance without having to acknowledge that their corruption has impeded good governance. Within the US government, histor-ically, it has also been easier to create—and to get approval for—aid programs that address petty corruption, because such programs tend to have very specific, definable goals with clear metrics and are generally time-limited. Aid budgets are proposed and approved on an annual basis. So while some multi-year projects do go forward, agencies tend to gravitate toward projects that can fit neatly into those budgets and, often, have a short-term bias.

An emphasis on petty corruption, however, can leave the elites free to pursue more illicit gains. The programs described here can bring about improvements related to health and the environment, and they can elevate the rule of law and bring about fiscal reform. But technocratic solutions aren't enough to ensure the advancement of democracy. They can't necessarily undo entrenched grand corruption that keeps self-interested groups in power. The US and other donors have spent billions in governance and anti-corruption work in too many countries that have readily accepted the aid dollars and yet failed to make any real progress toward liberal democratic governance. This work can catalyze reform, but fundamental cultural shifts require strategic engagement and long-term commitment, grounded in a commitment to improving governance and promoting democracy.

For a time, when the New Directions program determined US development priorities, governance and democracy took a back burner to basic human-needs assistance. Things began to change in the 1980s, around the time of the establishment of the National Endowment for Democracy, when new democracies were beginning to flower around the world. More fledgling democracies came into being during the 1990s, after the fall of the Berlin Wall, but all were fighting an uphill battle. Free elections and new constitutions did not suddenly erase existing problems or conflicts, and in some ways, increased openness aggravated them further. New governments faced tremendous expectations from their people, but very few had knowledge of or experience with democratic institutions. In too many cases, populist leaders seized on the opportunity to present themselves as alternatives to dysfunctional or failing governments or institutions.

Governance, anti-corruption, and democracy promotion come together in the effort to build functional political institutions. Former Ambassador James Michel has written extensively about the "fundamental need for competent, fair, and accountable public institutions" to ensure good governance that can enable economic development." The United States has tried to advance democracy in developing countries by providing support to and sharing experience with reformers and local actors working to establish the machinery of democracy and a working political system. For instance, democratic systems, whether a two-party system like in the US or a multiparty parliamentary system, need functioning political parties that can draft and communicate meaningful platforms. People who have never participated in a representative government need to learn how to function as legislators or members of parliament and run public agencies and offices. Elected officials need to research and hire staff and cabinet ministers. Accountable governance demands a free and engaged press, which can be established more quickly if benefiting from the advice and assistance of external organizations like Internews, an international NGO that supports independent media in more than one hundred countries. Groups like IFES (the International Foundation for Electoral Systems) help set up and monitor fair elections.

Why are some countries moving ahead while their neighbors are falling behind? The Baltic states are fast becoming important players in the European Union, while some neighboring countries are lagging, owing to inconsistent progress toward democracy. For instance, in Belarus, the democratic transition never got off the ground, and economic development has been slowed in the context of continued authoritarianism. In Central America, we want troubled countries of the Northern Triangle to develop along the path of Costa Rica or Panama; in South America, progress in Chile, Uruguay, and Colombia contrast with regression in Venezuela and Bolivia, where economic decline is tied to backsliding in democracy. In Africa, we look to democratic Botswana's remarkable economic growth after emerging from colonialism while watching South Africa, after a promising beginning during the presidency of Nelson Mandela (who left office in 1999, observing his principled commitment to serve only a single term), tread water for an extended period. In his important book, *Emerging Africa: How 17 Countries Are Leading the Way*, Steven Radelet discusses five major breakthroughs for those seventeen leaders, the first among them being the rise of democracy. In Southeast Asia, notable economic success stories like Singapore and Vietnam do not demonstrate adherence to democratic ideals, but those countries do have functional governing institutions that are enabling economic growth and delivering for their people.

If the development goal for emerging nations is to achieve self-reliance, it must be assumed that can only be achieved in the context of an effective and capable state that provides security, establishes and maintains regulatory standards, enables a formal economic and monetary system, delivers justice for its citizens, builds trust, and promotes a vibrant private sector and civil society.

Building strong institutions and the framework of good governance is, of course, only one piece of the puzzle. James Michel reminds us that "efficient and trustworthy public institutions are necessary but not sufficient to achieve a culture of lawfulness and integrity. Additional factors such as economic policies, access to technology, press freedom, public education, visible centers of moral authority and role models, an engaged civil society, and media attention are all important to achieve a broad shift in values, beliefs and behavior."

Supporting democracy isn't easy. Former Secretary of State Madeleine Albright was known to say that imposition of democracy is an oxymoron, that democracy is about choice. Look to the 2021 presidential elections in Honduras. The United States has poured in billions of dollars, both in direct humanitarian aid and in soft-power assistance over the years, none of which stemmed the tide of corruption, poverty, and social chaos that made the country one of the region's major sources of mass migration. The former president, who was tied to a member of a family of drug traffickers, steadily dismantled democratic institutions during his twelve years in office, a period marked by graft and violence.

The election came down to a choice between the mayor of the capital city, Nasry Asfura, representing the conservative governing party, and the leftist opposition candidate, Xiomara Castro, married to a former president who had been driven out of office. Castro campaigned on a platform of ending the cycle of organized corruption and crime, restoring order to civil society, going after the drug cartels, and rebuilding a functional and participatory government. She wanted Hondurans to come home from abroad. It seemed like an easy choice if the goal was to advance good governance and democracy to facilitate economic development. But the situation was far from simple. While in office, Castro's husband had espoused an affinity for the policies of Hugo Chavez, the socialist leader who had presided over the economic and social collapse of Venezuela, and Castro herself was a self-proclaimed socialist. Chavez and his Bolivian counterpart, Evo Morales, had been voted into power democratically before taking their countries down the road of authoritarianism in the name of socialism. The world watches to see if Castro's government will keep her campaign promises about fighting corruption and giving the country back to the people, or if she will take Honduras down the path of Venezuela.

A situation like this raised difficult questions about how US foreign policy should address development issues. Would the United States revise its aid policy toward Honduras depending on the outcome of the election? Such decisions arise constantly in development work. Do you support the devil you know—a government you know is corrupt—rather than take the risk of supporting leadership that might make needed reforms but might also veer off into authoritarianism, as has happened elsewhere in the region? Will the new government work with democratic allies in the West? Will it seek to build institutions that can survive the next regime change, guaranteeing some long-term stability? Will it play by the rules set by multilateral organizations and accept their input, advice, or monitoring? In short, will the country move in a direction that strengthens the liberal world order or weakens it? And how can the United States best engage on that basic question?

Questions like these are particularly vexing when it comes to Latin America, where the clear goal of aid and development assistance has been to address the conditions that have sent waves of migration north toward the United States. Throughout the region, emerging nations share borders with oppressive authoritarian regimes or criminal regimes masquerading as democracies. Countries once considered development successes seem to hang in the balance. In Chile, a bastion of democratic governance, a recent election revealed a country polarized between a far-left movement leader and a very conservative candidate who extolled the virtues of a long-deposed dictator.

Foreign policy, of which aid is but one component, has always involved certain convenient trade-offs and somewhat fluid priorities and standards. In the Middle East, for instance, the United States has maintained relationships with nondemocratic regimes in order to maintain strategic positions or protect access to natural resources. "But the broader shift in U.S. foreign policy today, with its stress on both great-power competition and short-term domestic priorities, has made those tradeoffs more frequent and acute," writes Richard Haass, president of the Council on Foreign Relations. "In China's neighborhood, for example, the Biden administration set aside concerns about human rights violations by Philippine President Rodrigo Duterte in order to make it easier for the US military to operate in his country, and it has worked to bolster ties with Vietnam, another autocracy ruled by a communist party. With Russia, it signed an arms control accord while overlooking the imprisonment of the opposition leader Alexei Navalny. It has largely ignored the rise of Hindu nationalism in India in favor of stronger ties with the country to balance China." In such cases, the US can use its soft-power tools to support local reformers seeking to establish or enhance the mechanics of good governance to build the rule of law into political life and an effective state. At all times, the US has to be clear in its belief in and support for democratic governance.

This is often unglamorous work that gets little attention. You will not make headlines with short-term projects, such as financing the building of polling stations to make voting more accessible or the use of an app to circumvent an informal system of bribes to police officers, or technical assistance to the writers of a tax code, or the designers of a municipal budget system, as you might with higher-level diplomatic actions. Foreign assistance to help local actors build institutions—a somewhat vague and imprecise phrase that denotes writing the rules of a functioning political system, creating effective governments, and cementing the rule of law—involves sustained effort over a long time. Success is often incremental and almost always difficult to measure. But without sound laws and institutions, it can be difficult for countries to manage their rise up the development chain.

While it is true that the developing world has become freer and more politically adept in many ways, the anti-corruption work and democracy promotion done by the development community takes on a new urgency in the context of great-power competition. We have seen that the Chinese are willing to literally bribe their way around the world, although their bribes may be accompanied by burdensome debt or white-elephant infrastructure projects. Fighting corruption means bringing governmental processes out into the open, making it more difficult for the Chinese and other bad actors to bribe or bully. Homegrown entrepreneurs and companies, or other outside investors that abide by the rules, have a fair shot at doing business in a clean way. It also means becoming much more vigilant about filling voids in global trade and international relations that bad actors will rush to fill. The point of good governance and of maintaining international standards and practices is to make it harder for the bad guys to be bad.

In particular, the US and its allies will have to step up their game regarding vigilance, governance, and corruption in the area of minerals and extractive mining. Even as the international community plans its transition away from fossil fuels, many lower- and middle-income countries have been outspoken in their resistance to that movement. At the 2021 UN Climate Change Conference in Glasgow, India joined with China, the world's largest burner of coal, in insisting that the group water down the anti-coal agenda in its resolutions. India's drive to bring more of its population up to some minimum standard of living depends on cheap fuel to power its rapidly growing economy. Countries across the developing world find themselves in a similar position, without access to the array of options available to wealthier nations. The global carbon transition will likely take much longer than planned—if it happens at all. In addition, as we make a transition, the levels of mining are going to more than double, especially in developing countries. Managing the mineral wealth, along with ongoing oil and gas extraction, which will continue for the next several decades at high levels, is going to be a major governance challenge, a major potential source of corruption, and a major source of profligacy.

Perhaps more important, much of the mineral resources that will power the coming transition are found in some of the poorer countries of the developing world. The most vivid case in point is the Democratic Republic of the Congo, ranked on numerous indices as the first or second poorest country in the world by per capita GDP but rich in resources, particularly newly valuable rare-earth metals. In the fall of 2021, China concluded a deal to take over control of an enormous cobalt mine in Congo, where the majority of the world's cobalt is mined. The mine had previously been owned by an American company, and according to reporting in *The New York Times*, US diplomats and even the manager of the mine raised alarms at the US State Department in hopes of the US reinvigorating its long relationship with Congo and possibly preventing China from cornering the market on this valuable element. Cobalt, along with lithium and copper, is an essential component of batteries for electric cars. While American and Asian automakers were racing to get affordable electric cars into the market, China—that is, Chinese companies often working in partnership with the government in Beijing—were buying up most of the world's supply of the minerals needed to power those cars. In addition to cobalt, Chinese interests control copper and lithium mines from Chile to Australia, as well as the mines within their own national borders. A conventional internal combustion car might use roughly twenty to forty pounds of copper in its engine and electrical system, but a fully electric vehicle can contain close to ten times that amount. And it isn't only electric vehicles that will require these batteries. Already, societies are growing increasingly dependent on smart devices that rely on rechargeable battery power.

China already produces more electric vehicles than any other country, selling cars, buses, and trucks throughout the world. The world's largest maker of electric car batteries, which supplies batteries to most of the world's largest auto manufacturers, is also based in China; and though the company is not owned by the government, Beijing has taken steps to support it. Many observers see a national master plan at work. That isn't surprising for a country with a state-controlled economy, substantial investment capital, a strong existing manufacturing base, and a ready workforce. What the world should be worried about is one nation's ability to control access to, and the prices of, natural resources that are essential to powering the future. As *The New York Times* noted in late 2021, "That dominance has stirred fears in Washington that Detroit could someday be rendered obsolete, and that Beijing could control American driving in the 21st century the way that oil-producing nations sometimes could in the 20th."

Imagine Congo or other countries very far down on the development scale, newly flush with income, but likely with weak governance, institutions, and civil society. Such countries are vulnerable to what is often referred to as the "resource curse"—the paradox of a country or region with significant resource wealth becoming poorer, less stable, and more corrupt due to the resource endowment. These are exactly the kind of countries that have been caught in Chinese debt traps before. If more of these countries enter into extractive arrangements with China, Beijing's influence will loom larger, making it all the more necessary for aid from the West to promote good governance and democracy and make sure that new wealth gets channeled appropriately into roads, schools, hospitals, and a social safety net, rather than feathering the nests of the elite or building up an overblown and unnecessary military. It could even go toward the creation of a sovereign wealth fund—a state-owned investment fund—like in Norway or Botswana. Beijing has shown its willingness to use its economic muscle to bully and intimidate smaller countries in pursuit of its ambitions. What makes us think they would not hold resources hostage in order to strengthen Chinese industries vis-à-vis foreign competition? And why stop at rare-earth metals and car batteries?

The multilateral system can help establish and maintain governance safeguards in this area: the Extractive Industries Transparency Initiative. Fifty-one participant nations, nearly half of which are in Africa, signed on to the principles set forth in 2003. EITI is an alliance between stakeholders from business, government, and NGOs to push for a complete and transparent accounting of the taxes and fees collected by governments from extractive industries. I wrote in *Forbes* magazine about EITI, identifying it as "an example of international standard setting, or 'soft law,'" part of a larger global trend toward increased accountability, transparency, and engagement related to technology on the part of civil society, business, and government. EITI can provide significant protection against the resource curse in that "it enhances a country's international standing as a more stable destination for foreign direct investment while promoting a positive international image. EITI boosts transparency and spreads awareness on how governments are utilizing resource related incomes."

In a short-sighted move, the Trump administration withdrew from EITI in 2017. It is imperative the United States rejoin this initiative at the earliest opportunity, lest it cedes totally its voice in mining and mineral extraction in the developing world. Pacts like EITI represent the critical value of multilateralism going forward, especially with regard to global development, climate change, and the carbon transition. As I wrote seven years ago, EITI serves a profoundly "important function in developing countries as often it provides the first opportunity for constructive multi-stakeholder dialogue and this in itself can have a positive effect on effective governance."

I believe that all developing countries share some long-range universal aspirations, including security, independence, a sense of agency, and national pride, but that specific needs, challenges, and immediate goals are unique to each country. The balance of short-term projects to improve governance and long-term democracy promotion, between fighting petty corruption versus grand corruption, will be different for every society, as will the cultural and political context in which development takes place. Twenty years ago, Plan Colombia helped turn around a deeply troubled political and economic situation. It was a country-specific, multi-year plan drawing on elements of the three Ds of foreign policy—*diplomacy, development, and defense.* Most importantly, Plan Colombia assembled the expertise of all the relevant agencies and departments of government in a carefully coordinated strategy with clear long-range goals.

A version of that plan is contained within the previously discussed Global Fragility Act of 2019, which explicitly calls for ten-year whole-of-government aid plans, beginning with at least five individual pilot countries or regions to establish better governance and build democratic institutions. The Global Fragility Act's framework can provide a useful model for much broader application. As mentioned previously, the United States has identified as the initial priority countries and region for implementation of the Act Haiti, Libya, Mozambique, and Papua New Guinea—along with the region of coastal West Africa, which includes Benin, Côte d'Ivoire, Ghana, Guinea, and Togo.

But the US is not limited to those specified countries in its use of coherent, all-of-government strategies for soft-power development efforts in furtherance of our foreign policy objectives. Too often, assistance is planned, budgeted, and staffed on a short-term basis, making it vulnerable to changes in administrations and political priorities, thereby impeding long-range planning or integration with other tools of soft-power in effective policy responses to complex challenges.

.   .   .   .   .

The development work that will add partners to the liberal world order will require an entirely new kind of budgeting process that can finance plans and programs that will survive changes in government. We will need to find and train and incentivize personnel with more specified skill sets, especially linguistic and regional knowledge, and make use of their expertise in high-level policy planning. There must be top-level coordination, not only among government agencies and NGOs but across the multilateral system. It will also require the United States and its allies to keep a collective finger on the scales at multilateral organizations, especially the standard-setting bodies, so that maturing governments can have a globally accepted set of norms and metrics to which to conform.

Good governance and democratization are vital to economic progress. The next chapter will outline soft-power tools to help invigorate the private sector in a developing economy, create productive public-private partnerships, and facilitate innovation and entrepreneurship. The surest way to mitigate migration is to raise incomes or per capita GDP. Citizens need opportunity, not handouts, and opportunity for all is most vibrant in a well-governed free-market democracy in which the rule of law ensures a level playing field.

As the development community resets its priorities for the coming decade, working in concert with the other legs of the policy tripod, diplomacy and defense, we need to focus our attention on these critical areas in coherent, whole-of-government and whole-of-society initiatives that can be sustained over time. We need to renew our commitment in the area of "closed spaces," that is, conditions where the power elites of a country, whether in government or business, are free to make decisions and to take action with little or no input or consultation with the general population. We have to level the playing field on technology, leveraging digital media as a positive force for freedom by enabling access wherever it may currently be unavailable, limited, or used to restrict rather than expand freedom.

The United States must work together with global partners to build the apparatus that enables an aggressive international anti-corruption and integrity agenda. That agenda must include keeping our own house in order. The published USAID Anti-Corruption Strategy talks about modeling behavior within the organization and via all the overseas projects it sponsors. The US government, as a whole, bears the same responsibility. The country identifies with a high ethical standard but has too often been a flawed and imperfect vessel when it comes to corruption or self-interest at the expense of others. The global stakes at present are too high to lower our standards or aspirations, given the pace of political, technological, social, and environmental change. The international community must work together to help developing countries productively manage the coming carbon transition, particularly its impact on extractive industries in developing economies. It also needs to focus on setting the rules of the game on large-scale procurement, that is, the big infrastructure initiatives so critical to progress in developing countries.

None of this work can be shouldered by the United States or any other country acting unilaterally. It will require the coordinated participation of USAID and its counterpart agencies, multilateral institutions like the World Bank and all the regional development banks, the Quad and G7 countries, and all our OECD partners.

My colleague, Ken Wollack, longtime head of the National Democratic Institute[2], where he worked with Secretary Albright, offers an apocryphal story that circulates around contemporary Russia, illustrating the necessity of making the machinery of democracy and governance commonplace and accessible in the developing world. The story involves an accomplished Russian concert pianist who was condemned to internal exile by the government. Held without access to a piano, he marked off a keyboard on a plank of wood, on which he practiced, hearing the music only in his head. The practice paid off. His return to the concert stage upon his release years later was met with rave reviews. Democratic activists in Russia today, often forced into secrecy by the gangster regime of Vladimir Putin, like to say that they are "playing on their planks"—staying engaged, practicing for democracy.

---

2   Like the International Republican Institute, NDI is an independent organization operating under the umbrella of the National Endowment of Democracy.

Chapter 8

NEW SCHOOL TIES

The Marketplace of Ideas

Through that education experience [in the United States], we actually have the ability to see how another society and country actually pursues their dream, and that will then provide us with the idea of how we can do the same for Indonesia.... We need a younger generation who have confidence and can inspire others so that they are going to be able to continue building this country better and stronger.

—Sri Mulyani Indrawati, Minister of Finance for Indonesia and former managing director of the World Bank

P atrick Awuah came from Ghana to study in the United States
in the 1980s. He graduated from Swarthmore College with
degrees in both engineering and economics. After Swarthmore, Patrick spent eight successful years working for Microsoft
before enrolling at the Haas School of Business at the University
of California at Berkeley. At business school, he worked on a feasi-
bility study and a business plan with the goal of bringing that experience of American education to other Ghanaians like himself. He
raised money, returned to Ghana, rented space, and started Ashesi
University, a private institution based on the liberal-arts model
of Swarthmore. Today, Ashesi University has 1,200 undergradu-
ates and is recognized as one of the finest institutions of higher
education not only in Ghana but in all of Africa. Ashesi's success
mirrored the transformation of Ghana itself, which is now a functioning democracy with a rapidly rising per capita income.

Not every international student in the US transforms the
experience as directly and productively as Patrick Awuah did. But
his story validates the high value of access to education for development progress. Over the last sixty years, the United States has
remained open to international students, many of whom return to
their home countries to take up leadership positions in government,
business, and culture—and in building local educational institutions. At the same time, the US has sent educators and trainers
and administrators into the developing world to assist in the establishment of schools and institutions of higher learning. The goal
has been to "prepare institutions and individuals to become actors
in supporting their countries' path to development," according to
USAID. As with most other development efforts, enabling education at all levels empowers people in developing countries to
acquire and then use knowledge to address the unique challenges
in their societies and create solutions appropriate to those societies.
Educated leaders drive success.

Since the early 2000s, no country has taken better advantage of
America's eagerness to welcome and educate foreign students than
China. In 2019, before the COVID-19 pandemic upended visiting
student programs around the world, there were more than 372,000
Chinese students at US universities, representing more than a third
of the total number of international students in our country. No

country has emulated this essential soft-power technique more effectively than China, which has nearly doubled the number of universities in the country and opened its doors to students from all over the world, including from the United States. It is no exaggeration to say that, in some ways, China is beating the US at its own game while simultaneously raising concerns about its reach into American academia via the multitudes of Chinese students on United States campuses.

Since the enactment of the Foreign Assistance Act in 1961, the United States, through USAID and other government departments, created programs to attract highly qualified students to its universities, building on programs dating back to President Truman's Point Four initiative. At the height of the Cold War, these exchange programs supported some 18,000 to 20,000 international students each year. In those days, with so much concern about the global food supply in the context of a population explosion, educational initiatives tended to focus on agriculture. American overseas assistance in education concentrated on helping the establishment of higher-ed institutions comparable to the land-grant universities in the US, which were originally designed to emphasize practical sciences and engineering in addition to the basic liberal arts.

As the priorities shifted over the next several decades, how the United States addressed international education assistance also evolved. In the 1980s, US foreign assistance for education remained strong. In addition, American universities, aware that attracting foreign students could burnish their global brand and shore up their finances, began actively recruiting and increasing scholarships overseas. But in the 1990s, aid budgets declined on the presumption that the end of the Cold War would bring a "peace dividend." And so, priorities in US education assistance were realigned. Aid spending dropped to its lowest levels, and its focus was narrowed to concentrate on basic education (elementary and secondary), with diminished support for higher education, including scholarships for promising students to study in the United States.

Some remaining funds were redirected toward the establishment of partnerships between US schools and institutions in developing countries. A new American Liaison Office for University Cooperation and Development (ALO) was set up in 1992 and would become HED, Higher Education for Development, in 2006. As countries rose up the development scale and graduated from assistance, many of the institutions that grew out of these partnerships would go on to educate a new generation of leaders without the need for US government funding. This is what development work seeks to achieve: that local institutions necessary for stability and progress become self-sufficient and self-perpetuating.

At the time of this writing, the prime minister of Bulgaria and the president of Moldova both hold advanced degrees from Harvard. Leaders of many African nations, including Ghana, Cote d'Ivoire, and Ethiopia, received their higher education in the US. Leaders over the first twenty years of the 2000s in Japan, Mexico, South Korea, Costa Rica, Thailand, Ecuador, Colombia, Greece, and other countries boast degrees from the United States. Notables in recent history, from Pakistan's Benazir Bhutto to the Philippines' Corazon Aquino and Ellen Sirleaf Johnson of Liberia, all had the benefits of their United States education experience as they undertook their transformative leadership in their home countries. Among the most respected leaders educated in the US is Sri Mulyani Indrawati, who received a doctorate in economics from the University of Illinois before becoming a director of the World Bank and Indonesia's Minister of Finance. Another fascinating example is Sergio Fajardo, the mayor who led the renaissance of Medellin in Colombia, who earned his PhD in mathematics from the University of Wisconsin.

Other students from developing countries who were educated in the United States have then started businesses or other institutions that have been central to economic growth in their home countries. The contacts made while studying and working in the US, whether in economics or public policy, engineering, or health science, have constituted an important international network of counsel and influence. For Patrick Awuah, it was not just the knowledge or practical expertise he acquired in the US that made his Ghanaian university start-up possible. He also relied on the goodwill—and the financial support—of the social and professional relationships he established in this country.

Ambassador James Michel, who chaired the OECD's Development Assistance Committee and held senior positions in the

State Department and at USAID, describes another dimension of networking that drives development. One initiative helped promising students in Latin America to earn advanced degrees in economics, providing a boost to human capital available to help accelerate progress in the region. Rather than bring those future leaders directly to the US for their studies, the initiative provided scholarships for study at Latin American universities while mounting efforts to shore up the quality of those institutions. Only a few top students each year would be selected for their final advanced studies in the US. Another initiative was to rely on a leading university in the region to be a hub for learning where students from several neighboring countries could concentrate. The networks that grew out of those efforts extended far beyond relationships with American colleagues and supporters, as students in Central and South America came together to share insights, strategies, and contacts.

For more than fifty years, the United States has attracted more international students than any other country in the world and helped bolster education systems around the world, all of which served to share expertise, values, and appreciation for the American ethos. However, the number of international students in the US has decreased, as have American aid budgets and resources in education. The global middle class has grown considerably and has more options when it comes to education. Quality higher-ed institutions have emerged across the developing world, while established universities in many wealthier nations have recognized the value of attracting international students. Additionally, some observers wonder if perhaps the "bloom is off the rose" when it comes to the attractiveness of the American educational experience. They suggest that the national brand has been tarnished by the public paroxysms over race relations, political polarization, accusations of "economic imperialism," as well as some language from our political leaders, which can sound, at the very least, as if we do not welcome foreigners.

Of course, the most significant new player on the global education scene, both in terms of young people going abroad to study and in bringing international students into its university system, is China. In 2019, before closing its borders during the pandemic, China welcomed close to a half-million foreign students, the majority coming from neighboring Asian countries, like South Korea and Pakistan, but a surprisingly large percentage of which were from the US. It should come as no surprise that Beijing saw the influx of foreign students as an opportunity to build relationships from which it would benefit in the future. After all, the US has done much the same thing for decades.

The experience of studying in China is poorly understood, but a wealth of anecdotal accounts paints a worrisome picture. Generally, university life adheres to the regimented and restricted conditions that seem to pervade society as envisioned by the Chinese Communist Party. In the words of one Chinese education minister, the fundamental objective of the education system is "to make all our students qualified to inherit and build up socialism with Chinese characteristics." All Chinese college students are required to take classes in basic military training and in Marxist ideology. The challenging standardized college entrance exam, the *gaokao*, which notoriously prioritizes the ability to memorize facts about Chinese history over aptitude or problem-solving, reflects the emphasis on tedious rote learning and a propagandized curriculum, particularly in the humanities. Many students report that the exam is the most difficult part of the higher-education experience, that once they've been accepted, it's relatively easy to coast through to graduation. Performance on the exam is essentially the only criterion used in admissions decisions. The students with the highest scores receive appointments to the elite schools, maybe 100 out of more than 2,500 universities. Those schools receive the bulk of government funding, leaving the smaller schools, usually in smaller cities or rural areas, to struggle financially. These factors and others have had a cooling effect on the fierce competition to get into Chinese schools, causing many to seek their education elsewhere. "Many Chinese youths see their own universities as diploma mills, churning out graduates whose earnings potential is often bleak," reported *The Wall Street Journal*.

Perhaps most disturbing is the crackdown on academic freedom in China. *Foreign Policy* covered this in some depth, including in an investigative series titled "China U." Multiple Western media outlets have documented numerous cases of Chinese academics losing their jobs or being shunted aside at their universities after publishing research that somehow did not conform to the party's messaging. The *FP* series noted, "The CCP's regime is essentially anti-intellectual. Whenever it senses a political, financial, or ideological crisis, it launches a war on thought, reproducing and updating the 1957 purge of intellectuals." Certain subjects are off-limits, not only in academia but in the general public discourse—most notably the "three T's," Tiananmen, Tibet, and Taiwan—but the censorship does not stop there. *Foreign Policy* asserted that "…the recent escalation in political control of the academy spans the entire ideological spectrum and affects nearly all social scientists and humanities scholars working on the mainland." The consensus is that the erosion of intellectual freedom in higher education mirrors the political repression that exists across contemporary Chinese society.

Objectively, such restrictions stifle innovation and creativity and are antithetical to the goals of higher education. It's unclear how that kind of academic environment is going to produce the flexible and adaptable workforce that the future will demand. But it's not our purpose here to fret over the next generation of Chinese workers. What's most pernicious is that the repressive practices of the Chinese Communist Party are now reaching deep into universities in the United States and other Western countries. A number of American universities have established partnerships and exchange programs with Chinese universities that openly censor their curricula. Several professional associations in American academia have brought up cases of US schools acceding to the demands of their Chinese partners to alter their own curricula to conform with what's taught in China. In one episode, Cambridge University Press deleted hundreds of journal articles from its Chinese website under pressure from China, which objected to some of the content. The publisher eventually restored the articles after an outcry from Western academics, but the lesson was clear, and it was ominous.

The Chinese government has ample funds to spread around through these arrangements, and the Chinese students that they send to the US bring in money through high tuition fees. In December 2021, a prominent chemistry professor on faculty at Harvard was convicted in federal court of making false statements to the US government about his affiliation with a Chinese university and his participation in China's Thousand Talents Plan. They also found him guilty of failing to declare income earned in China and failing to report a Chinese bank account. It's impossible to track how pervasive such practices are, but it's clear that Beijing knows how to attract leading scientists, not only with money but with the promise of recognition and support. Working with China in this way is not necessarily illegal, but it can represent a very serious conflict of interest, and the failure to disclose is an offense. In fact, an initiative was launched under the Trump administration to uncover US scientists who might be sharing sensitive information with China.

"This is what is happening at U.S. universities," says Rayhan Asat, a Uyghur scholar, "they are self-censoring themselves in order to recruit Chinese students for economic benefit." Asat found herself at the center of another Chinese incursion into American education, when activists believed to be plants of the CCP sabotaged a presentation she was giving at Brandeis University on the plight of the Uyghurs, literally hacking into her PowerPoint presentation and defacing the graphics. As the numbers of Chinese students grew on US campuses, so did the presence of observers surveilling their activities. Reporting from multiple sources has shown that Chinese embassy and consular personnel have worked with student groups to organize protests of campus speakers, including the Dalai Lama, and to gather information on the social and political activities of students.

In a well-documented case at Purdue University, a visiting Chinese student posted an open letter in tribute to the students killed in Tiananmen Square. Not only was he harassed on campus by other Chinese students who accused him of working for the CIA and threatened to report him to Chinese authorities, but he began receiving calls from his family in China who had been visited and warned by state security officers. The student had to face the harsh reality that even at an American university, the eyes of the Chinese government were on him. The incident provoked the president of Purdue, Mitch Daniels, to issue a letter to the university community, promising disciplinary action against any student who "reported another student to any foreign entity for exercising their freedom of speech or belief."

Few of these incidents come to the attention of the media in this country, but authorities within the US Justice Department say that organizations and associations linked to the Chinese Communist Party and the Beijing government exist on many campuses. US authorities acknowledge that because they generally are not violating any laws, there's little direct action that can be taken against these Chinese groups, and that the universities themselves have been reluctant to interfere.

The most notorious manifestation of China's infiltration into campus life is a network of language and cultural education organizations called Confucius Institutes. The controversial institutes, at least partially funded by the Chinese government, operate at dozens of American universities and in over 140 countries around the world. According to the Institutes' US Center website, they seek to deliver "educational and cultural programs that teach Mandarin, cultivate Chinese cultural awareness, and facilitate educational exchanges," as well as to "bring a little piece of China to everything we do." However, at least two prominent professional associations, the American Association of University Professors and the National Association of Scholars, took hard looks at the institutes and believed that they also sought to interfere in the recruitment of teachers, to restrict curricula, and to monitor the activity of Chinese students studying abroad.

In 2019, FBI director Christopher Wray told Congress that the Confucius Institutes "offer a platform to disseminate Chinese government or Chinese Communist Party propaganda, to encourage censorship, to restrict academic freedom." While the number of institutes operating in the United States dropped by more than two-thirds, they continue to proliferate globally.

It is not easy to determine the appropriate response to China's increasing encroachment into American higher education. No doubt, Beijing has, in many ways, turned the tables on the United States, both co-opting and exploiting this important soft-power tool. Of course, the US has to get more aggressive and consistent about policing Chinese influence in its universities, but I believe it is always beneficial to expose elite Chinese students to the US and the West, and specifically, to the free marketplace of ideas that American academia aspires to. Research indicates that 60 percent of those Chinese students said that their American education experience improved their view of the US. That statistic remains meaningful even after acknowledging that a large number of those students also reported that the experience also improved their view of the Chinese government once they had a chance to appreciate the challenges of managing a massive educational system. But we must remind ourselves that the young people studying in the US will occupy leadership positions in Chinese society down the road. China has not been engaged in the global community for that long, and very few members of the politburo in Beijing, for instance, had the chance to study abroad. Ten or twenty years from now, a significant number, perhaps even a majority, of the Chinese Politburo (if China is still a one-party communist state in twenty years) will have studied abroad. In spite of all the headaches described above, shutting down access to US higher education for Chinese students would be rash and premature. The world is full of leaders who can look back at the US experience as having helped shape their worldview and enabled their own success. Do we really want to exclude young Chinese from that possibility?

·   ·   ·   ·   ·

Education is a fundamental component of development. As a soft-power tool, it represents one of the thornier areas for which to devise a future strategy, and it has its share of skeptics. Some critics in the global development community insist that the "Global North" should not be enabling the creation of new higher education institutions in developing countries, nor should we be supporting private higher education institutions in those countries. These critics argue that any monies going to higher education are essentially a subsidy to the elites and the middle class of the developing world by creating universities or financing higher education, especially when those funds might be better spent on the basic human needs of the poorest of the poor. Many of these critics are vocal (or sometimes quiet) admirers of the publicly financed model of higher education in Europe that wealthier post-colonial countries have replicated, and these critics worry that any new education offering from private institutions erodes the value and impact of those public universities. Others have raised the concern that rather than return home where their countries and communities can benefit from this education, foreign students who study in the US using US taxpayer funds will decide to stay in the US or another partner country that made their degrees possible. From a development standpoint, that would be the worst outcome; the investment in education international students should pay off in their contributions back home, not enable the good life somewhere else. More importantly, those funds should not be facilitating a "brain drain" in the developing world.

There are few easy decisions, and any path forward will likely involve uncomfortable compromises. What is certain is that the United States is losing ground in an arena where it has previously dominated and must concentrate on offering a viable and attractive alternative to China's focused and aggressive strategy in higher education. United Nations data for 2020 showed that China had become by far the largest provider of college scholarships in the world, while the US did not even make the top ten. International enrollments in the US have declined by roughly 10 percent over the last five years, and not only because of the COVID-19 pandemic. Although the reasons for the drop-off are not clear, aside from the sudden decline during the pandemic, competition from institutions in other countries, including the UK, Canada, and Australia, and other social factors have likely contributed. Every time we contemplate restricting who comes to the US, we need to consider whether that action will discourage folks who have legitimate reasons for coming or who we should want to come and be influenced by American culture instead of China. Legitimate concerns about border security and about people entering the US with malign intent need to be weighed against the possibility that they will look elsewhere to get that degree in law or business or public health, which might not be in the long-term interest of the US.

China's global outreach in education is driven by Beijing and mirrors the calculated self-interest of many of its other initiatives, as was described in a report from my group at CSIS: "What is true of the Belt and Road Initiative is true of China's wider approach to exchanges: choosing the quickest route with the least amount of accountability prioritizes elites and leaves a trail of social and economic risks for those unable to access its benefits."

While certain steps should be taken in the short term to address foreign interference in American academics, any strategy to solidify the United States' leadership in global education must recognize that human capital is a long-term investment. Many policy makers in Washington and elsewhere resist funding higher education, specifically because the payoff on the investment may not manifest for as much as twenty years in the future. Sensible planning must accommodate a time horizon of thirty or forty years and must coordinate the missions and activities of multiple cabinet-level departments with public and private universities and research institutions. Taking the long view means supporting continuous education, in other words, expanding the US commitment to primary and secondary education, to building education infrastructure, including digital capacity, and to strengthening the partnerships that have sustained institutions of higher education in the developing world. These universities train the teachers and administrators who will educate future generations as countries move along the path to self-reliance. Basic education is connected in fundamental ways to other development efforts, in that as countries become richer and more capable, schools become a top internal spending priority. At the same time, the US can increase the education funding and resources available to countries other than China so that they can undertake the training of leaders and skilled workers on their own terms and according to their own specific needs.

The political culture and legislative bureaucracy in Washington have traditionally posed obstacles to the kind of long-term planning required to improve global education. The impact of extended programs can be hard to measure, which makes them difficult to justify and sell to a Congress that has more urgent priorities. But the US should take a page from history and remember that in the early days of the Cold War, there was a bipartisan consensus in Washington for foreign aid and development that supported our foreign policy.

The political reality is that the appetite for aid spending may not be great. If difficult choices have to be made, the United States would be wise to focus its immediate attention on Africa. Not only is sub-Saharan Africa in pressing need of education support, but it also is already becoming an important arena in which the great-power competition is playing out. It has the fastest-growing population of any continent, and the growth rate is projected to continue for at least another twenty years, with a pronounced youth bulge. There are not enough universities at present. And in many countries, domestic resource mobilization cannot generate enough money to create a publicly funded higher-education system such as that which exists in many European countries.

Beijing has wasted no time leveraging education in Africa. CSIS found that the number of African students enrolled at Chinese universities shot up from less than 1,300 in 2003 to more than 80,000 in 2017. China offered 50,000 scholarships to African students in 2018, and its relatively low tuition fees enabled an additional influx of self-funded students from Africa's rising middle class. Arab students from North Africa and the Middle East are also supported by the Chinese Scholarship Council. Students who cannot or do not choose to study in China are often still exposed to Chinese language and cultural education through Confucius Institutes, which continue to proliferate throughout the world.

Ideally, the US and its allies should be helping African countries build first-class, self-sustaining higher-education systems. USAID should be partnering with other bilateral donors, major philanthropies, and US educational institutions to set up a network of at least twenty new pan-African universities that would become self-sustaining over time. This system might resemble the network of management institutes established in India, which benefited in the early days from relationships with elite American universities. Development professionals today talk a lot about building local capacity in recipient countries as a critical step toward self-reliance. A high-quality higher-education system in students' home countries would go a long way toward keeping the most talented and aspirational future leaders from seeking their fortunes elsewhere. Just as importantly, having more educational opportunities at home would mitigate somewhat the fierce competition for overseas scholarships in which the elites almost always have an unfair advantage.

Washington can also take steps to free up aid money. Specifically, the government can reconsider some of the budgetary directives already in place. For instance, the US has committed substantial funds to certain African countries, but much of it—in some cases as much as 95 percent—was earmarked for combating HIV/ AIDS. As it happens, the United States' efforts to support HIV/ AIDS work in Africa, largely via the PEPFAR program of the George W. Bush administration, have been tremendously effective, making it now possible to redistribute some of those funds by allocating health monies not to direct service provision but to long-term training in medicine or public health either in the US, the local country involved, or elsewhere. It would not be unreasonable to start thinking about a 5 to 10 percent "tax" on out-of-date "earmarks" as a way to redirect these monies to capacity-building and long-term training.

It might be gratifying to think that emerging global powers enabling education in lower- and middle-income countries contributes to development and accelerates the arrival of more countries as burden-sharing partners. It would also be somewhat naive. As my colleagues wrote, there is a qualitative difference between the United States and its strategic competitors in education, primarily having to do with the standards on which it is based: "The United States' competitive advantage remains its high-quality education, fair and transparent recruitment processes, and exposure to civic-minded curriculum. These values must be contrasted against the competing models. In the same way that bridges and roads do not automatically make good development, nor do hefty scholarships and language centers replace strong education systems and reforms." The report we issued goes on to make a series of recommendations for a strategic review of education as a political tool, including:

- Align the diplomatic and development objectives driving education exchanges and access and amplifying the critical differences between what the US can offer and what competing countries have made available.

- Clarify the metrics and indicators of both short-term and long-term success to present convincing data to Congress and the executive branch in support of additional funding.

• Reevaluate and restate all assumptions of needs and "best value" in a rapidly evolving geopolitical landscape on a country-specific basis.

• Develop innovative partnerships with the private sector, particularly in the area of digital learning. This effort would involve USAID's New Partnership Initiative, which aims to engage non-traditional and local collaborators.

• Step up the emphasis on youth programming in the context of the demographic youth bulge throughout the developing world. These efforts would connect to the Global LEAD Initiative (Leadership and Educating Advancing Development) within USAID, which, the agency states, "aims to mobilize one million young leaders over the next five years to guide their countries' development on issues of education, civic engagement, and leadership development."

• Ensure that education exchange programs keep pace with skills and knowledge relevant to a rapidly evolving workplace and formalize the establishment and maintenance of networks to facilitate the integration of new cohorts of graduates into the labor force.

Building support for some of these action steps will take time, as will implementation. It may be a generation before anyone can measure or even discern the results, but that should not deter policy makers. Prompt action and commitment are imperative. Patrick Awuah, the visionary entrepreneur who founded Ashesi University in Ghana, makes the case succinctly. "The most important natural resource that we have on this continent is the human intellect. It is not gold in the ground or oil under the seabed." Awuah understands that development success depends on educating Africa's future leaders. "Today, there is a significant push for other regions to engage with Africa. China is looking to engage with Africa. The West is looking to engage with Africa. We need to make sure that whatever change happens in Africa is African-led and not led from somewhere else. To do that, we need to be educating people on our side of the table who can engage in those conversations and make sure that the best interests of African citizens are front and center. We need to get to a place where the educational system here matches anywhere in the world."

Chapter 9

JOBS, JOBS, JOBS

Economic Growth from the Inside Out

> Developing countries want to engage the world
> as trading partners and economic peers, not as aid
> recipients. U.S. development agencies must embrace
> this shared opportunity. To do so, they will need the
> private sector as a full and willing partner.
>
> —"Our Shared Opportunity: A Vision for Global
> Prosperity," CSIS

There is no more transformational force in development than broad-based economic growth. That assumption underpinned the recommendations from the CSIS Executive Council on Development, which included senior government figures as well as executives from major US corporations. Two additional assumptions also informed the council's work. The first is that responsible business investment can drive country growth, creating jobs and lifting community living standards. I devoted a lot of time early in my career to evangelizing for multi-stakeholder partnerships involving government aid agencies, private sector actors, development finance institutions, NGOs, and others, as a pathway to more efficient and affordable development. Twenty years ago, career foreign services officers recognized how the changing world presented new challenges that would require new forms of partnership, whether to feed millions of hungry people, supply power and electricity, manage new and complex global supply chains, or close the growing digital divide. One of the conclusions, in addition to the prospect of increased global trade and flows of private capital into the developing world, was that aid agencies needed to work with more intentionality and coordination with the private sector to meet these challenges. With the support of Secretary of State Colin Powell and the energetic sponsorship of Andrew Natsios, USAID administrator at the time, the agency launched the Global Development Alliance, dedicated to building public-private partnerships. It was my honor to work in the group steering this initiative and later to lead it. Hundreds of relationships and partnerships were established, and the Global Development Alliance continues to play a vital role in US development efforts.

Now more than ever, the broad-based economic growth that lifts countries out of poverty and serves as the primary pathway to self-reliance will rely on the full engagement of the private sector. The best social program is a job. In addition to providing income that circulates through an economy, work builds self-esteem. It gives them a bigger stake in current and long-term trends relevant to their well-being and that of future generations. It grounds people and offers direction and the opportunity for growth. It is antithetical to crime and corruption and can provide a deterrent to extremism. An International Finance Corporation (IFC) study in 2013 estimated that the world would need 600 million new jobs by the end of the decade just to keep up with population growth. We likely need more than that between now and the end of this decade. Further, that IFC study confirmed that nine out of ten new jobs in the developing world are created by the private sector.

．　．　．　．　．

Fifty years ago, more than two-thirds of US financial flows to the developing world were in the form of official direct assistance (ODA)—loans and grants from wealthy nations to governments and NGOs. In developing countries today, except for the poorest countries, the balance has shifted. Private and commercial flows far exceed official flows from donors or from the multilateral organizations such as the World Bank, IMF, and regional development banks. And all international flows to developing countries are dwarfed by the public and private domestic resources generated by the economies of developing countries, such as taxes, savings, private bonds, and capital investments.

While ODA now accounts for a much smaller percentage of developing countries' resource streams, it continues to act as an agenda-setter and catalyzer of private investment. In the last ten years, developing economies have absorbed more foreign direct investment (FDI) than developed counterparts.

The United States has aspired to make broad-based growth a central organizing principle of its development policy, but economic growth has taken a back seat to competing development priorities. USAID has recently updated its Economic Growth Strategy to acknowledge a basic assumption: "More sustainable, inclusive, and resilient economic growth—especially growth in the income of individuals—through enterprise-driven development is central to USAID's strategy of eliminating poverty, building self-reliance, and reducing dependence on foreign assistance.... As a country's per-capita income rises, its financial and taxation systems grow and mature, which enables private and domestic resources to replace foreign assistance."

Another operating assumption is that a transparent, accountable, and capable public sector creates an environment conducive to private investment and can help ensure that resulting benefits are widely spread. The development community talks about this component as the "enabling environment," that is, the hard and soft infrastructure that allows entrepreneurs to access financing and other resources, allows international firms to establish themselves in emerging markets and tap into underutilized workforces, and encourages businesses of all sizes to grow and mature. Here is where economic growth and good governance—the two most important elements of development—intersect in a kind of symbiotic relationship. Corruption, in either the public sector or the private, stymies business, which requires transparency and adherence to the rule of law to flourish. As former secretary of state Colin Powell put it, "Capital is a coward. It flees from corruption, bad policies, conflict and unpredictability." Look no further than Myanmar for confirmation: less than a year after the coup that restored a repressive military junta to power in February 2021, its upward economic progress completely reversed itself. International firms from France, the US, Australia, India, and even China were packing up their operations there as employment fell and poverty levels at least doubled.

At the same time, as domestic businesses grow and gain momentum, they can help foster the very conditions they—and other firms—need to prosper further. Ambassador E. Anthony (Tony) Wayne, a veteran of the US diplomatic corps and a keen observer of international economic affairs, argues that forward-looking local private-sector actors that fuel the economic engine in developing countries can simultaneously become prime drivers of reform. Successful business leaders who are creating jobs and contributing to the tax base can influence government agencies and civic organizations like chambers of commerce. They can establish public-private networks that can reach out to civil society groups, such as labor unions or the media, to catalyze political and social change. In addition, leaders in the local private sector have the unique knowledge required to help guide and manage the relationships between developing countries and donor countries or institutions. The private sector can even play a critical role in emergency response or disaster relief, for example. Think back to the destructive tsunami in Indonesia in 2004. The US government, through USAID and in partnership with former presidents George W. Bush and Bill Clinton, was able to mobilize support from a large network of private companies with a diverse array of capabilities to assist in rescue and rebuilding. Ambassador Wayne believes that in the context of great-power competition, such coalitions can support reforms in line with US and OECD values that can foster economic growth and prosperity. They can engage collectively with other countries, development banks, and other multilateral institutions, which will become ever more significant as China moves to play a more central role in those organizations.

External private sector actors have just as important a role to play, according to former ambassador James Michel. Foreign firms can bring established behaviors and values, as well as international standards and practices, to the new environments. In this way, broad-based economic growth, in addition to eradicating poverty, can be fundamental to achieving peace and stability, even as it depends on reliable governance and accountable institutions. It will rest on the pillars of vibrant markets, human capacity, modern infrastructure, peace and justice, safety nets, and social protection. The OECD is on the bandwagon as well, asserting that "Effective governance is a necessary condition for economic prosperity and social cohesion," in its Strategy on Development.

The Center for International Private Investment (CIPE), one of the constituent organizations of the National Endowment for Democracy, agrees that "constructive investments support broader economic and social goals, such as integrating marginalized groups into the economy, connecting regional markets and boosting integration, or ensuring compliance with environmental or labor regulations…. Over time, the strengthening of governance and markets that foster a supportive ecosystem of laws, regulation, culture, and institutions that foster innovative enterprises and create wealth for a broader section of society."

CIPE frames the conversation about development investment in terms of "constructive" capital and "corrosive" capital. Constructive capital "has clear terms, is market oriented and accountable to stakeholders," while corrosive capital "crowds out constructive capital, corrupting the market." Constructive capital thrives in a context of strong institutions that require and enable transparent public procurement and spending, support corporate governance ethics and fair dispute resolution, and encourage competition. By highlighting private-sector champions and increasing global awareness, constructive capital can on its own function as an advocate for reform.

Andrew Wilson, CIPE's executive director, explains constructive and corrosive capital in the context of the great-power competition. In the past, he says, the US and its partner countries focused
development finance strategy on creating an attractive environment
for foreign investment, believing that to be the route to economic
growth and a vehicle for spreading free-market democratic principles. But the West no longer has a monopoly on overseas investment.
China offers an attractive alternative asking for little if anything in
return in the way of good governance or compliance with global
standards. Simply put, overseas investment is now an arena of open
competition between constructive and corrosive capital, as defined
by CIPE. If the US and its allies want to enable a better offer,
we have to do a better job of demonstrating what's at stake and
creating awareness of the costs of relying on corrosive capital from
China, Russia, or other countries. "When opaque finance enters
recipient countries through governance gaps, it commonly has
negative impacts on human rights, the environment, small business
and labor, not to mention exacerbating governance challenges." To
demonstrate the point, CIPE points to Venezuela and Colombia.
Only a few decades ago, Venezuela was a rapidly advancing emerging
market while the latter was stymied by internal conflict. The Vene-
zuelan government then allowed the flow of corrosive capital from
within and without amid a breakdown of democratic governance.
Investors ran, and the economy collapsed. Colombia, on the other
hand, encouraged constructive capital and followed a more gradual
route toward sustainable growth, and in so doing, it built a strong
foundation for markets and capable institutions.

Michael Klein, professor and veteran of the World Bank,
IFC, and the OECD, writes that "the key to poverty reduction is
creating productive jobs where poor people live, which in statistics shows up as growth.... Because poor areas can benefit from
technical and organizational innovations made elsewhere in the
world, it is possible today to create productive jobs faster and in
greater quantity than ever before." Highlighting the link between
governance and growth, Klein argues further that "firms are the
vehicles that spread best practices and productive jobs.... Most if
not all governments try to help the process along not just by establishing the basics of property rights and contract security but also

by providing special support to small farmers and businesses or to larger ones under industrial policies that provide some protection from competition and easier access to credit."

* * * * *

The United States and its OECD partners must stand up for broad-based economic growth while, at the same time, encouraging a bias toward democratic governance. What will this growth environment look like, and how can the development "industry" help create it? Ultimately, broad-based growth has got to be an "inside job," driven by local actors for the benefit of local stakeholders. Foreign aid can be an important supporting actor through what are known as "economic-growth" activities to establish or support key elements, including:

- The enabling environment, competitive markets, governed by consistent and enforceable rules and regulations and accountable institutions.

- Functioning financial systems: banks and capital markets that can help move savings into investing

- Education and training linked to workforce development

- Inclusion: access to employment, business capital, and resources for women and other underrepresented groups within the population

- Infrastructure: both "hard" and "soft."

Given the challenges from the great-power competition and emerging from the pandemic, we need to refocus our development efforts. The West will not be able to compete dollar-for-dollar with

China, nor will it resort to coercive tactics like Russia. The building blocks of economic self-reliance represent the best competitive advantage for developing countries because they are the only sure pathway to sustainable growth, which, together with economic and political independence, is exactly what are never on offer from either of those powerful nations.

Funding for economic growth development activities can be a very tough sell in Washington. Like democracy and governance programs, economic growth activities can have long time horizons and results that are difficult to quantify or measure. So instead of recommending an entirely new pool of money be created for this work, the CSIS Executive Council on Development recommended a reallocation of hundreds of millions of dollars from other foreign aid accounts. The kinds of economic-growth activities carried out by aid agencies—fixing laws or strengthening legal systems—are not that expensive relative to other development programs, and a little bit of money can go a long way. This reallocation should occur in conjunction with a major education campaign involving the executive branch and senior representatives of US development, diplomatic, and economic agencies to reorient policy around poverty reduction through broad-based growth. The campaign would target members of Congress, NGOs, universities, and the business community.

In addition, the CSIS group urged the US government to promote entrepreneurship on a global scale, first by working to identify and reduce barriers to new business enterprises. In this context, we must revitalize the Doing Business report that was "paused" by the World Bank in 2020 after allegations that senior bank officials had pressured staff to alter data for certain countries. The Doing Business project, which quantified and reported the risk level of starting or operating businesses in 190 countries around the world, was a uniquely valuable reference, not only for prospective entrepreneurs but also for established firms interested in expanding into new venues and markets. Finance institutions of every stripe—government assistance agencies, foundations, development banks and development finance institutions, private equity, and so on—relied on the data supplied by the Doing Business project.

Next, the report suggested that the United States should align its development efforts more closely and efficiently with the private sector. In addition to reallocating money to economic growth activities, the US might aspire to allocate as much as 25 percent of all its development resources to support partnerships while streamlining the process for establishing, planning, and coordinating those partnerships. Since the publication of that report, the US has never allocated that level of resources in alignment with other partners. We have more work to do here. Plenty of precedent exists, such as when the tech giant Cisco partnered with USAID and other development organizations to bring more digital connectivity to Africa. In a win-win for all parties, an American firm expanded its reach and brought technological capability and Western standards to an underserved region. The government catalyzed the arrangement and brought expertise and authority to the table, which allowed the harnessing of private financing. Similarly, Mars, the food company, worked with development agencies to support the shrinking numbers of cocoa growers in West Africa and other countries. The cocoa business was threatened by climate change, urbanization, local conflicts, and disease, while a growing global middle class triggered an increase in demand.

The administrator of USAID, Ambassador Samantha Power, expressed her intentions in 2021 to explore more partnership initiatives, suggesting that development projects could piggyback on the international supply chains, infrastructure, and networks already established by companies like Google or Coca-Cola. Large corporations can be game changers in emerging economies. Some in the development community have an outmoded understanding of job creation, perhaps envisioning a collective of rural artisans empowered by microloans. And no doubt, a great deal of development assistance has historically focused on small and midsized enterprises (SMEs), which account for more than half of formal employment worldwide, according to the IFC. If informal employment is included, that number goes up to two-thirds of permanent, full-time employment in the developing world. At least half the jobs in the developing world are in the informal economy, some in small or midsized firms, but many as "micro" enterprises, a single person, a family, or a small, loosely organized group. But data show that most of the SMEs have a hard time growing, while jobs in smaller and micro-businesses are often at the low end of the wage scale and can be insecure. It can be useful to make capital available for those successful SMEs which are often too large for microloans and too small for traditional bank financing. It's equally important to ensure enabling environments that keep them healthy and stable and to view firms of any size as part of an ecosystem of firms in which the driving force for increasing productivity and income often comes from the larger players that have better access to new knowledge, skills, and technologies.

A major report from the World Bank made the case for larger enterprises as drivers of sustained economic growth. "Large firms represent important vehicles for change by contributing to an important share of net job creation and labor productivity across different contexts." Workers in large firms earn, on average, 22 percent higher hourly wages based on data from thirty-two low- and middle-income countries and have an even higher advantage in lower-income countries.

Whether these enterprises are offshoots of established firms seeking new ventures or partnerships or the product of local entre- preneurial efforts, they create jobs both directly and indirectly through the supply and value chains in which they participate and put goods into circulation. This, in turn, invigorates markets, improves worker incomes and conditions, and contributes to local tax bases. Additionally, successful large firms almost always generate spinoffs and copycats, creating a healthy cycle of compe- tition and innovation. For these reasons, the World Bank report encouraged governments and development finance institutions to "actively work to spread the benefits from production at scale across the largest possible number of market participants." Larger firms, especially multinational ones, present opportunities for exactly the kind of partnerships that Ambassador Power envisioned.

A truly well-rounded economy, of course, consists of enter- prises of every shape and size, from a family of shopkeepers to a local construction company to a textile conglomerate with multiple factories. All must be enabled, encouraged, and accommodated. Employment has a way of sparking a virtuous cycle of economic growth. That is, jobs often create more jobs. There is the "indirect employment," meaning new jobs up and down the supply chains that support ongoing businesses, and the "induced employment," meaning the jobs created by higher demand for consumer goods and services created by increased employment and higher wages.

.   .   .   .   .

Working with the private sector involves supporting trade as well as investing. As the amount of official development assistance diminishes and the nature of bilateral donor relationships evolves, trade becomes an ever more important development tool.

The United States had made significant progress in forging international trade agreements. But it withdrew from entering into the Trans-Pacific Partnership (TPP) during the Trump administration while renegotiating NAFTA, the North American Free Trade Agreement, now the US-Mexico-Canada Agreement, and concluding a trade agreement with South Korea. Our pullout from TPP was a mistake; the agreement entered in force without us, greatly diminishing US influence in a region of tremendous geostrategic importance and remaining a positive instrument of cooperation among its eleven members (Australia, Brunei, Canada, Chile, Japan, Malaysia, Mexico, New Zealand, Peru, Singapore, and Vietnam). When viewed through the lens of the great-power competition, TPP could have significant implications for foreign policy and national security. The US holds itself outside the pact at its own peril. The Biden administration has considered rejoining the agreement or possibly renegotiating some of its terms, but we need to act to become active participants. The United States should be leading on international trade instead of letting others set the agenda. When it comes to making policy and setting global standards, we should be "makers," not "takers." The US and its neighbors would also benefit from a trade agreement encompassing the whole of the western hemisphere, as was proposed at the Summit of the Americas in 1994, but never realized due to opposition from Cuba, Nicaragua, and Venezuela. Any of these pacts should reflect a post-COVID-19 opportunity to build new, resilient supply chains.

Trade also offers tremendous, mutually beneficial opportunities for the United States and developing countries by helping the latter into the international economy. The United States and its OECD partners occasionally get myopic when strategizing in this area and can lose sight of the fact that some of the less wealthy signatories to the big multilateral trade pacts need assistance to take advantage of these trade agreements. Many lower- and middle-income countries, while enthusiastic about the potential benefits of trade alliances, lack the capacity to make them fully operable and to meet global standards. A task force convened at CSIS summarized the problem: "Trade and investment agreements encompass an expanding range of nontariff, regulatory and investment barriers that impact the ability of developing countries to participate in regional and global supply and value chains. In this sense, the counties that stand to gain the most from increased international economic engagement are often ill-equipped to capture the benefits of trade."

In such circumstances, public money can help accelerate two-way trade, through what is known as "trade capacity building," to help countries negotiate and implement trade agreements and assist firms in those countries to trade successfully, generating jobs and income. TCB includes any "reforms to build the physical, human and institutional capacity to benefit from trade and investment opportunities, including transparent regulatory and tax regimes to ensure a level playing field for entrepreneurs and other businesses." Assistance for TCB must be part of every trade agreement going forward.

Another task force convened by CSIS recommended specific steps to promote trade capacity building, starting with the formation of a permanent interagency committee within the US government to coordinate the TCB activities in all relevant agencies. This committee could determine the criteria for selecting developing country partners and prevent needed funds from being diverted to other priorities. This would also enable Congress to create a single line item in the Foreign Operations budget for all these activities without having to allocate additional monies.

Multilateral support for trade capacity building took the form of the World Trade Organization's Trade Facilitation Agreement (TFA), designed to reduce red tape and remove unnecessary holdups at customs and borders. I helped the United States think through which commitments it would make to this important agreement, which, when it went into force in 2017, was projected to produce as much as a trillion dollars in global export gains and potentially create 20 million jobs. At the time, I argued that the US should dedicate $150 million over five years in support of TFA to demonstrate our commitment to ensuring its thorough implementation and to spurring comparable investments from allies and multilateral institutions like the World Bank. Several institutions came together to create a public-private platform called the Global Alliance for Trade Facilitation to help implement the agreement, helping countries from Colombia to Vietnam and Sri Lanka ease the movement of goods across borders.

Contained within the US government are a number of institutions that support overseas trade and investment in ways that bolster American business interests while also contributing to global development. The Trump administration had slated two critical agencies for closure, but they were rescued and arguably even made stronger in the past few years. First is EXIM, the Export-Import Bank of the United States. EXIM is the country's official export credit agency and describes its mission as "supporting American jobs by facilitating the export of U.S. goods and services." When risks in fragile or conflict-ridden countries make American firms skittish about new ventures, the government, via EXIM, can assume some of the risk with its own financing tools, enabling those companies to compete in global markets.

Although expanding markets drive increased output, which means more American jobs, some in the Republican party have seen EXIM as a form of corporate welfare, with the government underwriting the overseas profits of a few large companies. By the time Trump came into office, the bank was effectively dormant. Those of us who worked hard to support EXIM's revival made the case that the sale of American goods and services accelerates economic growth in the developing world. The export of engineering and construction services facilitates the delivery of electricity to rural communities, for example, or the sale of American locomotives enables the expansion of railway infrastructure in several African countries. But what really got EXIM's detractors to reconsider was the looming specter of China as a massive exporter of subsidized hard goods and infrastructure. By the time Washington started paying attention, China's own EXIM bank was doing more business than all the other export agencies in the world combined.

Some US businesses had felt hamstrung by EXIM's strict eligibility requirement regarding domestic content. If an American manufacturer was seeking export credit for machinery, but a large percentage of the components used to make the machinery come from outside the US, export of that product could not receive EXIM support. Given the interconnectedness of the global economy, that ruled out a lot of companies. Our efforts to revive EXIM, made with support from the bank's leaders from previous administrations, involved reducing that domestic content requirement to accommodate the changing nature of global supply chains. By 2019, EXIM had awoken from its slumber, but much more needs to be done to further empower the bank for the twenty-first century.

EXIM can become more dynamic by continuing to adjust content requirements, coordinating more effectively with other agencies, and expanding programming and outreach to small- and medium-sized American enterprises (SMEs). Lower domestic content requirements, along with a more dynamic set of indicators and criteria for a transaction's support of the US economy, would help protect American manufacturing while facilitating the export of more goods and services. To compete effectively with China, EXIM must play to the strengths of the US export economy. There is great opportunity for expansion within the rapidly growing US service sector—banking and finance, engineering, computing, health care, hospitality, and so on.

Another agency targeted for shutdown by the Trump administration was the Overseas Private Investment Corporation (OPIC). The US government's development finance institution functioned in many ways like larger multilateral investment banks, mobilizing and encouraging development by supporting private investment overseas through loans and guarantees, risk insurance, expertise, and guidance. OPIC had been the primary vehicle for building public-private partnerships to build industry and infrastructure and create jobs in the developing world, and for establishing a presence of both US government and business in emerging economies. In contrast to the EXIM bank, which specifically supports US exports, a development finance institution helps mobilize capital for new business ventures overseas.

My colleagues and I provided analysis that made the case to reauthorize and strengthen OPIC as early as 2011 and went all in after 2016. I personally threw myself into this effort, helping to architect legislation to keep the US in the development finance game. The result was the BUILD Act—Better Utilization of Investments Leading to Development—of 2018. BUILD rescued OPIC by absorbing it, along with USAID's Development Credit Authority, into a single agency, more streamlined but also stronger, called the United States International Development Finance Corporation (DFC). DFC's charter is to "facilitate the participation of private sector capital and skills in the economic development of countries with low- or lower-middle-income economies." The DFC can also work in upper-middle-income countries, under limited circumstances, including national security concerns, or if there are developmental imperatives in a discrete underdeveloped part of that country.

BUILD authorized DFC to make equity investments in businesses, provide technical assistance, increase acceptable risk levels by providing "first-loss guarantees" to raise the spending cap when necessary, and establish a "preference" for US investors rather than a requirement. Most importantly, BUILD's seven-year authorization meant that OPIC, long a target for budget hawks in Washington, would not have to fight for its life on a year-to-year basis.

The success is preserving and enhancing a US development finance capability represented only one small step toward strengthening the global development finance machinery. Institutions like DFC cannot, on their own, fuel the growth of emerging economies or even come close to matching the investment capital that China has been providing. They are, however, invaluable in that they mobilize private capital through partnerships with corporations, foundations, entrepreneurs, and innovators. "DFIs [development finance institutions] at their best can 'prime the pump,' supporting revolutionary businesses like Celtel [Mo Ibrahim's telecommunications infrastructure company across Africa], and opening economies to global trade and investment.... Based on the other tools available, as well as the changing world confronting policy makers, expect DFIs to be utilized more not less."

Not surprisingly, the COVID-19 pandemic took its toll on development finance, as it has in so many other spheres. Soren Andreasen, the CEO of the Association of European Development Finance Institutions, points to a "stagnation" in flows of money from the private sector, as occurred after the global financial crisis, which made development finance institutions all the more vital. However, with all the negative effects on the global supply chains and value chains, the developing world is going to need greater inflows of private capital than DFIs are expected to enable. While countries were able to access some investment capital through DFIs, that has not necessarily led to the growth they wanted. Andreasen believes the focus has shifted from "growth" to "quality," meaning investment in the developing world should reflect the values currently occupying the wealthier nations: sustainability, resilience, and inclusion.

The unique value provided by development finance institutions is described as "additionality," which can take several different forms. *Demonstration* additionality refers to a DFI making money in an emerging sector or region, spurring other private enterprise and investment. *Financial* additionality can mean enabling longer loan periods, which allows investment into projects requiring longer time horizons, such as infrastructure. DFIs also offer *design* additionality, meaning investing in projects, like factories or processing plants, whose success can be copied or repeated by others. Finally, DFIs provide *policy* additionality because they can accelerate reform through the deals they finance. Development finance institutions can put a project in front of policy makers and say: "If you make this change in policy, we can make this investment, and 1,000 private-sector jobs will be created."

In addition to multinational companies and governments (via DFIs), the private-equity community has also gotten into the act through "impact investing." The vision statement of Total Impact Capital, an investment fund founded by John Simon, a former executive vice president of OPIC and US ambassador to the African Union, speaks of the intention "to unite impact capital with high-quality investment opportunities that are financially sound, make the planet a better place, and have the potential to scale significantly."

The fund's strategy is to "focus on basic human needs and partner with proven implementers who bring knowledge, experience and a demonstrated track record of social and financial performance." Simon also reinforces the importance of domestic resource mobilization, pointing out that while development finance and overseas direct assistance provide important catalytic capital, neither will have the long-term impact of local capital. Local investment generates "country ownership," the idea that development should reflect the priorities of an engaged and enabled population—a country taking responsibility for its own development.

*   *   *   *   *

One hears three buzzwords more than ever in the context of development: sustainability, inclusion, and resilience. Sustainability generally refers to the climate and the environment, and the careful management of natural resources that often drive economic growth. (Think of the rare-earth metals needed for clean energy or timber in the Amazon.) Inclusion is, of course, about ensuring that women and previously underserved population groups have full access to employment, economic opportunity, and civic institutions. But it must also encompass equality of access to rights and protections outlined in global labor standards and ensure that all business and industry operations are consistent with international standards.

Resilience is a more complex and nuanced concept. National economies need to be resilient on a macro scale, which requires both diversification and vibrant domestic resource mobilization that can provide protection when any one sector of the economy is threatened. But a mature economy that can withstand crises and disasters must also create social safety nets to protect individuals. "As countries become wealthier and collect more taxes, populations demand greater accountability and expect their governments to address social challenges through social programs and spending." Research shows that implementing a social safety net program has a direct impact on reducing poverty and boosting prosperity. While direct assistance and other development resources can support the design of such programs, they need political and financial commitment from the governments of those emerging countries. Certainly, some ambitious programs have earned criticism for placing an undue burden on a country's economy, but they contribute to a national sense of cohesion and pride. The popularity of Brazil's Bolsa Familia program and Mexico's Prospera serve as important models for other aspiring countries.

. . . . .

The vision of prosperity espoused by my colleagues and myself at CSIS is one in which US development policy aggressively pursues opportunities to create stronger economic bonds that boost well-being of citizens in developing countries and Americans. We can no longer hold the private sector at arm's length or dismiss the vital role that corporate actors can play. Americans—both policy makers and ordinary citizens—must understand that citizens of the developing world are hopeful, healthy consumers who want to have steady jobs with growing firms and to live in clean environments with access to the full range of consumer goods and services. We must engage with those people by appealing to their aspirations, not criticizing their deficiencies, and work to enable the best and quickest pathways to full agency and autonomy.

We know that private-sector job creation is inextricably linked to overall development and poverty reduction, but we also must be vigilant about the obstacles that limit job creation and growth. The World Bank has used the acronym MILES to describe the large-scale potential constraints: Macroeconomic policies; Investment climate, institutions, and infrastructure; Labor market regulations and institutions; Education and skills; and Social protection. On a more practical level, constraints include access to power, land, and other physical resources; access to finance, particularly for smaller firms; inadequately trained workforces; informality; tax systems; corruption; and political instability. It is in these areas that the supporting role of the public sector is most needed. Development finance institutions can support the public sector in this process in addition to working directly with private companies.

In addition to the specific actions outlined here, such as renewed support for DFIs, new resources and templates for private-sector engagement and public-private partnerships, and linking democratic governance to broad-based economic growth, Ambassador James Michel summarizes the general principles that should drive policy going forward. To support economic growth, first get the policies right, then court the private sector in the context of improved policies and incentives and build into all those policies basic commitments to inclusion and sustainability. To support the evolution of stable, participatory democratic societies, work to strengthen government institutions in which local populations can feel confident while encouraging pluralism, tolerance, and support for democracy in all nongovernmental entities. The most successful countries are invariably most often the freest. They have protected individual rights, enforced the rule of law, and created a welcoming environment for free enterprise. Economic freedom consistently lifts people out of poverty and can prevent them from sliding back into it.

Finally, we must acknowledge that if the well-being of populations depends on successfully stimulating broad-based economic growth, the development work in the immediate future is going to be concentrated in fragile environments and failing countries, where it will be very challenging. The next chapter explores ways in which we can upgrade the US development apparatus and personnel to best accommodate that work.

Chapter 10

FIXING THE PLUMBING

Building the Future of Development

Ultimately, putting American interests first means leading abroad. Any mission for U.S. foreign assistance should support the broader national security strategy to ensure that it maximizes its foreign policy impact and puts American interests first. The best, most effective foreign assistance has always been driven by a combination of enlightened self-interest and a desire to effect positive change in the world.

—Report of A Bipartisan Task Force Report of the CSIS Project on U.S. Leadership in Development, July 2017

I n 2012, a paper my colleagues and I published raised the hackles of influential members of the development establishment, not to mention some high-ranking administration officials. Rajiv Shah was the administrator at USAID, and like most of his predecessors, he had come in with big plans to reform the agency, bringing more efficiency and accountability and making significant changes to the ways in which development assistance would be delivered. No one who follows US foreign assistance closely would argue that the US assistance architecture is perfect. It is a system that was well-designed over sixty years ago, but it has been diminished, distorted, and fragmented over the six decade it has survived, sometimes through amendments to the charter of USAID and sometimes through the creation of competing alternative mechanisms. There are now more than twenty federal agencies delivering overseas aid in one form or another. The resulting cacophony of voices in internal US deliberations and in engagement with other countries is needlessly complicated, incoherent, wasteful, and inefficient.

Rajiv Shah's major initiative, USAID Forward, sought to align US assistance with principles set out in a series of high-level forums on aid effectiveness organized by the OECD in Paris (2005), Accra (2008), and Busan (2011). The principles, as set out in the Busan Partnership Agreement, were:

- Ownership of development priorities by developing countries

- A focus on results

- Partnerships for development

- Transparency and shared responsibility

In furtherance of those principles, Busan called for necessary assistance to strengthen country systems within the overall context of national capacity development for sustainable outcomes.

USAID Forward put that intent front and center. This was not the first time the agency had launched "localization" initiatives. During the George W. Bush administration, for instance, the New Partners Technical Assistance Project was intended to empower local actors, along with US faith-based organizations and other groups, to work on HIV/AIDS issues through PEPFAR. Rajiv Shah's plan sought to take this to a much more ambitious level and build it into the institutional DNA of USAID, which would move quickly to reduce its dependence on US-based outside implementers, that is, the network of nonprofit and for-profit organizations and consulting companies that comprise what many like to deride as the "development-industrial complex," and what might be more aptly called the "development-industrial base."

In the thirty years since the end of the Cold War, USAID had gone through a series of personnel reductions, even as the number of projects it was expected to carry out had increased. To bridge that gap, an ecosystem of international development assistance had arisen that depended increasingly on outside organizations to implement USAID programs. Most nettlesome in the political climate of the early 2000s were the ten to twenty large international development consulting firms and NGOs through which roughly three-quarters of the US foreign aid budget was by then distributed. Those organizations hired and managed the experts who implemented the projects that USAID financed because USAID could no longer hire the necessary staff itself. It's easy to sympathize with the impulse to break the cycle of corporatization of foreign aid and vilify the "Beltway bandits" who were seen to be prospering from contracts intended to help development in poor countries. Why should taxpayer dollars go to pay the overhead of these partner organizations? How did their continued dominance of the development effort increase local ownership or build local capacity? Why were consultants hired by contractors, rather than US government representatives, carrying out the dialogue and diplomacy about US policy in relation to the policies of the developing country?

The first goal of USAID Forward was to realign resources through "implementation and procurement reform." The new initiative set an explicit target of 30 percent of USAID's money allocated to country programs to be reserved for grants or contracts with local government or private organizations in developing countries rather than US-based firms or NGOs. Although the intent was admirable, my colleagues and I concluded that the plan was misguided. We thought it would not result in more effective delivery of aid, would not increase accountability and efficiency, and would neither decrease USAID's bureaucracy nor maximize the use of its personnel. Against the advice of influential development professionals and with some trepidation from senior people in my own organization, I published a report expressing those concerns.

Our argument was straightforward. To begin with, many smaller countries that are just beginning the climb up the development scale lack the experience, expertise, or transparency to manage large projects. In particular, they do not have adequate financial infrastructure or controls to ensure that the assistance money would be channeled properly and used efficiently for the intended purposes. Similarly, we thought that local NGOs or advocacy groups were also likely to be ill-equipped to carry out large-scale programs. To be clear, while this perspective might seem to some as paternalistic, it was instead the product of years of development experience, in which donor funds have gone missing and well-intentioned projects have failed to meet their goals. It's reasonable to argue that building local capacity means giving emerging countries the space to make mistakes from which they can learn, but that has to be balanced by the need to take the utmost care with American taxpayer dollars and delivering aid quickly where it is needed. In fact, one of the possible unintended consequences of USAID Forward that worried our team at CSIS was that properly monitoring the ability of local actors to account for the money allocated to them would necessitate, ironically, adding *more* bean-counters and bureaucrats to the US assistance apparatus, using up budget resources that should go to program designers, technical experts, and others who can do meaningful development work.

The drive to move resources away from the development-industrial complex and toward more direct support to local entities was based on some shaky assumptions. First, sending in a US development consultant does not automatically negate the possibility of improving local capacity. The goal of such projects is almost always to support local authorities or groups, not to supplant them. Outside implementers usually work in partnership with local actors on finite, time-limited projects that are designed to leave behind knowledge, expertise, and ownership of the result. Next, we must be expansive in our interpretation of that word, "ownership." Does it mean that a program must be conceived or originated, as well as implemented, by the recipient nation? Countries can "own" an idea without refining it in detail or controlling all the resources to implement it. As we said in our paper, "good, practical ideas are good, practical ideas regardless of their origin."

Finally, we asserted that rejecting large corporate development firms just because they come from the for-profit private sector would mean throwing the baby out with the bathwater. Have some of these firms grown complacent, not to mention excessively top-heavy and, in the process, rich? Yes. Can the processes for delivering assistance be streamlined in the same way that other parts of government can be streamlined? Of course. Is it possible that the current network of development firms has a disincentive to work themselves out of a job? Perhaps. Is it possible too small a group of implementers who deliver this work deprives the world of new, creative ideas? Quite possibly. And the US government should absolutely find ways to diversify its implementer base and, of course, hold them all accountable for their processes and results. But the reality is that these firms exist for a reason. They are good at delivering assistance, and they are good at running all the bureaucratic traps that have accumulated over forty years. And they often represent the best solution, even for building local capacity. I argued controversially that the US has a defense industrial base and that our defense industrial base was a strategic asset of the United States. We likewise had a "development industrial base" made up of this ecosystem of partners, and this ecosystem was a strategic asset of the United States as well.

Publicly challenging the popular reform initiative of a prominent and influential appointee of a popular president did not win me many friends. Within Washington circles, the report was condemned by the smart set as "partisan propaganda," and it was suggested that I was "shilling for private corporate interests." It was made clear to me that I would not be welcome in an important organization dedicated to modernizing the delivery of assistance, in which many of my peers in the development community held leadership positions. USAID Forward generated a lot of energy and attention but ultimately had a limited impact, partly because of resistance on the Hill, and partly because Rajiv Shah moved on before the programs were fully implemented, and the new subsequent administrator, Gayle Smith, had other priorities. Shah was one more in a succession of USAID administrators who have tried to improve the effectiveness of US foreign assistance in changing geopolitical circumstances and uncertain support and commitment. One can see elements of USAID Forward brought back to life in Samantha Power's stated goals for changing the way USAID does business during the Biden administration.

· · · · ·

With that initiative from ten years ago still percolating through foreign assistance reform efforts, let's now break down the challenges inherent in the current aid mission and delivery systems and some ways to strengthen this vital component of America's soft power.

The internal inconsistency of development work is that the universal ambition is to pursue development objectives so effectively that we will work ourselves out of a job, whether we work for the government, an NGO, or a for-profit consulting firm. USAID administrator Mark Green asserted that the purpose of our foreign assistance is to one day end the need for it to exist. Under his direction, the agency formulated a new policy framework in 2019 that envisioned aid as being in service of a "Journey to Self-Reliance." This framework emphasized "enabling locally led— and, increasingly, locally financed—problem-solving for enterprise driven growth; inclusive societies; and transparent, accountable governance." It defined self-reliance as embracing two elements: "Self-reliance entails a capacity to plan, finance, and implement solutions to local development challenges and a commitment to see these through effectively, inclusively, and with accountability" (emphasis added).

Self-reliance is an aspirational goal, of course, and one likely to take decades to achieve, depending on the circumstances in any particular country. The more immediate, practical goals of foreign assistance align with more general foreign policy goals. Five years after our report that took on USAID Forward, CSIS convened a high-level, nonpartisan task force to make recommendations for reforming and reorganizing foreign assistance in response to the Trump administration's request that all departments of government submit plans for improving efficiency, effectiveness, and accountability. While CSIS prides itself on the nonpartisan nature of its work—the co-chairs of this task force came from both sides of the Senate aisle—we must also be sensitive to the political moment. We knew this report would be read by an inward-looking administration that was ostensibly very skeptical of all or almost all foreign assistance, and so the report emphasized more nakedly self-interested language than we might customarily have used.

The advice in that report was premised on three goals for assistance:

1. Prevent conflict and respond to humanitarian disasters.

2. Forge new international economic relationships to create American jobs and markets for American goods.

3. Make our borders secure and America safe.

Working within these broad goals, our task force set out a series of principles to guide reform, each of which opens up a discussion of one or more of the basic "plumbing" issues related to the planning and delivery of foreign assistance.

> *Development must remain an effective instrument of US national security and foreign policy as part of the 3Ds, integrated coherently with military and diplomatic engagement.*

Any mission for US foreign assistance should support the broader national security strategy to ensure it maximizes its foreign policy impact and puts American interests first. It could be useful, for instance, to introduce and periodically submit to Congress classified national diplomacy and development strategies. Another important step would be to allow the USAID administrator to also wear the hat of deputy secretary of state for development and have authority over all the many agencies within the government involved in soft-power activities. Moreover, that person should be confirmed by Congress.

> *Development is a distinct discipline that requires distinct skills and approaches; maintaining a skilled and experienced professional staff of development experts is essential.*

This assertion has ramifications on an organizational level and for the personnel within the organization. The first and most important point is that USAID must remain an independent agency within the US government and not be folded into any other department, such as the Department of State. That idea has been floated more than once in Washington, most recently during the Trump administration, and my vocal opposition helped prevent that from happening. We've been down this road before: In 1999, the United States Information Agency (USIA), the primary vehicle for public diplomacy, was folded into the State Department. With the Cold War over, many in Washington argued that USIA's mission had become obsolete. The move was disastrous. Years later, during the debate of merging USAID into State in 2017, I wrote, "Dismantling USIA and shifting its primary functions to the State Department crippled US public diplomacy operations in ways that have been lasting and profound—a self-inflicted wound from which the United States is still recovering." The work of USIA involved highly specialized skills and experience that were not commonly found at State.

Diminishing USIA was shortsighted, given that a new war of ideas began two years later with the 9/11 attacks. The US would spend the next fifteen years trying to rebuild that public diplomacy capacity but without recreating a dedicated cadre of relevant expertise within the foreign service. Development, too, demands specialized training and a variety of skill sets unique to the field. It should not have to compete with diplomacy for funding and resources. The USAID culture and mission are different from those of the State Department. Its brand has currency and allows countries that may be leery of diplomatic or security ties to the US to partner with us on development challenges. It's also a fact that USAID funds, in part-

nership with others through its Global Development Alliance partnership initiative, often catalyzes or leverages so much more from
others in terms of monies, expertise, or market power. And USAID
has a strong brand that represents an important seal of approval.

The continued success of many developing countries will require
us to rethink how we recruit, train, and maintain uniquely skilled
professional development staff. Staffing issues are becoming more
and more critical as the developing world continues to separate into
two distinct camps: the rising middle-income countries on the road
to self-reliance; and those fragile states, often in conflict zones, that
are inhospitable or dangerous for aid workers. Many of these fragile
countries also have tribal, ethnic, or cultural groups that are little
studied or poorly understood and that speak obscure dialects. The
expectation is that the richer and more capable countries will need
less direct assistance and embedded aid workers. Many will "graduate" from foreign assistance and forge new kinds of relationships
with the countries that had once been donors. At the same time, the
fragile or failing countries will continue to need more from us, and
the work will demand more from aid personnel.

The aid community should look to examples like Carter Malkasian, who spent two years on the ground in Afghanistan as a State
Department political officer, working closely with the local population of a remote corner of Helmand province and chronicled his
experience in a book, *War Comes to Garmser: Thirty Years of Conflict
on the Afghan Frontier*. As a trained historian with knowledge of the
region and of warfare, and a fluent speaker of the Pashto language,
Malkasian brought specialized skills and a rare sense of commitment to his assignment. In his book, Malkasian wrote about how
he worked to ensure that the specialized military operations the
American mission required did not unfold in a vacuum but that
they worked in harmony with the needs, customs, and aspirations
of the population. American forces had to buttress all manner of
isolated local efforts while simultaneously working to stabilize a
central government. Most importantly, our commitment needed to
be long-term and genuine.

To attract more people like Malkasian, the aid community
must look to other sources and routes to employment. It is significant that he had a doctorate in military history and understood

the interplay of defense, diplomacy, and development. If more and more foreign aid work is going to be in war-torn regions or countries torn by civil unrest, that kind of cross-cutting experience is going to be increasingly useful. There is a long tradition of young Americans going into the Peace Corps after college, then moving into either the foreign service or into USAID, but there has not been enough effort to recruit aid workers from the ranks of military veterans. Not only have these young men and women demonstrated their willingness to accept challenging assignments, but many, like the US Army Special Forces or Green Berets, have exactly the kind of specialized training and experience in local language and custom that prepares them for careers in development or diplomacy. Lester Munson, a former deputy assistant administrator at USAID and now the top lobbyist in Washington specializing in foreign affairs, observed that USAID has been among the worst in Washington when it comes to hiring veterans, when in fact it should be leading. Bringing in more veterans would "change the culture at USAID in three years," says Munson.

Many people in Washington have advocated for developing staff with a more fully rounded set of skills and experience, a concept known as "jointness," which could be achieved through a policy of secondment and rotation between the three Ds—USAID, the State Department, and the Department of Defense. A deeper understanding of what other agencies do, and how all the pieces of the puzzle can fit together, can improve individual performance and increase inter-agency cooperation. Munson cites the example of the Goldwater-Nichols Act of the 1980s, which mandated joint military operations as a means of breaking down inter-service rivalries that had become counterproductive. The Global Fragility Act of 2019, with its mandate for holistic ten-year country-specific development programs, could provide both an impetus and a framework for bringing together teams with diverse skill sets, especially for work in challenging environments. We do not want to suddenly clean house and replace good people trained in the social sciences with a cadre of military personnel, but there is value in the varied experience and training of the different services, and it would be wise to seek a constructive balance.

The last piece of the personnel puzzle is to rethink the full life cycle of employment, especially as it relates to challenging environments. We should seek people who can commit to longer-term assignments in difficult locales in order to build constructive relationships and develop useful institutional memory. That kind of service might be uncomfortable or even impossible for people with families. Nor can the mental and physical health impacts of hostile environments be overlooked. Longer commitments, however, must be matched by incentives and rewards as well as more specialized training, especially in languages and specific cultures. For example, instead of being rotated out of an assignment after one or two years, why can't an aid worker work toward early retirement by completing two seven-year tours of duty over the course of his or her career in adverse environments? The one thing we know for sure about development is that it takes time and requires both patience and dedication. In the same way that we must rethink the foreign assistance budgeting process to enable longer-term commitments, we must build a workforce for the long haul. This does not automatically mean maintaining a permanent presence of aid workers from wealthy nations in the developing world; it means giving those workers the time and the tools to identify and work with local actors to strengthen local capacity and build institutions.

> *Foreign assistance should be allocated to further US capacity to mitigate threats; respond to humanitarian needs; and advance peace, security, and economic cooperation with friendly countries.*

The last three decades have seen a significant increase in budgetary directives in the foreign assistance portion of the State, Foreign Operations, and Related Programs Appropriations Bills and Act, commonly referred to as the "150 account" by Washington insiders. Directives are spending targets attached to specific purposes in appropriations bills and are separated into hard directives, which state that an amount of funding "*shall* be made available," and soft directives, that state that an amount "*should* be made available"—a subtle distinction, perhaps, but an important one.

People in and around government working on foreign assistance generally refer to these directives as "earmarks."

Tessie San Martin, the CEO of FHI360, a large nonprofit human development organization, describes earmarks and directives as a "Faustian bargain" to save foreign aid in the context of relaxed global tensions at the end of the Cold War. With so many in Congress eager to capitalize on the presumed "peace dividend," directives became a way to ensure that some monies would be committed to assistance and development by dedicating them to either specific countries or regions or sectors like agriculture, higher education, biodiversity, or democracy. In 1999, the majority of directives were country/regional, but by 2020, the overwhelming majority were sector directives. Examples might be the money appropriated for PEPFAR, the initiative to address HIV/AIDS, or money that goes to basic education. With so much of the foreign aid budget committed by statute to specific purposes, the US had, in San Martin's words, "created a monster." That is, the government had very little flexibility to adapt its assistance expenditures to suit changing circumstances. Directives had reduced the United States to pivot quickly with non-humanitarian assistance funding to address a crisis or take advantage of an opportunity for development. Of course, there is always a need for aid to address basic human needs. But if, as I believe, the core drivers of development are good governance and economic growth, we have to be flexible enough in our budgeting to accommodate those priorities. At present, there is no Congressional directive (earmark) for supporting economic growth, and funds available for promoting democratic governance are constrained by the earmarks and directives for activities that Congress has given higher priority.

One reason the phenomenon of directives has persisted is actually built into the American system of government. There is sometimes a conflict of interest or a level of distrust between the executive and legislative branches. The executive may want to align development spending with its foreign policy agenda and, thus, focus more on country/regional directives, whereas Congress may incline toward sector-based programs. An administration may fear that Congress will decide against appropriating funds for a favored cause or initiative and, therefore, may set aside money by executive order. Or conversely, Congress might want to protect a program the administration has targeted for cutbacks. This is not necessarily a function of partisan politics; it happens often enough when both branches are controlled by the same party.

The risk is that rather than building a foreign aid budget that best serves to advance an agreed-upon set of goals, USAID must essentially work backward, piecing together a strategy and program that fit within the budgetary constraints created by predetermined earmarks and directives. So how to work with a cumbersome system that has evolved haphazardly over thirty years? It will not be easy. Reforming the Foreign Operation Appropriation must start with rebuilding trust between the executive and legislative branches. A process must be established to facilitate significant and sustained dialogue between the two entities. Both the State Department and USAID need to be more transparent about how, where, and what money is spent, and where the expenditures paid off and where they did not; which means doing a better job of measuring and evaluating. Congress should look at larger and fewer sectoral directives and seek to find ways to give the government more flexibility to respond to changing conditions and respond to opportunities, bearing in mind the long-term, non-linear nature of the development process. And while there is a legitimate place for presidential initiatives, whole-of-government initiatives are always preferable and must be prioritized.

Ideally, we need a process through which a classified national diplomacy and development strategy can be periodically submitted to Congress. Approval of such a joint strategy would establish a framework for budgeting resources and a context in which to evaluate the continued validity or efficacy of existing directives or the need to establish new ones. At the same time, Congress must have access to comprehensive performance metrics with which to track and enforce sector development progress so that data, rather than directives, can drive the planning process. The lack of such metrics has plagued the development effort for years, although important progress is being made.

The point is that the United States must be more agile and flexible about foreign aid spending. Think about a country like Moldova, newly vibrant, with a leader educated in and supportive

202 Daniel F. Runde

of the US, but in a politically charged corner of Eastern Europe. Or consider Laos, a country on the precipice of vassal status to China, and with which the American engagement over the last fifty years has focused almost exclusively on landmines left over from the Vietnam War. In such countries, a smart and creative realignment of our aid priorities could reset our relationships with potential geopolitical benefits.

> *Organizational efficiencies can be achieved by establishing clear responsibilities and division of labor between functions and offices in the State Department, USAID, and other development agencies, thereby eliminating unnecessary duplication.*

Critics of the development-industrial complex worry about the US tax dollars that go to cover the administrative costs of for-profit implementers. Nobody likes to think about the sometimes-fancy offices or the occasional comfortable lifestyles afforded these consultants at the public's expense. It's a reasonable concern, especially in the context of the push to use funds to enable local actors in the developing world, but it may also be something of a red herring. Those that argue that for-profit contractors may not share the ethic of working to put themselves out of a job make a valid point. A lot of great development work comes out of these firms, but one could argue that their strongest expertise lies in winning government contracts. They have mastered the intricate web of rules and regulations established by the Federal Acquisition Regulation, or FAR, which itself represents a barrier to entry to new players in the development space. We don't want to throw the baby out with the bathwater and stop tapping into this valuable resource. A better approach would be to make the FAR more streamlined and navigable, reducing the advantage of these entrenched firms and allowing the inclusion of a greater diversity of implementers.

The costs of bureaucracy within the government itself may be even more crippling. In 2010, former USAID administrator Andrew Natsios published an important paper in which he railed against the complex and crippling "counter-bureaucracy" that had come into being around the foreign assistance enterprise.

Natsios used the phrase obsessive measurement disorder (OMD) to describe a syndrome based on the idea that counting everything in government programs (or private industry and increasingly some foundations) will produce better policy choices and improved management. He described agencies overwhelmed by budgeting, oversight, accountability, and measurement systems that had arisen gradually over decades. "The compliance side of U.S. government aid programs had grown at the expense of the technical, program side," effectively "turning the means into an end." The central problem with the counter-bureaucracy is that it ignores a fundamental principle of development—that the most precisely and easily measured programs are the least transformational, and those programs that are most transformational are the most difficult to measure. The government is by nature risk-averse, but most of the most important aid programs in fragile states are almost by definition high-risk and resistant to measurement. Natsios worried that programs with measurable outcomes were crowding out riskier programs with less tangible results, not only in the US agencies but in many of the large multilateral organizations.

It's important to keep these concerns about bureaucracy as an impediment to effectiveness in the context of the push to funnel more direct aid to governments and local actors in the developing world—a well-intentioned initiative that could easily necessitate even more bureaucratic processes and staff. No one would argue against the need for accountability, but the command-and-control system has outgrown its usefulness. The federal government must undertake a comprehensive review of effectiveness, outside the political arena so that it can be objective and free from partisanship, with the goal of developing measurement systems that allow for exemptions from quantitative milestones that are inappropriate to many delicate and vulnerable programs.

There's another way to increase organizational efficiency while simultaneously bringing the soft-power initiatives of development in line with broader US foreign policy and the national security strategy. This involves a federal budgeting device known as the "F process" or "F office" (sometimes inaccurately referred to as the "F Bureau"), about which many in Congress, especially newcomers, may be unaware, but which holds a lot of significance to the aid community. The major offices with the highest status within the State Department are designated by a single letter—S for the secretary, P for the undersecretary for political affairs, E for the undersecretary for economic affairs, and so on. F (as opposed to "FA," which would denote a less important function) refers to the US Office of Foreign Assistance, out of which most assistance funds within USAID and the State Department are allocated. The F bureaucracy dates to the George W. Bush administration when Condoleezza Rice was secretary of state. Prior to that time, USAID controlled its own budgeting process with the executive branch. Final control of the aid budget was subsumed into the "Office of Foreign Assistance," reporting to the secretary of state in the hopes of the State Department getting a clearer picture of how foreign assistance funds were being spent and getting some further control on how that money was spent. When the process was set up, it was originally controlled by the USAID administrator. The "dual-hatted" status of that position only lasted a couple of years, however, before the F office was put in the hands of the State Department. Most of the aid community began to see this setup as a way of having State babysit USAID, and they felt constricted by it.

Since the Truman administration, many had tried to address the question of who controls—or who should control—the overall foreign assistance effort. The Foreign Assistance Act of 1961 was intended to consolidate in one agency, USAID, what had been the work of five predecessor agencies whose roles overlapped, causing a loss of cohesion and effectiveness. There was a time, thirty or forty years ago, when the overwhelming majority, perhaps 90 percent or more, of foreign assistance money was spent by USAID, with the small amount remaining coming from State. According to data from 2019, around 60 percent of foreign assistance dollars is disbursed by USAID, with the rest coming from State and the multitude of other agencies doing work in this area. Moving the F process back into State created a variety of inefficiencies that should not be hard to correct. The budget process has become too cumbersome and time-consuming, and the USAID administrator has less control over how assistance funds were allocated, which has sometimes meant leaving long-term development programs at the mercy of short-term foreign policy objectives.

In 2017, I wrote in favor of restoring to USAID the budget authority of the F bureau. "There exists an inherent tension, one that is not solvable, between using foreign assistance used for strictly foreign policy reasons (at times a good thing) and foreign assistance used strictly based on needs (a good thing at other times). Few want malaria and food aid moneys, for example, used in a Machiavellian way. In F's current form, foreign assistance objectives have at times lost out to foreign policy objectives. This may produce outcomes counterproductive to both foreign policy and long-term development objectives…. The best outcome would be that the top person has the authorities of USAID, control of the F office at State, and a title that gives him or her the coordinating authorities for all 18 agencies' international soft-power activities."

That recommendation also appeared in the report of our CSIS task force in the same year, which made the case that "moving the functions of the F office to USAID would create efficiencies and facilitate closer coordination between the USAID administrator and the secretary of state on issues of foreign assistance. F would also provide secretariat support for the USAID administrator in his or her role in coordinating federal foreign assistance." Giving the agency head a senior-level title, such as deputy secretary of state for development and USAID administrator, would formalize the important role of coordinating soft-power assistance efforts across the government. It would also institutionalize the relationship between State and USAID, ensuring that the department continued to have input into foreign assistance expenditures while maintaining the independence of USAID as a stand-alone agency.

The United States should be systematic and selective in choosing the countries where our assistance will best serve the national interest.

The ability to assess more accurately and meaningfully the development progress of recipient countries would be universally welcomed by both critics and supporters of foreign-assistance spending. Virtually every reform recommendation regarding development in general and USAID specifically involves developing a more finely tuned system of metrics. Gauging effectiveness enables us to adjust priorities and redirect resources as necessary. And although Andrew Natsios was not wrong in his observation that the most transformational assistance may also be the most resistant to quantitative measurement, we must continue to refine the process.

In fact, a significant amount of theoretical work has been done in the area of metrics and assessments since we issued our report in 2017. In 2019, the Nobel Prize in Economics went to three economists who proposed a novel way to assess development outcomes through a model called randomized controlled trials. The Nobel committee credited their theories with helping to channel direct aid better, but one would be hard-pressed to come up with examples outside of a handful of specialized practitioners and researchers who use "RCTs" in their day-to-day development work. Policy makers in Washington and elsewhere have put more and more pressure on the aid community to present demonstrable results to prove the impact of its work. And in fact, there have been great advancements in theory, technique, and data collection, but a serious lack of implementation, diffusion, and learning of new insights. Among my colleagues, one hears stories about research studies made available on the website of, for instance, the World Bank, but with literally zero downloads. Some of this is a failure of folks like me in the think-tank world who are supposed to be transmission belts among researchers, practitioners, and policy makers.

To get the most value of new and innovative measurement and evaluation (M&E) techniques, we need to translate more effectively what might be arcane data into real learning. We need to bridge the gap between the researchers, practitioners, and the policy makers and appropriators in government. Those of us in the influence-and-persuasion business—that is, in the think-tank world—can and should be doing a better job in the role of interlocutor, processing the information into useful insights for those in a position to take action.

USAID has made progress in M&E by developing what could be one of its flagship tools: Self-reliance country roadmaps, comprised of "objective third party metrics that measure national capacity and commitment, plus hundreds of curated secondary metrics and financing profiles measuring economic freedom, democracy and citizen-responsive governance, environmental and social conditions (including indicators in health and education), human rights, equality, and other factors." These roadmaps are still evolving, and no doubt a debate will ensue about the metrics and thresholds used, but they constitute the start of an important conversation. The roadmaps could provide a more nuanced and sophisticated assessment of a country's place on the development spectrum than more simplistic metrics that have long been used, such as per capita GDP. The hope is that all decision-makers can incorporate the data into their decisions in the coming years.

With many countries moving into the middle-income ranks, it has become more and more pressing that the aid community develop "graduation" strategies on a country-specific basis. If delivering direct humanitarian aid becomes less of a priority, assistance efforts might emphasize support for domestic resource mobilization efforts that will enable a transfer of responsibility to host countries. We might consider limiting or ending small assistance programs, replacing entire foreign aid programs with a single development attaché, or working with selected countries through a regional mission rather than directly. We can also seek a better division of labor with other bilateral donors and MDBs, which would be tied to renewed US leadership at the World Bank and other multilateral institutions.

Certain emerging countries could be eligible for a new bilateral relationship with the United States. Brazil, for example, has become the most dynamic economy in the western hemisphere, after the US, but still receives aid in various forms. It would benefit both countries to form a binational institution that would foster stronger ties, at all levels, in selected areas like education, technology, trade, and governance. As my colleague Arianna Kohan and I wrote in 2021, the "two regional powerhouses, Brazil and the United States have a unique ability to effect policies and implement programs that have national, regional, and global impacts. Such an institution would reinforce diplomatic ties between the two countries, allowing for stronger positioning on regional issues." A binational institution built for the long haul could facilitate long-term strategies for cooperation in multiple sectors and would have the benefit of remaining independent of changing administrations in either country. In addition to strengthening the ties between the two nations, it could facilitate greater regional coordination and integration.

There is precedent for this kind of institution, including the Luso-American Development Foundation (FLAD) for Portugal and the Costa Rica United States Foundation for Cooperation (CRUSA), both established to facilitate continued cooperation after US aid programs ended. We can borrow from the lessons learned from such organizations to establish something uniquely tailored to Brazil. The United States could consider a binational institution with India, as well. Deepening the long-term relationship with both countries will prove particularly relevant in the context of the global power competition. China wields influence in Brazil as its largest trading partner, and in India, too, as its third-largest trading partner but, more importantly, as a regional heavyweight.

There is no single right way to deliver foreign assistance or to support development. The debate over reform begins again with every new administration. In November of 2021, the newly appointed administrator of USAID, Samantha Power, delivered an address at Georgetown University's School of Foreign Service, in which she detailed her vision for modernizing the agency, both in its makeup and in the way it does business. Her speech reprised some of the goals of her predecessors while confirming the challenges we had identified in those goals.

"In the last decade, despite numerous efforts, initiatives, and even support from Capitol Hill, the amount of USAID dollars going to local partners increased only from four percent to six percent. As recently as 2017, 60 percent of our assistance was awarded to just 25 partners. This is because, a number of reasons, it's largely because working with local partners, it turns out, is more difficult, time-consuming, and it's riskier. Local partners often lack the internal accounting expertise our contracts require, or they might lack the legal counsel needed to shape their contracts, many of which can run hundreds of pages long. So, clearly this status quo, as in the percentages that illustrate this, is tough to shift. There is a lot of gravity pulling in the opposite direction. But we have got to try."

Ambassador Power outlined the priorities for the foreign assistance apparatus: ensure that decisions are driven by data rather than intuitions or assumptions; establish an emergency fund for countries hardest hit and least equipped to deal with immediate effects of climate change; improve both national and global pandemic readiness; support anti-corruption initiatives; and create new mechanisms to safeguard journalists and protect a free press. She also wants to start a centralized fund for private-sector engagement that can tap the resources of American corporations with global reach.

What did not come through in Power's statement was the urgency of the mission. America's soft-power needs are arguably as important now as at any time in our history because of the great-power competition with China. The United States must rebuild its capacity, its primacy, as a driver of global progress. We cannot ignore the importance of public diplomacy—of branding and messaging that keeps the US front and center as the partner of choice for emerging countries. In late 2020, the Trump administration issued an executive order calling for a "re-brand" of US foreign assistance. As more and more agencies took over elements of soft-power assistance, there was no longer a single entity with which to associate the work. The brand got diluted, and the new order sought to unite all foreign assistance programs under one logo. President Trump left office before taking action on it. It will be up to the Biden administration or another administration, but there does not seem to be any branding solution that will satisfy all agencies. Furthermore, the State Department may not be able to "force" agencies that it does not control to comply with a new executive order overseas. Several ideas have been floated, and no decision has been made, but the most sensible choice is to maintain the USAID handclasp logo that has been existed since USAID was launched in 1961, and which generations of people around the world associate with US assistance. It may not seem like the most important issue facing development, but if the US is serious about retaking the high ground as a force for good in the world, it needs to get behind the right unifying image.

In the Venn diagram of priorities for foreign assistance, the main intersecting elements are delivering aid where needed, eliminating corruption, building capacity, and ensuring America rightly "gets the credit." We have to do the job and do it well, and while it sounds nice to say that the intrinsic value of the work is enough, we cannot forget that assistance is also motivated by enlightened self-interest, and part of its value lies in disseminating values through American leadership.

While few, if any, argue against the need for reform in the US development system, there has to date been a lack of political will to follow through on the tough political choices it will surely entail. The last meaningful revamp of the Foreign Assistance Act came in 1985. And in what was essentially a unipolar world since then, little has happened to motivate lawmakers to look at the mechanics in the processes with fresh eyes. As a new era of great-power competition unfolds, the time has again come to recognize the benefits of foreign assistance to the United States and its partner countries, to align its structure with its goals, and to ensure a positive legacy at home and abroad. The world ten or fifteen years from now will look dramatically different than it does today. Because there are important challenges that will not be met fully by private-sector finance, remittances, philanthropy, and developing country governments, foreign assistance will prove ever more vital to the stability and security of the United States and of the world.

Conclusion:

ENABLING A
TRANSFORMATIONAL
ALTERNATIVE

At the end of the Cold War, many American policy makers saw a unipolar world led by the United States and the liberal democracies of the West, a world that would allow us to redirect some portion of the time and resources we had committed to foreign assistance to other things. Such a world may never have been anything more than a comforting fantasy. Sadly, it is certainly not the world we live in today. The fact is that while the West relaxed a little and enjoyed the fruits of its putative victory, an entirely new bilateral competition took shape, catching many policy makers unaware. We certainly began to reengage after 9/11, but we need to allocate more effort and attention to a series of different challenges today. No one wants to think of today's situation as a new Cold War, and hopefully, that's not what it is, but we are going to need to look at the entire world through the lens of great power competition. Whatever we want to call this age, we have moved beyond the twenty-five-year period that might be considered the post-Cold War era, and the time has come to update our soft-power tool kit to meet the new challenges of today.

The stakes have changed, as have the rules of engagement and the field of play. The global competition won't play out directly in Moscow or Beijing or Washington. Instead, it will primarily play out in countries like Ukraine and in Southeast Asia, Latin America, and especially Sub-Saharan Africa. It won't be mainly about aircraft carriers or missile defenses or night-vision goggles, but rather about trade and infrastructure, digital connectivity, the standards for technology and commerce, training and education, and economic development. Great-power competition will also be about ideas and values, which I believe are communicated and spread through every social, commercial, and political interaction between nations. The Biden administration is on the right track by standing up for democratic ideals through its new anti-corruption initiative and convening a global democracy summit. Most significantly, it will be about forming lasting and productive partnerships that can help empower countries to realize their greatest aspirations. That's where the soft-power tool kit is of paramount importance. Whichever global power leads in these nonmilitary spheres of soft power will lead the twenty-first century. If one can be sure of anything, it will be that if the US doesn't take the lead, some other nation will, and there can be little doubt that the resulting world will be much less free than it might otherwise have been.

Two authoritarian behemoths, China and Russia, are actively working to assert their influence and authority. Russia never posed a serious economic threat to the West, and still probably doesn't, rarely looking to involve itself beyond the former Soviet space and other near neighbors in Asia and the Middle East. Moscow's soft-power offer is limited, largely restricted to mining and energy. In the military assistance sphere, Russia offers a product that is not quite first-class by US standards—"Chevy" military gear, as opposed to our "Cadillac" military equipment. But governments on a tight budget might decide Russia's "Chevy" military gear is their best option. Buying Russian military equipment often comes with training, Russian "experts" who are sent over to help run and maintain the systems. These military deals often come linked with political support at the United Nations, or elsewhere. China, on the other hand, has the capacity and the economic mass to displace the United States from its position of leadership. And in the eyes of more than a few nations, it is already on its way to doing so, spreading its reach through hard and digital infrastructure projects, especially its monumental Belt and Road Initiative. If we do nothing, over time, China will replace us as the world's leader.

China mushroomed into the world's second-largest economy while too many Western policy makers were looking the other way. At the same time, the developing world also underwent phenomenal change, much of which also went largely unnoticed. Conditions in the developing world are vastly different than they were even as recently as the Clinton and George W. Bush administrations. The last twenty years have seen an immense reduction in poverty and huge progress across a range of social, economic, and political metrics. In his book, *The Great Surge*, the economist Steven Radelet asserts that roughly a billion people have been lifted out of poverty during that time, owing primarily to three great catalysts. (Granted, Radelet's book came out before COVID-19, and there have been major economic setbacks in the developing world, but two or three years from now, we should hope that many of these countries will bounce back.) First, major political shifts occurred, especially the end of the Cold War, a decline in autocracy, and a widespread belief that free markets rather than centrally planned socialism (as practiced by the Soviet Union), could reduce poverty. That created a fertile environment for economic development and political self-determination. Second, globalization and the spread of technology and connectivity helped drive prosperity through increased productivity and newly enabled trade relationships. And third, energetic and enlightened developing country leadership, often educated in the West, carried out economic policies, invested in human capital, and built more capable institutions that could sustain economic growth.

Over the course of this book, I've tried to lay out the kinds of soft-power development tools and foreign assistance that have helped facilitate these shifts and can continue to do so in the future. Ensuring that these countries maintain that upward trajectory will speed the arrival of more global partners and burden-sharers to meet global challenges. History bears out that assertion. While it's true that global development always comes, at least in part, from enlightened self-interest, it's also true that many of our most important trading partners today were at one time recipients of our aid. But that amazing positive change doesn't tell the whole story. For all the progress that we've seen, there remain thirty to forty fragile or failing countries in which so many ills are concentrated, and which will continue to cause or exacerbate problems on a global scale: conflict, uncontrolled migration, radicalization, and the acceleration of health emergencies.

These challenges must be addressed in the context of two major current phenomena: seismic demographic shifts around the world, especially the youth bulge in the world's poorer countries, and the post-COVID-19 response of the US and others to the developing world.

Research suggests that there will be 3.2 billion people in the world under the age of twenty-five by the year 2030, most of them living in Asia and Africa. Already, 1 in 5 young people globally are considered "disengaged," meaning young people without a job, not in school, and without other training. In other parts of the world—not just in the wealthier countries of West and parts of Asia but in China as well—a new "global aging" wave is about to hit in Southeast Asia, China, Latin America, and most of the countries in the former Soviet space. Roughly one billion people over sixty-five are in need of some kind of care or access to social safety nets. The number of aging people is going to rise quickly with very serious implications, including the possibility that many middle-income countries might face shortages of workers and may remain stuck in the "middle-income trap" because of this demographic change.

A report from CSIS declared: "If economies do not produce enough good jobs, and if institutions do not prepare the labor force for the needs of the labor market, national, regional and global stability will be compromised." Rising middle-income countries are hungry for trade and technology, infrastructure, and stability; but countries struggling at the lower end of the development scale need jobs, jobs, jobs, and an enabling environment to drive economic development and increased capability. Countries that cannot move in that direction will never be in a position to become meaningful trading partners or allies.

Foreign aid will never create the hundreds of millions of jobs required. Nor can infrastructure projects financed by China that use Chinese workers and benefit Chinese companies. But as I've described, direct assistance, in partnership with the private sector and with able partners on the ground, can catalyze the investment, entrepreneurship, and innovation that leads to inclusive home-grown economic development. It can also help spur improvements in local capacity and help establish capable institutions that are vital to social and economic stability.

There are some caveats to keep in mind related to job creation and development. The first has to do with technology and auto-mation. I've heard some in the development community voice despair over the idea that the kind of manufacturing labor that drove China's growth and, it is hoped, would drive the growth of other low-income nations are jobs threatened by automation. But the reality is that automation is much less of a factor where labor costs less and where the population skews younger. Manu-facturers are more likely to turn to automation in more expen-sive labor markets with aging populations. In India, for example, where about 90 percent of jobs are still in the informal economy, it's hard to imagine workers being replaced by robots any time soon. There are going to be plenty of speed setbacks along the way to the fourth industrial revolution, having to do with the wildly uneven distribution around the world of digital infrastructure, networking technology, training, and other factors.

The second caveat is about the major contradictory demo-graphic trends just mentioned, which will have as profound an effect on the future of work as automation and technology. Not only does a growing economy need workers willing to commit themselves to a future in their home country rather than go the route of migration, but institutions must be in place to prepare and equip those people for the workplace of the twenty-first century. Third, societies need a system of social safety nets to support the labor force. As important as it is to grow the formal economy in developing nations, we also have to acknowledge that the so-called "gig economy" is here to stay. As workers follow geographic shifts in the labor market, move from project to project in the creative economy, or try to launch small businesses, local services and institutions, from housing to health care to transportation infrastructure, will have to adapt.

The COVID-19 pandemic, still ongoing at the time of this writing, has disrupted progress and accelerated challenges, shining a light on the chasm between rich and poor countries. A lot of lip service was paid in wealthier nations about the inequality of vaccine access in the developing world, but a certain amount of vaccine nationalism remained the reality. Even the most well-intentioned elected officials are going to prioritize Pittsburgh over Paraguay, or Berlin over Burundi, when push comes to shove. But this is not enough. Even if wealthy nations achieve high vaccination rates and tamp down the virus within their borders, they can't bounce back fully while partner countries remain mired in disease. Maybe we will put COVID-19 in the rearview mirror, but that will not be the end of pandemics. Health crises like COVID-19 that reach across borders are going to be part of the landscape in the future, and we must do a better job of preparing for the next one. That means working in partnership with multilateral organizations to stockpile medicines and supplies, training medical staff and upgrading health-delivery infrastructure, and participating in the establishment of some form of pandemic early-warning system, as has been approved by agencies around the world.

The lagging distribution of vaccines in poorer countries is one of the gaping voids created by the pandemic. Another was the realization that we needed to rethink global supply chains. Countries such as Mexico and the countries of Central America and Southeast Asia should all be beneficiaries of the inevitable shifts in supply chains away from China toward somewhere else. The US, through new trade agreements, commercial diplomacy to engage private enterprise, and its foreign aid, should accelerate and consolidate these shifts. And, most ominous for the future was the ever-widening digital divide. The ability to cope with the challenges of the pandemic was directly related to the level of digital technology and connectivity. Digital access will be to development in this century what electricity was to the previous one.

These are the kind of vacuums that powerful nations rush to fill when they seek to expand their reach and influence. Any place the US and its partners have failed to show up, China is there. In the digital space, this means that where we don't show up, Huawei and ZTE, with their ties to the government in Beijing and their lack of adherence to global standards, will fill the space. To address supply chain shortages, we must use soft-power tools to bring about new trade alliances that can reduce dependency on China's manufacturing capacity. And as the world moves toward battery-powered devices and electric vehicles, we already see China moving to control the natural resources that will power the energy transition.

*   *   *   *   *

The new bilateral power competition cannot be—must not be—a fight to the finish. We have to ask ourselves how we want this power struggle to end. It is in no one's interest to escalate tensions, but nor can the West continue to cede ground when it comes to leadership and influence around the world. Assuming we can avoid open conflict, perhaps China's problems and internal contradictions will catch up with the Chinese Communist Party and the government that it runs in the "People's Republic of China." It may sound almost crazy, but we should remain quietly hopeful for a day—perhaps far off—when we have functioning democracies in Russia and on the Chinese mainland. Our challenges are with the governments of China and Russia, not with the Chinese or Russian citizens, and we should find ways to maintain ties to the people of those two countries.

In the meantime, we should seek to prevent China and Russia from filling vacuums that we leave unattended in developing countries, whether those vacuums are in the digital, commercial, infrastructure, training, or vaccine realms. The further China and Russia extend their reach, the more developing countries will find themselves tied to autocracies that do not respect human rights, do not tolerate dissent, and greatly limit individual opportunity. Maybe China has more cash to throw around, for now, and maybe Russia is more willing to use aggression to try to achieve its goals; but neither seems able to offer a transformational opportunity for developing countries. Either we speak to the deepest hopes and aspirations of developing countries, or these countries will take those hopes and aspirations to the Chinese Community Party or, occasionally, Vladimir Putin. We must make a better offer, or we have to enable someone other than China or Russia to make a better offer. That's the basis on which we must update our play-book for this new era.

China may build a road for a rising country, but American leadership, exercised through soft-power, can put that country on a path to a full partnership. When I meet with government officials from the developing world, they are clear about the difficult choices they face. They want to work with the US and with countries in the OECD, but if the West does not show up, these countries will have no other choice than to work with Beijing. China is spending money hand over fist, building dams and ports and railways, but always getting something concrete in return that will sustain its own economy. China has a lot to offer but has yet to move beyond a coldly transactional relation-ship with the countries in which it invests. We need to move these countries beyond the transactional paradigm offered by China and move to a truly transformational paradigm. What we should all want is a meaningful and constructive partnership and inclusion in a community of nations that can address the great challenges of the future together.

There is a lot of bad news in the world, but I would urge that we remain optimistic and hopeful. The launch of the Marshall Plan and the challenges we responded to at that time were as great or arguably greater than the challenges we have before us. We should not downplay the challenges ahead, but we have confronted big challenges before, and we should be able to do it again. As long as we can enable a positive offer responding to the aspirations of other countries, most other countries would prefer to go with the US and our allies. For all our imperfections as a society and the imperfections of our political system, the United States has a lot of cards to play. We have many friends, and if we treat our friends well, they will stay with us. We will need to get a consensus on not only the challenges before us but also on the solutions and the constructive offer we can make to others. I hope this book will start a focused conversation toward those solutions. If we move swiftly, we can ensure that the twenty-first century is a century marked by increased prosperity and freedom in the world.

Notes

Chapter 1

The Hambantota Port Project: Maria Abi-Habib, "How China Got Sri Lanka to Cough Up a Port," *The New York Times*, June 25, 2018. https://www.nytimes.com/2018/06/25/world/asia/china-sri-lanka-port.html

The financial performance of the port: Colonel R. Hariharan, "Chinese trick: Unviable port turns strategic asset," *Times of India*, December 17, 2017. https://timesofindia.indiatimes.com/blogs/tracking-indian-communities/chinese-trick-unviable-port-turns-strategic-asset/

The financial performance of the port: Maya Majueran K., "Then and now: Hambantota International Port," *DailyFT*, August 2, 2021. https://www.ft.lk/columns/Then-and-now-Hambantota-International-Port/4-721196

Sri Lanka's already massive debt burden: Uditha Jayasinghe, "Explainer: Sri Lanka on the edge as debt burden mounts," Reuters, January 17, 2022. https://www.reuters.com/markets/rates-bonds/sri-lanka-edge-debt-burden-mounts-2022-01-17/

The poster child for China's: Brahma Chellaney, "Chinese Debt Trap Diplomacy," *Project Syndicate*, January 23, 2017. https://www.project-syndicate.org/commentary/china-one-belt-one-road-loans-debt-by-brahma-chellaney-2017-01

China-sponsored hydroelectric project: Tom Fawthrop, "Myanmar's Myitsone Dam Dilemma," *The Diplomat*, March 11, 2019. https://thediplomat.com/2019/03/myanmars-myitsone-dam-dilemma/

China-sponsored hydroelectric project: Thomas Fuller, "Myanmar Backs Down, Suspending Dam Project," *The New York Times*, September 30, 2011. https://www.nytimes.com/2011/10/01/world/asia/myanmar-suspends-construction-of-controversial-dam.html

US set about easing: Julie Hirschfield Davis, "Obama to Relax U.S. Sanctions Against Myanmar," *The New York Times*, May 17, 2016. https://www.nytimes.com/2016/05/18/world/asia/myanmar-burma-sanctions.html

Rethink its unyielding stance: Michael Green and Derek Mitchell, "Asia's Forgotten Crisis: A New Approach to Burma," *Foreign Affairs*, November/December 2007. https://www.foreignaffairs.com/articles/asia/2007-11-01/asias-forgotten-crisis

Hilary Clinton recognized the opportunity: Steven Lee Myers, "Clinton's Visit to Myanmar Raises Hopes and Concerns," *The New York Times*, November 29, 2011. https://www.nytimes.com/2011/11/30/world/asia/clintons-visit-to-myanmar-raises-hopes-and-concerns.html

Hilary Clinton, recognized: Gregory B. Poling, "Clinton's Myanmar Visit: The United States Responds to Reform," CSIS, December 5, 2011. https://www.csis.org/analysis/clinton%E2%80%99s-myanmar-visit-united-states-responds-reform

Myanmar's neighbors, soon followed suit: John J. Brandon, "ASEAN Chairmanship Offers Opportunity for Myanmar," *The Asia Foundation*, January 8, 2014. https://asiafoundation.org/2014/01/08/asean-chairmanship-offers-opportunity-for-myanmar/

As her government jailed: BBC News, "Myanmar's Aung San Suu Kyi: Journalists 'jailed over official secrets,'" September 13, 2018. https://www.bbc.com/news/av/world-asia-45506243

The China-Myanmar Economic Corridor: Lucas Myers, "The China-Myanmar Economic Corridor and China's Determination to See It Through," Wilson Center, *Asia Dispatches*, May 26, 2020. https://www.wilsoncenter.org/blog-post/china-myanmar-economic-corridor-and-chinas-determination-see-it-through

Just as China declined to join: Lucas Myers, "China Is Hedging Its Bets in Myanmar," *Foreign Affairs*, September 10, 2021. https://foreignpolicy.com/2021/09/10/china-myanmar-coup-national-league-for-democracy/

Just as China declined to join: Debby S. W. Chan, "Business as Usual: Chinese Investment After the Myanmar Coup," *The Diplomat*, September 2, 2021. https://thediplomat.com/2021/09/business-as-usual-chinese-investments-after-the-myanmar-coup/

Just as China declined to join: Ruosui Zhang, "Chinese Investment in Myanmar: Beyond Myitsone Dam," *The Diplomat*, July 22, 2020. https://thediplomat.com/2020/07/chinese-investment-in-myanmar-beyond-myitsone-dam/

Allow China to reap the rewards, Sreeparna Banerjee and Tarushi Singh Rajaura, "Growing Chinese investments in Myanmar post-xoup," Observer Research Foundation, November 9, 2021. https://www.orfonline.org/expert-speak/growing-chinese-investments-in-myanmar-post-coup/

Respects the right of the Afghan people: Zhou Bo, "In Afghanistan, China Is Ready to Step Into the Void," *The New York Times*, August 20, 2021. https://www.nytimes.com/2021/08/20/opinion/china-afghanistan-taliban.html

Faced a major humanitarian crisis: Jane Ferguson, "Afghanistan Has Become the World's Largest Humanitarian Crisis," *The New Yorker*, January 5, 2022. https://www.newyorker.com/news/

dispatch/afghanistan-has-become-the-worlds-largest-humanitarian-crisis

Beijing has begun paying some lip service: Beata Cichocka, Ian Mitchell, and Euan Ritchie, "Three Key Shifts in Development Cooperation in China's 2021 White Paper," Center for Global Development, February 9, 2021. https://www.cgdev.org/blog/three-key-shifts-development-cooperation-chinas-2021-white-paper

Myanmar's economic and political development: *The Economist*, "Myanmar's grinding conflict is at risk of being forgotten," January 29, 2022.

Chapter 2

Novel depicting the blunders: William J. Lederer and Eugene Burdick, *The Ugly American*, W.W. Norton & Company, 1958.

The 1944 Bretton Woods conference: "Bretton Woods and the Birth of the World Bank," World Bank archives. https://www.worldbank.org/en/archive/history/exhibits/Bretton-Woods-and-the-Birth-of-the-World-Bank

The 1944 Bretton Woods conference: "The Bretton Woods Conference, 1944," U.S. Department of State archive. https://2001-2009.state.gov/r/pa/ho/time/wwii/98681.htm

I look to Arthur Vandenberg: "The Vandenberg Resolution: The UN Charter and the Future Alliance," U.S. Department of State archive; The Origins of NATO. https://1997-2001.state.gov/regions/eur/nato/vandenberg.html

Under the leadership of Eleanor Roosevelt: Allida Black, "Eleanor Roosevelt and the Universal Declaration of Human Rights," U.S. National Park Service. https://www.nps.gov/elro/learn/historyculture/udhr.htm

JFK believing he could win over: BBC News, "John F Kennedy: When the US president met Africa's independence heroes," February 27, 2021. https://www.bbc.com/news/world-africa-56116383

JFK's successors: Office of the Press Secretary, the White House, "FACT SHEET: The United States and Central America: Honoring Our Commitments," January 14, 2016. https://obamawhitehouse.archives.gov/the-press-office/2016/01/15/fact-sheet-united-states-and-central-america-honoring-our-commitments

Reflecting this new perspective on aid: Investopedia team, "What Are the Criticisms of the Human Development Index (HDI)?" Investopedia, last modified February 24, 2022. https://www.investopedia.com/ask/answers/042815/are-there-critics-human-development-index-hdi.asp

The Caribbean Basin Initiative: Daniel F. Runde, Linnea Sandin, and Amy Doring, "Reimagining the U.S. Strategy in the Caribbean," CSIS, April 8, 2021. https://www.csis.org/analysis/reimagining-us-strategy-caribbean

On a much grander scale: "Address to Members of the British Parliament," Ronald Reagan Presidential Library and Museum, June 8, 1982. https://www.reaganlibrary.gov/archives/speech/address-members-british-parliament

Citizens Democracy Corps: "White House Fact Sheet on the Citizens Democracy Corps," The American Presidency Project, May 12, 1990. https://www.presidency.ucsb.edu/documents/white-house-fact-sheet-the-citizens-democracy-corps

EBRD actually cut off Russia: Paul Hannon, "EBRD to Stop New Investments in Russia," *The Wall Street Journal*, last modified July 23, 2014. https://www.wsj.com/articles/ebrd-to-stop-new-investments-in-russia-1406117154

Allocated continued assistance: Russian Democracy Act of 2002, Public Law 107-246, https://www.congress.gov/107/plaws/publ246/PLAW-107publ246.pdf

Executing those agendas to be contracted out: U.S. General Accounting Office, "Strategic Workforce Planning Can Help USAID Address Current and Future Challenges," GAO.gov, August 2003. https://www.gao.gov/assets/gao-03-946.pdf

Millennium Development Goals: World Health Organization, "Millennium Development Goals (MDGs)," WHO Newsroom, February 19, 2018. https://www.who.int/news-room/fact-sheets/detail/millennium-development-goals-(mdgs)

Sustainable Development Goals: United Nations, "The 17 Goals," UN Department of Economic and Social Affairs, Sustainable Development. https://sdgs.un.org/goals

Made possible by the Leland Initiative: Leland Initiative: Africa Global Information Infrastructure Gateway Project (Project No. 698-0565), United States Agency for International Development Africa Bureau, Office of Sustainable Development. https://pdf.usaid.gov/pdf_docs/PNABZ059.pdf

Chapter 3

In his history of USAID: John Norris, *The Enduring Struggle: The History of the U.S. Agency for International Development and America's Uneasy Transformation of the World*, Rowman & Littlefield, 2021.

Biden's precipitous pull-out: P. Michael McKinley, "We All Lost Afghanistan," *Foreign Affairs*, August 16, 2021. https://www.foreignaffairs.com/articles/united-states/2021-08-16/we-all-lost-afghanistan-taliban

Departure represents a human tragedy: Daniel Runde, "Immediate Steps to Respond to the Emergency in Afghanistan," CSIS, August 20, 2021. https://www.csis.org/analysis/immediate-steps-respond-emergency-afghanistan

When a grand council: Francesc Vendrell, "What Went Wrong After Bonn," Middle East Institute, last modified April 18,

2012. https://www.mei.edu/publications/what-went-wrong-after-bonn

Afghans owned cell phones: Broadcasting Board of Governors, "Media Use in Afghanistan," Gallup, https://www.usagm.gov/wp-content/uploads/2015/01/Afghanistan-research-brief.pdf

Non-military aid in 2019: World Bank Online Data Bank, "Net official development assistance received (current US$) – Afghanistan," https://data.worldbank.org/indicator/DT.ODA.ODAT.CD?locations=AF

The US facilitated talks: "U.S. experiments with three-way dialogue with Uzbekistan, Afghanistan," *Eurasianet*, May 28, 2020. https://eurasianet.org/us-experiments-with-three-way-dialogue-with-uzbekistan-afghanistan

The Taliban has made some concessions: Christina Goldbaum, "Taliban Allow Girls to Return to Some High Schools, but with Big Caveat," *The New York Times*, October 27, 2021. https://www.nytimes.com/2021/10/27/world/asia/afghangirls-school-taliban.html

Emigration decreases when countries: Michael A. Clemens and Hannah M. Postel, "Deterring Emigration with Foreign Aid: An Overview of Evidence from Low-Income Countries," Center for Global Development, CGD Policy Paper 119, February 20 https://www.cgdev.org/publication/deterring-emigration-foreign-aid-overview-evidence-low-income-countries

Decisions made by the US: Gary J. Bass, *The Blood Telegram: Nixon, Kissinger, and a Forgotten Genocide*, Alfred A. Knopf, 2013

A senior official: Dipanjan Roy Chaudhury, "Bangladesh: Henry Kissinger's basket case is an economic success story," *Economic Times*, February 1, 2021. https://economictimes.indiatimes.com/news/international/world-news/bangladesh-henry-kissingers-basket-case-is-an-economic-success-story/articleshow/80635079.cms

Bangladesh has a number of challenges: "Bangladesh's growth has been remarkable, but is now at risk," *The Economist*, March 27, 2021.

Roughly thirty states: OECD (2020), *States of Fragility 2020*, OECD Publishing, Paris, https://doi.org/10.1787/ba7c22e7-en.

That figure is unimaginable: The World Bank, "GDP per capita (current US$), World Bank DataBank. https://data.worldbank.org/indicator/NY.GDP.PCAP.CD

Most of the solutions are Bei: Daniel F. Runde and Mark L. Schneider, "A New Social Contract for the Northern Triangle," CSIS, May 8, 2019. https://www.csis.org/analysis/new-social-contract-northern-triangle

One development in Washington: Daniel F. Runde, "A New US Agenda for Central America," *Project Syndicate*, January 13, 2021. https://www.project-syndicate.org/commentary/biden-administration-central-america-northern-triangle-by-daniel-f-runde-2021-01?barrier=accesspaylog

Radelet argued that: Steven Radelet, *Emerging Africa: How 17 Countries Are Leading the Way*, Center for Global Development, 2010.

Chapter 4

Jack Ma was nowhere to be seen: Sam Peach, "Why Did Alibaba's Jack Ma disappear for three months?" BBC News, March 20, 2021. https://www.bbc.com/news/technology-56448688

A much lower profile: Raymond Zhong and Alexandra Stevenson, "Jack Ma Shows Why Chinese Tycoons Keep Quiet," *The New York Times*, April 22, 2021. https://www.nytimes.com/2021/04/22/technology/jack-ma-alibaba-tycoons.html

Deng came into power: Seth Faison, "DENG XIAOPING IS DEAD AT 92; ARCHITECT OF MODERN CHINA,"

The New York Times, February 20, 1997. https://www.nytimes.
com/1997/02/20/world/deng-xiaoping-is-dead-at-92-archi-
tect-of-modern-china.html

Jump-starting the country's devastated economy: Ezra Vogel,
Deng Xiaoping and the Transformation of China, Belknap Press/
Harvard University Press, 2013 (reprint edition).

Said bluntly that China's goal: Michael Hayden remarks at the
Boca Grande men's club.

The government established: Douglas Zhihua Zeng, "China's
Special Economic Zones and Industrial Clusters: Success
and Challenges," Lincoln Institute of Land Policy Working
Paper, 2012. https://www.lincolninst.edu/sites/default/files/
pubfiles/2261_1600_Zeng_WP13DZ1.pdf

Expansion had raised: The World Bank, "GDP per capita
(current US$) – China," World Bank DataBank. https://data.
worldbank.org/indicator/NY.GDP.PCAP.CD?locations=CN

The most far-reaching: Andrew Chatzky and James McBride,
"China's Massive Belt and Road Initiative," Council on Foreign
Relations, last modified January 28, 2020. https://www.cfr.org/
backgrounder/chinas-massive-belt-and-road-initiative

This massive undertaking: OECD (2018), "The Belt and Road
Initiative in the global trade, investment and finance landscape," in OECD Business and Finance Outlook 2018, OECD
Publishing, Paris, https://doi.org/10.1787/bus_fin_out-2018-
6-en.

From Sudan to Angola: George Tubei, "10 massive projects
the Chinese are funding in Africa – including railways and a
brand-new city," *Business Insider South Africa*, September 25,
2018. https://www.businessinsider.co.za/here-are-150-million-
rand-projects-in-africa-funded-by-china-2018-9

A double-edged sword: Wade Shepard, "What China Is Really
Up to in Africa," *Forbes*, October 3, 2019. https://www.forbes.

com/sites/wadeshepard/2019/10/03/what-china-is-really-up-to-in-africa/?sh=2cfd1c315930

A billion-dollar expressway: Andrew Higgins, "A Pricey Drive Down Montenegro's Highway 'From Nowhere to Nowhere,'" *The New York Times*, August 14, 2021. https://www.nytimes.com/2021/08/14/world/europe/montenegro-highway-china.html

The Khorgos Gateway: Henry Ruehl, "The Khorgos Hype on the Belt and Road," *The Diplomat*, September 27, 2019. https://thediplomat.com/2019/09/the-khorgos-hype-on-the-belt-and-road/

China's widely discussed "debt bomb": William Pesek, "China's $18 Trillion Ticking Time Bomb Threatens 'V-Shaped' Boom," *Forbes*, May 25, 2021. https://www.forbes.com/sites/william-pesek/2021/05/25/chinas-18-trillion-ticking-time-bomb-threatens-v-shaped-boom/?sh=2392e040814a

China's widely discussed "debt bomb": Edna Curran, "China's Debt Bomb," Bloomberg Business, last modified September 17, 2018. https://www.bloomberg.com/quicktake/chinas-debt-bomb

The writing on the wall: Mark Dillen and Cameron Khos-rowshahi, "From Addis Ababa: A Power[ful] Africa Message," USAID, August 28, 2013. https://blog.usaid.gov/2013/08/from-addis-ababa-a-powerful-africa-message/

The signs of debt stress: Thomas J. Duesterberg, "The Slow Meltdown of the Chinese Economy," *The Wall Street Journal*, December 20, 2021. https://www.wsj.com/articles/slow-melt-down-of-china-economy-evergrande-property-market-col-lapse-downturn-xi-cewc-11640032283

Others outside of China: Keith Bradsher, "China's Economy Is Slowing, a Worrying Sign for the World." *The New York Times*, last modified January 17, 2022. https://www.nytimes.com/2022/01/16/business/economy/china-economy.html

Construction began in 2009: Dominique Fong, "China's Ghost Towns Haunt Its Economy," *The Wall Street Journal*, June 15, 2018. https://www.wsj.com/articles/chinas-ghost-towns-haunt-its-economy-1529076819

The problems of Evergrande: Alexandra Stevenson and Cao Li, "Evergrande Went From China's Biggest Developer to One of Its Worst Debtors," *The New York Times*, last modified October 11, 2021. https://www.nytimes.com/2021/08/10/business/economy/china-evergrande-debt-property.html

The problems of Evergrande: Alexandra Stevenson and Cao Li, "With Property Sales Plunging, China Evergrande Faces More Protests," *The New York Times*, January 4, 2022. https://www.nytimes.com/2022/01/04/business/china-evergrande-protests.html

The disconnect between the uneducated: Scott Rozelle and Natalie Hell, *Invisible China: How the Urban-Rural Divide Threatens China's Rise*, University of Chicago Press, 2020.

Robert Zoellick gave a speech: Robert B. Zoellick, "Whither China: From Membership to Responsibility," Remarks to National Committee on U.S.-China Relations, September 21, 2005, https://2001-2009.state.gov/s/d/former/zoellick/rem/53682.htm

Beijing cracked down: Coco Feng and Xinmei Shen, "China tech crackdown: in 2021, technology giants came under intense scrutiny after sleeping watchdogs awakened," *South China Morning Post*, December 22, 2021. https://www.scmp.com/tech/big-tech/article/3160529/china-tech-crackdown-2021-technology-giants-came-under-intense

The Swedish clothing retailer: Elizabeth Paton, "H&M responds to a firestorm in China over Xinjiang cotton," *The New York Times*, March 31, 2021. https://www.nytimes.com/2021/03/31/business/hm-responds-to-a-firestorm-in-china-over-xinjiang-cotton.html

Met with the greatest alarm: Lisa Friedman, Hiroko Tabuchi, and Winston Choi-Schagrin, "Climate Change Is a 'Hammer Hitting Us on the Head,' Developing Nations Say," *The New York Times*, August 9, 2021. https://www.nytimes.com/2021/08/09/climate/climate-change-UN-report.html

Chapter 5

Walt Rostow: W. W. Rostow, *The Stages of Economic Growth: A Non-Communist Manifesto*, Cambridge University Press, 1960.

Other economic theorists: Douglass C. North, John Joseph Wallis, Steven B. Webb, Barry R. Weingast, 2007. "Limited Access Orders in the Developing World: A New Approach to the Problems of Development." Policy Research Working Paper; No. 4359. World Bank, Washington, DC. 2007. https://openknowledge.worldbank.org/handle/10986/7341

The economist Paul Collier: Paul Collier, *The Bottom Billion: Why the Poorest Countries Are Failing and What Can Be Done About It*, Oxford University Press, 2008.

Another great thinker: Daren Acemoglu and James A. Robinson, *Why Nations Fail: The Origins of Power, Prosperity, and Poverty*, Crown Business, March 20, 2012.

One step in the right direction: Erol Yayboke, Annie Pforzheimer, Janina Straguhn, and Daphne McCurdy, "The Policy Maker's Guide to the Global Fragility Act," CSIS, May 6, 2021.

A supporting player: Development Assistance Committee, "Shaping the 21st Century: The Contribution of Development Cooperation," OECD/DAC, 1996. https://www.oecd.org/dac/2508761.pdf

The landmark 2008 report: Commission on Growth and Development, "The Growth Report: Strategies for Sustained Growth and Inclusive Development," The International Bank for Reconstruction and Development/The World Bank, 2008.

The Sustainable Development Goals: United Nations, "The 17 Goals," UN Department of Economic and Social Affairs: Sustainable Development, https://sdgs.un.org/goals

Kofi Annan defined: Report of the Secretary General (Kofi Annan), "The Rule of Law and Traditional Justice in Conflict and Post-Conflict Societies," United Nations Security Council, August 23, 2004. https://www.un.org/ruleoflaw/blog/document/the-rule-of-law-and-transitional-justice-in-conflict-and-post-conflict-societies-report-of-the-secretary-general/

There exists today: WJP Rule of Law Index, World Justice Project, https://worldjusticeproject.org/rule-of-law-index/

One great setback: Daniel F. Runde, "World Bank must keep 'Doing Business,'" *The Hill*, September 20, 2021. https://thehill.com/opinion/finance/573010-world-bank-must-keep-doing-business/

Makes a compelling case: Development Initiatives, "Investments to End Poverty, 2018: Meeting the Financing Challenge to Leave No One Behind," 2018. https://devinit.org/documents/728/Investments-to-End-Poverty-2018-Report.pdf

Andrew Natsios made the point: 2021 Global Development Forum, CSIS, October 15, 2021. https://www.csis.org/events/2021-global-development-forum

A comprehensive paper from CSIS: Johanna Nesseth Tuttle, Thomas J. Pritzker, Daniel F. Runde, "Our Shared Opportunity: A Vision for Global Prosperity," CSIS, March 4, 2013. https://www.csis.org/analysis/our-shared-opportunity

Another important paper: Daniel F. Runde, Conor M. Savoy, Erol Yayboke, Jeanne Shaheen, and Todd Young, "Reforming and Reorganizing U.S. Foreign Assistance: Increased Efficiency and Effectiveness," CSIS, July 24, 2017. https://www.csis.org/analysis/reforming-and-reorganizing-us-foreign-assistance

Chapter 6

Brazil has a working relationship: Daniel F. Runde, "Brazil's OECD candidacy is best chance for reform," *The Hill*, October 21, 2020. https://thehill.com/opinion/international/522024-brazils-oecd-candidacy-is-best-chance-for-reform/

According to reporting: Colum Lynch, "China's Soft-Power Grab," *Foreign Policy*, August 14, 2020. https://foreignpolicy.com/2020/08/14/china-soft-power-united-nations-hong-kong-crackdown/

While not perfect: Daniel F. Runde, "Defending the 'Global Spoils System' of Leadership Jobs in Multilaterals Is in the U.S. Interest," CSIS, April 24, 2020. https://www.csis.org/analysis/defending-global-spoils-system-leadership-jobs-multilaterals-us-interest

My intent was to clear away: Daniel F. Runde, "Time for the world to get behind David Malpass for World Bank president," *The Hill*, February 5, 2019. https://thehill.com/opinion/international/428590-time-for-the-world-to-get-behind-david-malpass-for-world-bank-president/

Withholding support: Daniel Runde, "A Fight Over a Trump Official Could Block Aid to Latin America," *Foreign Policy*, February 12, 2021. https://foreignpolicy.com/2021/02/12/trump-latin-america-foreign-aid-idb-inter-american-development-bank/

A strongly worded op-ed: Daniel F. Runde, "Senate should confirm Biden picks for top multilateral postings," *The Hill*, November 28, 2021. https://thehill.com/opinion/international/583294-senate-should-confirm-biden-picks-for-top-multilateral-postings/

I wrote extensively: Daniel Runde, "Approve IMF Quota Reform as Part of Ukraine Rescue Package," *Foreign Policy*, March 12, 2014. https://foreignpolicy.com/2014/03/12/approve-imf-quota-reform-as-part-of-ukraine-rescue-package/

The same cannot be said for China: Daniel F. Runde, "An Economic Crisis in Pakistan Again: What's Different This Time?," CSIS, October 31, 2018. https://www.csis.org/analysis/economic-crisis-pakistan-again-whats-different-time

Took the U.S. government to task: Colum Lynch and Robbie Gramer, "Outfoxed and Outgunned: How China Routed the U.S. in a U.N. Agency," *Foreign Policy*, October 23, 2019. https://foreignpolicy.com/2019/10/23/china-united-states-fao-kevin-moley/

I concluded that a Chinese director: Daniel F. Runde, William Alan Reinsch, and Rachel Abrams, "Why the United States Should Care about the WIPO Election," CSIS, December 12, 2019. https://www.csis.org/analysis/why-united-states-should-care-about-wipo-election

Which ultimately prevented China: Daniel F. Runde, "Trump administration wins big with WIPO election," *The Hill*, March 9, 2020. https://thehill.com/opinion/international/486590-trump-administration-wins-big-with-wipo-election/

Laid out the worrisome specifics: Kristen Cordell, "How to Win at the International Telecommunication Union," CSIS, May 20, 2021. https://www.csis.org/analysis/how-win-international-telecommunication-union

To ensure future effectiveness: Daniel F. Runde, Romina Bandura, Kristen Cordell, Shannon McKeown, "The Future of U.S. Leadership in Multilateral Development Institutions: A Playbook for the Next 10 Years," CSIS, September 28, 2021. https://www.csis.org/analysis/future-us-leadership-multilateral-development-institutions-playbook-next-10-years

Chapter 7

Agenda for Sustainable Development: Department of Economic and Social Affairs, "Transforming our world: the 2030 Agenda for Sustainable Development," United Nations, 2015. https://sdgs.un.org/2030agenda

The World Bank defines: Worldwide Governance Indicators, World Bank, 2021. http://info.worldbank.org/governance/wgi/

Going a bit deeper: United Nations, "Governance and Development: Thematic Think Piece," The UN System Task Team on the Post-2015 UN Development Agenda, May 2012. https://www.un.org/millenniumgoals/pdf/Think%20Pieces/7_governance.pdf

Posits four universal principles: World Justice Project, "What Is the Rule of Law?" https://worldjusticeproject.org/about-us/overview/what-rule-law.

Where democracy is less liberal: "Foreign Aid in the National Interest," USAID, 2002. https://rmportal.net/library/content/higherlevel_fani/at_download/file

Let's not mince words: Rex Nutting, "World Bank chief charges 'corruption,'" UPI, October 1, 1996. https://www.upi.com/Archives/1996/10/01/World-Bank-chief-charges-corruption/4876844142400/

Corruption constrains economic growth: Daniel F. Runde and Christopher Metzger, "Fighting Corruption for U.S. Economic and National Security Interests," CSIS, April 13, 2020. https://www.csis.org/analysis/fighting-corruption-us-economic-and-national-security-interests

The recent discontinuation: Daniel F. Runde, "World Bank must keep 'Doing Business,'" *The Hill*, September 20, 2021. https://thehill.com/opinion/finance/573010-world-bank-must-keep-doing-business/

Look at Singapore: University of Gothenburg, V-Dem Institute, "Autocratization Turns Viral: Democracy Report 2021," V-Dem Institute, March 2021. https://www.v-dem.net/static/website/files/dr/dr_2021.pdf

The strategy paper: "UNITED STATES STRATEGY ON COUNTERING CORRUPTION," The White House, December 2021. https://www.whitehouse.gov/wp-content/uploads/2021/12/United-States-Strategy-on-Countering-Corruption.pdf

The United Nations and OECD: United Nations, "UNITED NATIONS CONVENTION AGAINST CORRUPTION," United Nations Office on Drugs and Crime, 2004, https://www.unodc.org/documents/brussels/UN_Convention_Against_Corruption.pdf

The United Nations and OECD: OECD, "CONVENTION ON COMBATING BRIBERY OF FOREIGN PUBLIC OFFICIALS IN INTERNATIONAL BUSINESS TRANSACTIONS and Related Documents," https://www.oecd.org/daf/anti-bribery/ConvCombatBribery_ENG.pdf

We've elaborated: Daniel F. Runde and Christopher Metzger, "Fighting Corruption for U.S. Economic and National Security Interests," CSIS, April 13, 2020. https://www.csis.org/analysis/fighting-corruption-us-economic-and-national-security-interests

Larry Cooley: interview with D. Runde.

Has exercised soft power: USAID, *Handbook on Legislative Strengthening*, Center for Democracy and Governance, 2000.

Modernization and computerization: James Michel, "Institutional Integrity: An Essential Building Block of Sustainable Reform," Tetra Tech, October 2018. https://www.tetratech.com/en/documents/institutional-integrity-an-essential-building-block-of-sustainable-reform

Presidential elections in Honduras: John Lee Anderson, "Is the President of Honduras a Narco-Trafficker?" *The New Yorker*, November 8, 2021. https://www.newyorker.com/maga-zine/2021/11/15/is-the-president-of-honduras-a-narco-traf-ficker

OECD has encouraged attention: "OECD Recommendation on Public Integrity," OECD, 2017. https://www.oecd.org/gov/ethics/recommendation-public-integrity/

Writes Richard Haass: Richard Haass, "The Age of America First," *Foreign Affairs*, November/December 2021. https://www.foreignaffairs.com/articles/united-states/2021-09-29/biden-trump-age-america-first

The mine had previously been owned: Eric Lipton and Dionne Searcey, "How the U.S. Lost Ground to China in the Contest for Clean Energy," *The New York Times*, last modified December 7, 2021. https://www.nytimes.com/2021/11/21/world/us-chi-na-energy.html

That dominance: Keith Bradsher and Michael Forsythe, "Why a Chinese Company Dominates Electric Car Batteries," *The New York Times*, December 22, 2021. https://www.nytimes.com/2021/12/22/business/china-catl-electric-car-batteries.html

An example of international standard setting: Daniel Runde, "EITI's Silent Revolution," *Forbes*, October 3, 2014. https://www.forbes.com/sites/danielrunde/2014/10/03/eitis-si-lent-revolution/?sh=c49e24238c47

Chapter 8

Through that education experience: AmCham Indonesia, "AmCham Education Summit 2021: Sri Mulyani on the Bene-fits and Relevance of a US Education," YouTube, 23:54, August 18, 2021. https://www.youtube.com/watch?v=sF-QgmP5SCQ

The goal has been: Morgan McMaster, Alejandra Guevara, Lacey Roberts, and Samantha Alvis, *USAID Higher Education: A Retrospective, 1960-2020*, United States Agency for International Development, 2019. https://www.edu-links.org/sites/default/files/media/file/USAID_HE_Retrospective_FINAL.pdf

The number of international students: Laura Silver, "Amid pandemic, international student enrollment at U.S. universities fell 15% in the 2020-21 school year," Pew Research Center, December 6, 2021. https://www.pewresearch.org/fact-tank/2021/12/06/amid-pandemic-international-student-enrollment-at-u-s-universities-fell-15-in-the-2020-21-school-year/

Those schools receive: David Matthews, "News blog: what it is like to study in a Chinese university," Times Higher Education, September 9, 2015. https://www.timeshighereducation.com/blog/news-blog-what-it-study-chinese-university

Many Chinese youths see: Te-Ping Chen and Miriam Jordan, "Why So Many Chinese Students Come to the U.S.," *The Wall Street Journal*, May 1, 2016. https://www.wsj.com/articles/why-so-many-chinese-students-come-to-the-u-s-1462123552

The recent escalation: Sarah Biddulph, Donald Clarke, Jerome A. Cohen, Margaret Lewis, Taisu Zhang, Teng Biao and David Yeliang Xia, "Winter Settles on Chinese Universities," *Foreign Policy*, April 1, 2019. https://foreignpolicy.com/2019/04/01/winter-settles-on-chinese-universities/

Sharing sensitive information: Ellen Barry, "In a Boston Court, a Superstar of Science Falls to Earth," *The New York Times*, last modified December 22, 2021. https://www.nytimes.com/2021/12/21/science/charles-lieber.html

Promising disciplinary action: Sebastian Rotella, "Even on U.S. Campuses, China Cracks Down on Students Who Speak Out," ProPublica, November 20, 2021. https://www.propublica.org/

article/even-on-us-campuses-china-cracks-down-on-students-who-speak-out

Offer a platform to disseminate: Gary Sands, "Are Confucius Institutes in the US Really Necessary?" *The Diplomat*, February 20, 2021. https://thediplomat.com/2021/02/are-confucius-institutes-in-the-us-really-necessary/   .

Improved their view: Tea Leaf Nation Staff "Do Years Studying in America Change Chinese Hearts and Minds?" *Foreign Policy*, December 7, 2015. https://foreignpolicy.com/2015/12/07/do-years-studying-in-america-change-chinese-hearts-and-minds-china-u-foreign-policy-student-survey/

China's wider approach to exchanges: Richard Crespin, Kristen Cordell, and Colleen Waterston, "Winning the Great Power Education: Revamping the U.S. Approach to Education Exchange," CSIS, January 13, 2021. https://www.csis.org/analysis/winning-great-power-education-revamping-us-approach-education-exchange

Today, there is a significant push: Interview with Anne Backhaus, "Educating the Leaders of Tomorrow's Africa," *Der Spiegel*, May 12, 2019. https://www.spiegel.de/international/globalsocieties/ashesi-university-is-among-the-best-in-africa-a-1299802.html

Chapter 9

That IFC study confirmed: "IFC Jobs Study: Assessing Private Sector Contributions to Job Creation and Poverty Reduction," International Finance Corporation, January 2013. https://www.ifc.org/wps/wcm/connect/a93ef4fe-8102-4fc2-8527-5aff9af7f74f/IFC_FULL+JOB+STUDY+REPORT_JAN2013_FINAL.pdf?MOD=AJPERES&CVID=jMRYe5J

Developing economies have absorbed: Daniel F. Runde, "Development Finance Institutions Come of Age," *Forbes*, Oct. 17, 2014. Development Finance Institutions Come of Age

Ambassador Wayne believes: interview with D. Runde, January 6, 2022.

Former Ambassador James Michel, (interview with D. Runde, January 6, 2022)

Constructive investments support: Eric Hontz, "Building a Market for Everyone: How Emerging Markets Can Attract Constructive Capital and Foster Inclusive Growth," CIPE Insights, October 25, 2019. https://www.cipe.org/newsroom/ building-a-market-for-everyone-how-emerging-markets-can-attract-constructive-capital-and-foster-inclusive-growth/

Andrew Wilson: interview with D. Runde, January 6, 2022.

When opaque finance enters: Kim Eric Bettcher, "The Link Between Open Economies and Open Societies," CIPE Insights, October 21, 2021. https://www.cipe.org/newsroom/the-link-between-open-economies-and-open-societies/

Built a strong foundation: Eric Hontz, "Building a Market for Everyone: How Emerging Markets Can Attract Constructive Capital and Foster Inclusive Growth," CIPE Insights, October 25, 2019. https://www.cipe.org/newsroom/building-a-market-for-everyone-how-emerging-markets-can-attract-constructive-capital-and-foster-inclusive-growth/

The key to poverty reduction: Michael Klein, "Ways Out of Poverty: Diffusing Best Practices and Creating Capabilities— Perspectives on Policies for Poverty Reduction," The World Bank, Policy Research Working Paper, March 2003. https:// openknowledge.worldbank.org/handle/10986/18312

Actively work to spread the benefits: Andrea Ciani, Marie Caitriona Hyland, Nona Karalashvili, Jennifer L. Keller, Alexandros Ragoussis, and Trang Thu Tran, *Making It Big: Why Developing Countries Need More Large Firms*. World

Bank Group, 2020. https://openknowledge.worldbank.org/handle/10986/34430

A task force convened: Scott Miller, Daniel F. Runde, Charles Rice, and Christina M. Perkins, "Opportunities in Strengthening Trade Assistance: A Report of the CSIS Congressional Task Force on Trade Capacity Building," CSIS, February 2015. https://csis-website-prod.s3.amazonaws.com/s3fs-public/legacy_files/files/publication/150224_Miller_Strengthening-TradeAssistance_Web.pdf

The US should dedicate: Daniel F. Runde and Rachel Paige Casey, "The Clock Has Started on TFA Implementation," CSIS, July 17, 2017. https://www.csis.org/analysis/clock-has-started-tfa-implementation

Great opportunity for expansion: Daniel F. Runde and Alexander Mayer, "Moving Forward: An Ex-Im Bank for the Twenty-First Century," CSIS, March 2, 2021. https://www.csis.org/analysis/moving-forward-ex-im-bank-twenty-first-century

Soren Andreasen: interview with D. Runde, January 10, 2022.

DFIs at their best: Daniel Runde, "Development Finance Institutions Come of Age," Forbes, October 17, 2014. https://www.forbes.com/sites/danielrunde/2014/10/17/development-finance-institutions-come-of-age-dfi/?sh=49e65ae15c2c

Simon also reinforces, interview with D. Runde.

As countries become wealthier: Daniel Runde, "Social Safety Nets and Developing Countries: A Chance to Get It Right," Forbes, August 29, 2016. https://www.forbes.com/sites/danielrunde/2016/08/29/social-safety-nets-and-developing-countries-a-chance-to-get-it-right/?sh=5cd6c5121156

The acronym MILES: "RESILIENCE, EQUITY, AND OPPORTUNITY: The World Bank's Social Protection and Labor Strategy 2012–2022," World Bank, April 2012. https://openknowledge.worldbank.org/handle/10986/12648

Development finance institutions can support, "IFC Jobs Study: Assessing Private Sector Contributions to Job Creation and Poverty Reduction," International Finance Corporation, January 2013. https://www.ifc.org/wps/wcm/connect/a93ef4fe-8102-4fc2-8527-5aff9af7f74f/IFC_FULL+JOB+STUDY+RE-PORT_JAN2013_FINAL.pdf?MOD=AJPERES&CVID=-jMRYe5J

Chapter 10

Good, practical ideas: Daniel F. Runde, Conor M. Savoy, Asif Shaikh, and Nikki Collins, "The Ecosystem of U.S. International Development Assistance: A Development and Foreign Policy Strategic Asset," CSIS, October 24, 2012. https://csis-website-prod.s3.amazonaws.com/s3fs-public/legacy_files/files/publication/121024_Runde_EcosystemUSIDA_web.pdf

It defined self-reliance: Daniel F. Runde, "Whither the Journey to Self-Reliance?" CSIS, August 12, 2021. https://www.csis.org/analysis/whither-journey-self-reliance

We knew this report would be read: Daniel F. Runde, Conor M. Savoy, Erol Yayboke, Jeanne Shaheen, and Todd Young, "Reforming and Reorganizing U.S. Foreign Assistance: Increased Efficiency and Effectiveness," CSIS, July 24, 2017. https://www.csis.org/analysis/reforming-and-reorganizing-us-foreign-assistance

Another important step: Daniel Runde, "Absolutely Reorganize, But Don't Break Foreign Assistance," *Forbes*, March 23, 2017. https://www.forbes.com/sites/danielrunde/2017/03/23/absolutely-reorganize-but-dont-break-foreign-assistance/?sh=37310ee33521

Years later during the debate: Daniel F. Runde and Shannon N. Green, "The Folly of Merging State Department and USAID: Lessons from USIA," CSIS Commentary, May 26, 2017. https://

Daniel F. Runde

www.csis.org/analysis/folly-merging-state-department-and-usaid-lessons-usia

Lester Munson: interview with D. Runde.

Tessie San Martin: interview with D. Runde.

A function of partisan politics: Daniel F. Runde, Michael Casella, and Rodney Bent, "Earmarks and Directives in the Foreign Operations Appropriation," CSIS, February 26, 2021. https://www.csis.org/analysis/earmarks-and-directives-foreign-operations-appropriation

Congress should look at: Daniel F. Runde, Conor M. Savoy, and Shannon McKeown, "Increasing Flexibility and Responding to Global Challenges within the 150 Account," CSIS, February 11, 2022. https://www.csis.org/analysis/increasing-flexibility-and-responding-global-challenges-within-150-account

He described agencies overwhelmed: Andrew Natsios, "The Clash of the Counter-bureaucracy and Development," Center for Global Development, last modified July 13, 2010. https://www.cgdev.org/publication/clash-counter-bureaucracy-and-development

This may produce outcomes: Daniel Runde, "Let USAID Run USAID," *Foreign Policy*, Dec. 19, 2017. https://foreignpolicy.com/2017/12/19/let-usaid-run-usaid/

Self-reliance country Roadmaps:

Daniel F. Runde, "Whither the Journey to Self-Reliance?" CSIS, August 12, 2021. https://www.csis.org/analysis/whither-journey-self-reliance

An address at Georgetown: "Administrator Samantha Power on a New Vision for Global Development," USAID, November 4, 2021. https://www.usaid.gov/news-information/speeches/nov-4-2021-administrator-samantha-power-new-vision-global-development

The importance of public diplomacy: Daniel F. Runde, "Executive order to rebrand US assistance: Right question, likely wrong answer," *The Hill*, December 14, 2020. https://thehill.com/opinion/international/530087-executive-order-to-rebrand-us-assistance-right-question-likely-wrong/

Conclusion

Roughly a billion people: Steven Radelet, *The Great Surge: The Ascent of the Developing World*, Simon & Schuster, 2015.

If economies do not produce enough good jobs: Daniel F. Runde, Romina Bandura, "The Future of Global Stability: The World of Work in Developing Countries," CSIS Project on Prosperity and Development. https://www.csis.org/programs/project-prosperity-and-development/projects/education-work-and-youth/future-global

Acknowledgments

I 've been in the business of persuasion and influence for quite a
while. I have produced hundreds of essays, commentaries, and
reports; have organized hundreds of seminars and panels; and
have recorded more than a hundred podcasts on the subject of soft
power. But I nonetheless was unprepared for the undertaking of
putting my ideas into book form. I am grateful for the support
and collaboration of so many people, without whom this book may
never have come to fruition.

I wish to thank John Hamre, president and CEO, and Craig
Cohen, executive vice president of the Center for Strategic
and International Studies, for the opportunity to work in such
an exciting intellectual environment. My colleagues at CSIS,
including Conor Savoy, my longtime thought partner and one of
Washington's sharpest thinkers, Romina Bandura, Kristen Cordell,
Erol Yayboke, and all the staff members who have supported our
program over the years. I started this work at CSIS in partnership
with Johanna Nesseth when she was a senior vice president at
CSIS, and she has been a critical partner and collaborator since
she moved on to the private sector. The work I've done at CSIS
could not have proceeded without the ongoing and generous
support of the Chevron Corporation.

Two men, in particular, have helped shape my thinking on these
subjects and have been invaluable guides throughout the writing
of this book. Andrew Natsios, a former USAID administrator, has
been my most important professional mentor after giving me my

first break in Washington. I consider Andrew a hero for our time. Ambassador James Michel, senior advisor at CSIS and former head of the all-important Development Assistance Committee at OECD, has shared his wisdom and experience with me. Both men were generous with their time and guidance as I organized my thoughts and arguments, and Ambassador Michel provided a close and careful reading of the full manuscript.

I would be remiss if I did not thank Holly Wise, a retired foreign service officer who was my first boss at USAID and taught me so much.

Among the many other professional colleagues in the development community who were kind enough to share their ideas and to help me process mine were Larry Cooley, Ambassador Earl Anthony Wayne, Ambassador John Simon, Lester Munson, Tessie San Martin, Andrew Wilson, Stephen Hadley, Michael Klein, Soren Andreasen, Jerry Hyman, and Rich Bissel.

My agent, Tom Miller of Liza Dawson Associates, took me on before I even had a proposal to share and has shepherded me through the sometimes-daunting publishing process. Adam Bellow, my editor at Bombardier Books, also took a chance on me and has provided insight and direction. David Sobel's assistance crafting the manuscript reflected a true collaborative partnership. I am deeply grateful to all three.

Of course, no one writes a book without the love and support of those closest to him, beginning with the unfailing encouragement I received from my parents, Jim and Barbara Runde. I must also mention my grandfather, Orlin H. Runde, whose life, including his service during World War II, made a great and positive impression on me.

My wife, Sonia, the best thing that ever happened to me, has been endlessly patient and supportive, as have our three amazing children, Daniel, Ben, and Alex. Sonia's collaboration on a book with her own father, Domingo Cavallo, was a great inspiration and model. It is with my family in mind that I seek to advance ideas for a safer, healthier, more prosperous, and collaborative future through this work.

Index